LOVE
BUSTERS

REVISED AND EXPANDED

LOVE BUSTERS

PROTECTING your MARRIAGE from HABITS that DESTROY ROMANTIC LOVE

Willard F. Harley, Jr.

Revell

a division of Baker Publishing Group
Grand Rapids, Michigan

Published by Revell
a division of Baker Publishing Group
P.O. Box 6287, Grand Rapids, MI 49516-6287
www.revellbooks.com

Printed in the United States of America

Library of Congress Cataloging-in-Publication Data

Harley, Willard F.
    Love busters : protecting your marriage from habits that destroy romantic love / Willard F. Harley.—Rev. and expanded.
        p.   cm.
    Includes index.
    ISBN 978-0-8007-1894-7 (cloth)
    ISBN 978-0-8007-3214-1 (intl. pbk.)
    1. Marriage. 2. Communication in marriage. 3. Man-woman relationships. I. Title.
HQ734.H2852 2008
646.7′8—dc22   2007045356

In keeping with biblical principles of creation stewardship, Baker Publishing Group advocates the responsible use of our natural resources. As a member of the Green Press Initiative, our company uses recycled paper when possible. The text paper of this book is comprised of 30% post-consumer waste.

green press
INITIATIVE

CONTENTS

INTRODUCTION

Has a friend ever asked for your advice about his (or her) marriage? Where do you begin? How would you help him so that his marriage could be fulfilling instead of disappointing?

In describing the problem, your friend would probably tell you what his wife was **doing** that made him so unhappy. And then he would tell you what his wife was **not doing** that caused him to feel particularly unfulfilled in his marriage.

But if you talked to your friend long enough, you would probably discover that his problems go beyond what his wife is doing or not doing. You would discover what I have discovered in the majority of couples I've counseled—your friend has fallen out of love with his wife. Whatever feeling of love he once felt for her is now gone.

How would you help?

When it comes to solving marital problems, sometimes it's easier to see the solution when it turns out to be somebody else's problem. In your friend's case it might be clear to you that if his wife would stop doing the things that upset him and start doing things that would make him feel more fulfilled, his feeling of love for her might return. So you might begin by going to his wife with his complaints, and by trying to encourage her to make a few changes in her behavior.

But if his wife is like most of the wives (and husbands) I've counseled, you wouldn't get very far in describing those complaints. Assuming that she would even hear you out, after you had uttered your last word you'd be hearing *her* litany of complaints about your friend—how he's been doing all sorts of outrageous things to upset her, and how he'd failed

> How spouses affect each other has a tremendous bearing on the success or failure of a marriage.

miserably in making her feel fulfilled in their marriage. And if she were honest with you about her deepest feelings, you might also discover that she doesn't feel any more love for him than he does for her.

It wouldn't take long for you to discover that each of them understood the other person's problems, but not their own. And you would also discover that they did not understand how their mistakes contributed to their loss of love for each other.

When a couple first comes to my office, I do not talk to them together. That's because they are likely to spend the entire session criticizing each other. If I would let them talk to me together, they would leave my office in worse shape than when they arrived. Instead, I talk to them one at a time to gain insight into how they affect each other—how they make each other miserable and how they have failed to make each other happy. I also try to estimate how much love they have lost for each other.

During their very first counseling session, I make a very important point. It's a point I want you to fully understand: Just about everything that you and your spouse do affects the feeling of love you have for each other. What you do either builds your love for each other, or it destroys that love.

How spouses affect each other has a tremendous bearing on the success or failure of a marriage. If your friend's wife would simply stop doing the things that upset him and start doing the things that make him feel terrific, your friend's complaining would be over, and something else would happen too. Your friend would once again be in love.

Of course, your friend would also have to make some changes. He would need to take his wife's complaints to heart and accommodate her feelings as well. Then she would be in love with him too. But whatever it would take to restore their love would be worth doing because it would create something that they both want very badly—a fulfilling marriage.

A Fulfilling Marriage Requires Passion

Marriage is like an aircraft with exceptional performance—when it flies fast. But when it flies slowly, it cannot stay aloft—it stalls and crashes. When a husband and wife are in love with each other, they are happier, healthier, wiser, and more productive than ever. But when love fades, they lose everything that made them better people. What once seemed almost effortless becomes awkward and very difficult. Instincts that work *for* a couple who are in love work **against** them when they lose their love for each other. And in most cases, the relationship eventually becomes so bad that couples try to escape each other through divorce or permanent separation.

Take my word for it because it's based on years of experience: If you want a marriage that satisfies both you and your spouse, you must have a passionate marriage. (I will be using the phrase *feeling of love* and the word *passion* interchangeably in this book.) That's because a mediocre marriage lacking passion will not remain mediocre very long. Once you lose the feeling of love in your marriage, it's a slippery slope all they way down to disliking, or even hating each other. Instead of bringing out the best in each other, you will find yourselves bringing out the worst.

When a man and woman get married, they think their feelings of love will last a lifetime. The vows and commitments they make depend on that assumption. But their passion for each other is usually short-lived. Some couples sustain it for just a few months or years after the wedding. For others, it's only days. And when passion goes, the commitments of marriage usually go with it.

Some marriage counselors advise couples to accept the inevitable: Enjoy it while it lasts but don't expect it to continue forever. Some recommend rising to a higher form of passionless love, while others suggest divorce.

But I believe that couples don't have to accept the loss of love as inevitable. Instead, they can *restore* the love they once had for each other. And once it's back, all thoughts of divorce or passionless love vanish.

Impossible, you may say. And it may certainly seem that way. When you're in love, it seems impossible that you will ever lose that feeling; and when you're "out of love," it seems impossible to get it back. Most couples I counsel don't believe they will ever feel that love for each other again. But my methods for restoring passion do not require faith—they require action! When a

> If you want a marriage that satisfies both you and your spouse, you must have a passionate marriage.

couple follows my instructions, their love usually returns, ending the threat of divorce.

This book and its companion, *His Needs, Her Needs*, work together in helping couples build and sustain the feeling of love. While *His Needs, Her Needs* will help you *build* love by teaching you how to meet each other's most important emotional needs, *Love Busters* will help you avoid *losing* love.

During courtship, a man and woman create the feeling of love for each other by meeting each other's most important emotional needs. But after they get married, they usually develop habits that destroy their love for each other. I call those destructive habits Love Busters. And as long as Love Busters are tolerated, love doesn't have a chance.

The lessons of this book will teach you how to throw those rascals out. I'll identify the six most common Love Busters and explain how couples have learned to overcome them. Once they're gone, romantic love has free rein in marriage.

The assignments suggested in this book require the use of question-naires, inventories, worksheets, and other forms. But due to space and size limitations, I've had many requests to print them in a larger and more convenient form. In response to these requests, these forms are now available in *Five Steps to Romantic Love: A Workbook for Readers of* Love Busters *and* His Needs, Her Needs. I recommend it to you as a supplement to this book.

Additionally, you'll note that throughout this book you'll encounter ideas labeled as "Basic Concepts." These concepts will be numbered, but not necessarily in the order of appearance in this book. Rather, the number attached to each concept reflects its place within the context of my overall approach to marital counseling. A complete overview of my ten basic concepts for falling in love and staying in love is found in the back of this book.

I encourage you and your spouse to place great value on the passion you share for each other. The strength of your marriage depends on it. But if you have lost your passion, don't despair. It can be restored to your marriage if you follow my advice. And once it is restored, you'll agree that it is too valuable to ever lose again.

Part I

Setting the
STAGE

1

How Love Busters Can Wreck a Marriage

Karen couldn't even remember what it was like being in love with Jim. Whenever he was home, her stomach knotted up and she often felt sick. When they talked, which wasn't very often, she was usually defensive. Vacationing together was unthinkable—if she wanted to relax, he had to be far away. Could she survive this marriage long enough for her children to grow up? Her marriage was looking increasingly hopeless to her.

When I talked with Karen for the first time, she wanted a separation from Jim, one that would help her survive a few more years of their marriage. Their youngest daughter, Lisa, was thirteen. For Lisa's sake, Karen wanted to wait five or six years before divorcing Jim.

You may not be feeling as desperate as Karen felt that day, but perhaps you know what she was going through—the fighting, the sarcasm, the disrespect, and . . . the loneliness. But marriage isn't supposed to be like that. It should be a caring relationship, where a husband and wife treat each other with kindness and consideration, not with rudeness and anger.

Karen had expected her marriage to be caring and thoughtful. And while she was dating Jim, she had no reason to expect anything else. He talked with her almost every day, focusing his attention on what he could do to help her, and he was there for her whenever she had a problem. He even changed his plans whenever they conflicted with hers.

Arguments? They didn't have any because Jim was usually willing to try to see things from her perspective. Again and again he proved to Karen that caring for her was his highest priority—and that made her feel loved and very secure.

Jim had never known a woman as attractive to him as Karen, and—miracle of miracles—she loved him as much as he loved her! She showered him with affection and admiration. This was the woman he wanted for life; she seemed perfect in every way. Within a year they were married.

Jim's Neglect

Not long after the wedding, Jim began to feel the financial pressure of becoming a family man. Karen was pregnant and wanted to work fewer hours after their child arrived. Jim assumed that his income had to increase to make up the difference, so he decided to work longer hours.

With more of his time and energy spent at work, Jim's ability to meet Karen's emotional needs eroded. During her pregnancy, when she needed his emotional support more than ever, he now expected her to work things out on her own. Instead of making her the love of his life and center of his attention, he seemed to cut her adrift. At least that's how Karen felt about the way he treated her.

But from Jim's perspective, his neglect made sense. *After all,* he thought, *we're both intelligent adults. She can take the car to the garage just as easily as I can. Why should she expect me to drop everything at work to do something she can do for herself? Am I her servant? Is she a princess?*

At first, Karen was deeply troubled by his change of attitude, though she tried not to show it. She made a valiant effort to accommodate his new approach to their relationship, troubleshooting around the home, rearranging her schedule to fit his, but when she was alone, she cried. *Why had he changed so much? Is it because I'm pregnant? Am I ugly?*

By the time little Andrea arrived, Karen's conviction that Jim cared for her had been seriously damaged. He had not only failed to support her during pregnancy, but he made matters worse by having little to do with Andrea after her birth. He was so focused on becoming a success at work that he had become a failure at home. Karen felt utterly abandoned. *Maybe,* she thought, *he no longer loves me.*

As the chemistry of their relationship deteriorated, her care for him deteriorated with it. In response to Jim's neglect of her, Karen began to neglect him. She no longer asked him how his day went. She did not show him much affection or admiration anymore. And she wasn't very enthusiastic about making love either.

Karen's Loss of Sexual Interest

Jim didn't pay much attention to the fact that Karen had stopped being affectionate or that she wasn't as admiring. But he sure noticed her loss of sexual interest. When they were first married, she had looked forward to making love to Jim, and was very passionate whenever they did. Now it was something she tried to avoid. Whenever they made love, she felt used.

One day Jim got up the courage to ask her what was going on. "Karen, what's happening to you? Why do you keep pushing me away?"

"I'm sorry, Jim," she replied. "I just haven't been in the mood lately. I don't know why."

There were a host of common excuses that she could have used. After a child's birth the mother is usually exhausted much of the time, and sex requires energy. She could have used that as an excuse. Or she could have focused attention on the fact that Andrea took away their privacy. But deep down, she knew that her loss of sexual interest had something to do with her feeling of being neglected by Jim. But she didn't think there would be any point in discussing it. He was excited about his career, they needed his financial support, and he kept telling her that he was giving her as much of his time as he could afford. What was there to discuss? Why even mention his neglect?

"What do you think it would take to get you in the mood?" It was difficult for Jim to raise the subject. He felt like he was begging.

But Karen wasn't making it easy for him, either. "I don't know," she answered. "I just don't know."

The truth was that Jim had stopped doing the things that made Karen fall in love with him. He was not as supportive, not as accommodating, and worst of all, he spent very little time alone with her. Her emotional needs were not being met anymore. Consequently, she was not as motivated to meet any of his needs. Sex, it turned out, was something she felt like doing only when she knew that Jim loved and cared for her. Now she was feeling emotionally neglected, so what had been effortless became very difficult for her.

While Jim and Karen were dating, they often expressed their feeling of love for each other. That's because those feelings were so strong, they could hardly avoid mentioning it. But when Karen's passion for Jim began to erode, she did not warn him. In fact, she kept telling him she loved him, when deep down she knew her feelings were changing. Her married friends told her that loss of passion in marriage was something she had to expect. After all, they said, passion was for newlyweds, not for couples who become parents. So Karen focused her attention away from Jim, and toward Andrea. Her daughter became her highest priority in life.

From the beginning of their marriage, Jim and Karen had rarely discussed the growing problems with their relationship. When one offended the other, it was usually shrugged off. But now they had a problem they could not shrug off so easily—or at least Jim could not shrug off. He didn't want to go through life with a sexually reluctant wife and he didn't know how to fix the problem.

If Jim had understood what was bothering Karen, he could have solved their problem rather easily. He had simply failed to meet her emotional needs, and that had taken its toll on his sexual attractiveness. His career had become his highest priority instead of Karen. If he had gone back to doing what had drawn her to him in the beginning, cheerfully helping her whenever she had a problem, accommodating her in his schedule, and now that Andrea had joined them, taking an active role in the care of their new daughter, *presto*, sexual problem solved! (See chapters 16 and 17 for that solution to Jim's problem).

16

But Jim didn't understand how important it was to make Karen his highest priority. And his frustration introduced a new and destructive chapter in their marriage. He had a choice. He could solve his sexual problem with care and understanding or he could try to force the issue. Regretfully, he chose the latter.

The Road to Marital Disaster

One night, after Jim and Karen had gone to bed, he reached over to kiss her goodnight. Thinking he was trying to initiate lovemaking, she pushed him away. Jim's feelings of resentment had been building for some time and her rejection sent him over the edge. He was furious. Throwing her out of bed, he called her names and lectured her for half an hour about her bad attitude. All his pent-up resentment poured out in a moment of unrestrained rage.

Karen huddled in a corner, afraid he would hit her. She didn't dare say a word. Eventually he settled down.

When it was over, Jim felt much better. He had finally said what he had felt for such a long time. But Karen was a basket case. He started to apologize for losing his temper but then stopped himself. *I'm glad I had the courage to say what I felt,* he thought. *Now we're getting somewhere!*

They were getting somewhere all right but not where Jim wanted to go. They were now on the road to marital disaster.

Jim put his arm around Karen, telling her how much he loved her. Still in the corner, she didn't dare push him away now. All she could do was cry. As he became more amorous, she let him do anything he wanted—eventually they made love. Jim felt it was one of their best sexual experiences ever. Karen felt raped.

Many women would have gone straight to an attorney the next day to end the marriage, but Karen believed she had married Jim for life. So after she had time to reflect on the nightmare she had experienced, she made some decisions that she thought would help her survive.

First, she would never be found cowering in a corner again. Next time he lost his temper, she would fight fire with fire—let him know what a creep she thought he had become.

Second, because Jim got what he wanted by forcing his will on her, she would get what she wanted by forcing her will on him. In the past, when she needed something from him and he refused, she would do it herself. Now she would not accept no for an answer. She would *demand* what she wanted.

Third, she would learn to become emotionally distant from Jim. She would remain married to him but never again become so emotionally vulnerable. She had already been doing almost everything without him, but she had tried to be emotionally bonded to him in the hope that some day they would return to the passion they once had for each other. But now she was convinced that her only hope for survival was to create an independent life of her own that was completely separate from his, physically and emotionally.

Karen made one huge concession, however. What made him so angry was his unmet need for sex, so anytime he wanted sex, she would accommodate him. She felt it was her duty as long as they were married.

At first, Jim thought his prayers had been answered. Whenever he wanted sex, he got it. And Karen seemed more passionate. For the first week they made love every night.

But their relationship was actually going downhill fast. Karen had erected an emotional barrier around herself that Jim couldn't penetrate. Whenever Karen demanded help from Jim, even when he did what she wanted, she gave him no credit. He didn't help her because he cared for her, she reasoned. He helped her because she made him do it. Besides, she didn't let him to do anything that would meet her most important emotional needs, like being affectionate or talking to him about her deepest feelings, because that would make her too emotionally vulnerable.

Instead, Karen began to demand that Jim give her more freedom to do whatever she pleased. She demanded more money to spend on herself and she spent almost all of her leisure time with her friends. She began to think that, as a wife and mother, she had forgotten to care for herself all these years. So her own personal interests came in a very close second to those of Andrea. Jim's interests, of course, were near the bottom of her list.

Karen made her weekly schedule without any input from Jim. She encouraged him to leave for work early and come home late. If he planned to be home for the weekend, she would plan to do something with her friends. She did not even deposit her own check into their joint account. The money she earned went into her own separate account and she made Jim pay as many of their bills as she could.

Despite all this independent behavior, Karen stayed true to her decision to give Jim the sex he wanted—at least at first.

Though Jim now had no sexual complaints, he was still frustrated much of the time. He was particularly upset with Karen's failure to let him know where she was going or what she had been doing. And he didn't like the way she kept her income separate from his, and her spending a secret. Whenever he asked about her schedule or the money she was spending, she told him it was none of his business. When he argued with her about her secrecy, she would scream at him to leave her alone. If he persisted, she would threaten to leave him. That was usually effective in backing him off.

Jim might have been willing to suffer through the bad marriage for the rest of his life if Karen had made love to him regularly. But as it turns out, her commitment didn't last very long. At first, she allowed herself to say no once in a while, but within a few months she was saying no almost every time.

Actually, her commitment to lovemaking was poorly conceived. None of us can force ourselves to do something that's unpleasant indefinitely. Sooner or later we all find excuses to avoid it. There's hardly a woman anywhere who can consistently make love to a husband she dislikes. And Karen was beginning to hate hers. Eventually, she couldn't force herself to make love to Jim at all. Her stomach knotted up at the very thought of it.

The brief reprieve that had been brought on by frequent lovemaking came to an end. Jim and Karen were left with their independent lifestyles, demands, anger, disrespect, and dishonesty. No marriage can last very long with those weights dragging it down.

By the time they made their first appointment with me, they were not meeting any of each other's emotional needs. But what's worse, they were deliberately hurting each other. They could hardly remember what it was like being in love.

I Can't Take This Anymore!

Jim and Karen's experience is all too common in today's marriages. What starts out as a caring and thoughtful relationship often disintegrates into thoughtlessness. As a husband and wife stop meeting each other's needs and start hurting each other, their love turns into hate.

Some couples try to suffer through it for the sake of their children or their religious convictions. But most often, they decide that they can't take it anymore—they file for divorce. Unfortunately, divorce doesn't usually ease the pain. All exits lead to disaster for the couple and their family.

Since so much personal and familial happiness depends on the success of marriage, you'd think that couples would approach it with a careful plan to insure success. But sadly, most don't give their marriages much thought until it's almost too late. About half of all marriages end in divorce, and most of the others are a bitter disappointment. Very few marriages, about 20 percent or 1 in 5, turn out to be as fulfilling as they could have been.

> What starts out as a caring and thoughtful relationship often disintegrates into thoughtlessness.

I'd like your marriage to be one of these rare exceptions. I've written this book to help you avoid the tragedy of Jim and Karen's marriage and, instead, build a happy marriage that *stays* happy. If you are already feeling the way Jim and Karen felt, I'd like to help you recover in a spectacular way. If you follow my advice, you're likely to enjoy a lifetime of love. My recommendations have helped thousands of people replace marital pain with marital pleasure, and you can be one of them.

But before I show you how to make your marriage a happy exception, I must first explain why Jim and Karen reacted to each other the way they did. At first they loved each other, but eventually they hated each other. How did that happen? It's something you must fully understand if you want to avoid Jim and Karen's tragic experience.

Basic Concept #1: The Love Bank

My years of counseling experience have taught me that when you learn to behave in ways that make your spouse feel great, and you learn to avoid behaving in ways that make your spouse unhappy, he or she will be in love with you. That's how Jim and Karen first fell in love with each other—they made each other happy when they were together, and they did whatever they could to avoid upsetting each other.

To help couples understand this very important fact, I created the concept of the Love Bank. It helps me explain the rise and fall of **romantic love**—the feeling of passion toward each other that people should always have in their marriage.

Within all of us is a Love Bank that contains accounts in the names of all of the people we know. It's the way our emotions keep track of the way people treat us. When someone does something that makes us feel good, love units are deposited into their account. And when that person does something that makes us feel bad, love units are withdrawn. If someone consistently does things that make us feel good, that person builds a large Love Bank balance. If on the other hand he or she does things that make us feel bad and does very little to make us feel good, they end up with a negative Love Bank balance.

Love Bank

The way our emotions keep track of the way people treat us.

Our emotions check our Love Bank regularly to determine who is taking good care of us and who isn't. With that evidence, they encourage us to spend more time with those who make us happy and avoid those who make us unhappy. If someone has a large positive balance, our emotions encourage us to spend time with that person by making him or her feel attractive to us. On the other hand, if someone has a large negative balance, our emotions encourage us to avoid that person by making him or her feel repulsive to us. We have very little control over these feelings, and they are based almost entirely on Love Bank balances. People we like have accumulated positive balances and people we dislike have accumulated negative balances.

Once in a while, someone of the opposite sex comes along who makes us feel absolutely sensational. That's because they meet one or more of our most important emotional needs. When that happens, so many love units are deposited that his or her account hits what I call the **romantic love threshold**. Our emotions are so impressed with that high balance that they give us added incentive to spend more time with that person—they give us the feeling of romantic love. We don't merely find that person attractive—we find that person **irresistible.** And along with that feeling goes a desire to spend our lives with whoever has that high Love Bank balance. Marriage is an easy choice when Love Bank balances are above the romantic love threshold.

What Goes Up, Can Go Down

Before marriage, while a couple is dating, they usually deposit a tremendous number of love units because they're doing things that make each other very happy—they're meeting each other's important emotional needs. They also try to avoid doing whatever might make each other unhappy. They want to please each other and avoid anything that would be hurtful. This mutual effort deposits so many love units that their Love Bank balances rise above the romantic love threshold, and they're ready to marry—they find each other irresistible and they want to be together for the rest of their lives.

Romantic Love Threshold

The Love Bank balance needed to trigger romantic love—finding someone irresistible.

Unfortunately, after marriage most couples, like Jim and Karen, fail to keep their Love Bank balances above the romantic love threshold. They don't do as good a job meeting each other's emotional needs. And sometimes they begin doing things that are irritating and annoying. They don't try as hard to be thoughtful as they did before marriage. When that happens they lose their feeling of passion for each other.

But it gets worse. When a couple loses their romantic love for each other, they don't feel like meeting each other's important emotional needs as they did before. And their failure to meet those needs often leads to abusive tactics—they try to force each other to meet them. Such tactics not only fail to help them achieve their goal, but they also drive Love Bank balances below zero. What used to be a feeling of attraction turns into a feeling of repulsion. It's not uncommon for a couple who started out feeling that they would love each other forever to come to the conclusion that their marriage was the biggest mistake of their lives.

And it's all due to Love Bank balances. If Jim and Karen had simply been able to keep their Love Bank balances above the romantic love threshold, they would have had a marriage full of passion for the rest of their lives. But because they allowed their balances to drop below that threshold, they lost their feeling of passion for each other. And by allowing their Love Bank balances to keep falling until they entered negative territory, they eventually came to regret the day they met each other.

Marriage Can Make Us Hate the One We Once Loved

Of all the people you know, you are more likely to hate your spouse than anyone else. And your spouse is more likely to hate you than anyone else. What I am telling you is true, and because of it, I want you to take extraordinary measures to avoid this very real danger. Since you may not believe me or may think I am exaggerating, I will explain why this is the experience of most married couples.

Many of our relationships are voluntary. That is, we choose the people we'll spend our time with. Our emotions encourage us to select those who have deposited love units in our Love Bank, since they are the ones most likely to keep depositing. By surrounding ourselves with those who treat us well, they will keep depositing love units, so we come to like them more and more.

On the other hand, our emotions encourage us to avoid those whose Love Bank accounts are in the red. By avoiding these people, we prevent them from making even more withdrawals. So most people who make us unhappy don't have an opportunity to withdraw as many love units as they might, because we try to avoid them once their account is negative. That's why we usually don't dislike very many people—we "close their account" before things get that bad.

> A couple who thought they would love each other forever can come to the conclusion that their marriage was the biggest mistake of their lives—all due to Love Bank balances.

But there are some people who are not easy to avoid. At work, at home, in our churches, clubs, or community activities, we have to deal with certain people whether we like them or not. And these are the ones we can grow to hate, because they have an opportunity to keep withdrawing love units until their account reaches the hate threshold. That's the negative balance that our emotions use to trigger an intense feeling of repulsion toward someone who has consistently and repeatedly made us unhappy. Just as our emotions give us added incentive

> The person in the best position to withdraw unprecedented numbers of love units is your spouse.

(the feeling of love) to be with those with accounts over the romantic love threshold, our emotions give us added incentive (the feeling of hate) to avoid those with accounts under the hate threshold.

You might find another job or switch churches to avoid someone who treats you badly enough. Uncles, aunts, cousins and other members of your extended family can be avoided, at least for most of the year. With greater effort it is possible to avoid brothers and sisters, or even parents.

But a spouse is almost impossible to avoid unless you divorce, especially if you have children. So it should come as no surprise that the person in the best position to withdraw unprecedented numbers of love units is your spouse. And for that reason, you are more likely to hate your spouse than anyone else. Your spouse is the person hardest to avoid—regardless of how miserable he or she makes you feel.

Day after day, month after month, year after year, your spouse can withdraw love units by making demands of you, criticizing you, lying to you, annoying you with disgusting habits and thoughtless activities, calling you disrespectful names, and even being physically or verbally abusive to you. And what can you do about it? What can you do to get him or her to stop?

You do what most people do: Dish it back as fast as it comes. If you're miserable, then, by golly, you'll *both* be miserable. Your instinct is to destroy the one who is upsetting you, and almost all couples respond that way when Love Bank accounts fall into the red.

When a married couple's relationship starts on a downward slide, the loss of love units usually gains momentum. Instead of caring for each other, spouses devise increasingly painful strategies to pay each other back for the last thoughtless act. As negative Love Bank balances increase, the feeling of anger and disrespect increases. Because they live together, a couple cannot avoid each other, and withdrawals continue unabated. The end result is often the violence that comes from a deep and pervasive hatred.

> All the best intentions, sincere vows, and honest efforts cannot substitute for a substantial Love Bank account.

The secret to avoiding this tragedy, of course, is to keep Love Bank balances above the romantic love threshold. And if they happen to drift below that threshold, couples should make a special effort to avoid losing any more, and start re-depositing.

All the best intentions, sincere vows, and honest efforts cannot substitute for a substantial Love Bank account. The Love Bank determines whom we marry and it usually determines whether or not we'll

Love Busters

Habits that drain the Love Bank.

be divorced. Therefore it is tremendously important to understand how to build Love Bank accounts and how to avoid withdrawals once deposits have been made.

Basic Concept #5: Love Busters

Whenever you do something that makes your spouse unhappy, you withdraw love units. But let's face it, it's impossible to avoid all the bumps and bruises of life, especially *marital* bumps and bruises. Even in the best marriages, spouses hurt each other now and then.

But occasional mistakes do not drain a Love Bank as long as they're seen as mistakes. An apology quickly heals the wound and the deposits continue unabated.

It's when a mistake turns into a habit, repeated again and again, that Love Bank balances are at great risk. In these situations, apologies mean very little because the same mistake keeps being repeated. Nothing is done to keep love units from flowing out of the Love Bank. I call these habits that drain the Love Bank **Love Busters,** because they do more to ruin romantic love than anything else.

Through years of marriage counseling, I've been made aware of a host of Love Busters that all fall into six categories: selfish demands, disrespectful judgments, angry outbursts, dishonesty, annoying habits, and independent behavior. Because each of these categories is so important, I will discuss them one at a time in the following chapters and show you how to overcome each of them.

Then, in the second part of this book, I will show you how these Love Busters prevent couples from resolving common marital conflicts. You'll also see how easy it is to resolve these conflicts once Love Busters are eliminated.

The Chapters of Jim and Karen's Marriage

Let's think once more about Jim and Karen's marriage. Their story consisted of five stages—chapters, we'll call them. They progressed through the first three chapters even before I counseled with them. In the **first chapter** they met each other's emotional needs, deposited love units, and were in love with each other. In the **second chapter** they stopped meeting some of these important emotional needs and, as a result, their deposits were few and far between. Their frustrations with unmet needs opened the **third chapter**. Instead of solving their problems thoughtfully, they chose to hurt each other. This selfish strategy poked gaping holes in their Love Bank accounts, and love units poured out.

The Parable of the Net

Marriage is like a fishing net. Each day fishermen use their nets to catch fish and sell them at the market.

One fisherman takes his fish from the net every day but lets debris from the ocean accumulate. Eventually so much debris is caught in the net that he can hardly cast the net out of the boat, and when he does, it's almost impossible to retrieve. Finally, in a fit of anger, he cuts the net loose and goes home without it. He's unable to catch and sell fish again until he buys another net.

Another fisherman removes debris every time he retrieves the net with the fish he caught. Each time he casts his net, it's clean and ready to catch more fish. As a result, he catches and sells enough fish to support himself and his family.

In this parable, the fish are emotional needs met in marriage and the pieces of debris are Love Busters, habits that cause unhappiness.

Bad marriages are like the first fisherman's net. Selfish demands, disrespectful judgments, angry outbursts, annoying habits, dishonesty, and independent behavior accumulate over time. The burden of the unhappiness they cause ruins a couple's willingness and ability to meet each other's emotional needs. Eventually the marriage supplies no benefits to either spouse and ends in divorce or emotional separation.

Good marriages are like the second fisherman's net. Love Busters are eliminated as soon as they appear, making it easy for the spouses to meet each other's emotional needs. Love is sustained because the Love Busters are tossed overboard.

But there are very important fourth and fifth chapters to Jim and Karen's story. In the **fourth chapter** they learned to stop hurting each other. They no longer made demands, showed disrespect, or became angry when they didn't get their way. They also learned how to get what they needed from each other by making thoughtful decisions that took each other's feelings into account. And they learned to be honest with each other instead of creating secret and independent lives.

This book will teach you the lessons that Jim and Karen learned in the fourth chapter of their book of life—the lessons of avoiding Love Busters. Before you can ever hope to rebuild your Love Bank balances, you must first learn to stop making Love Bank withdrawals.

But to make their book of life complete, in the **fifth chapter** Jim and Karen relearned how to meet each other's important emotional needs. That helped them deposit so many love units that they both broke through the romantic love threshold once and for all. The lessons that they learned in their fifth chapter of life are described in this book's companion, *His Needs, Her Needs*.

If you find yourselves in Jim and Karen's third chapter of life, with an unfulfilling marriage that has led you to respond with demands, disrespect, and anger, or if you have just given up on ever having the kind of marriage you need, and have created an independent lifestyle that ignores each other's feelings, this book is for you. Throughout this book I will focus your attention on the tragic mistakes that Jim and Karen made and the steps they took to overcome those mistakes and allow their love to be restored.

In marriage you have an unprecedented opportunity to make your spouse happy. You do that whenever you meet his or her most important emotional needs. But you are also in a position to make your spouse miserable, more miserable than anyone else can. In all too many marriages, people choose to make each other miserable. When they come to me with their marital problems, my ultimate goal is to teach them how to make each other happy. But before I can get to that goal, I must first teach them how to stop hurting each other.

By the time you finish this book, you will know how to protect your spouse from your Love Busters. You'll be able to plug up the leaks in your Love Bank so that deposits will accumulate until you are passionately in love with each other—essential for a happy and fulfilling marriage. Once you learn these lessons, your efforts to meet each other's needs will reap huge dividends. The love units you deposit in each other's Love Banks will break through the romantic love threshold, and just like Jim and Karen, you'll be in love with each other again.

Key Principles

All of us have within us a **Love Bank** (Basic Concept #1) that keeps track of the way people treat us. When someone does something that makes us feel good, love units are deposited into their account. And when he or she does something that makes us feel bad, love units are withdrawn.

Our emotions check our Love Bank regularly to determine who is taking care of us and who isn't. With that evidence, they encourage us to spend more time with those who make us happy, and to avoid those who make us unhappy.

When someone of the opposite sex makes us feel absolutely sensational by meeting one or more of our most important emotional needs, so many love units are deposited that his or her account hits the **romantic love threshold**. Our emotions are so impressed with that high balance that they give us added incentive to spend more time with that person—they give us the feeling of **romantic love**. We don't merely find that person attractive—we find that person **irresistible**.

Our emotions encourage us to avoid those whose Love Bank accounts are in the red. But some people, like our spouse, are not easy to avoid, so they may keep withdrawing love units until their account reaches the **hate threshold**.

Just as our emotions give us added incentive (the feeling of love) to be with those with accounts over the romantic love threshold, our emotions give us added incentive (the feeling of hate) to avoid those with accounts under the hate threshold.

It's not uncommon for a couple that started out feeling that they would love each other for eternity to come to the conclusion that their marriage was the biggest mistake of their lives. And it's all due to Love Bank balances.

Love Busters (Basic Concept #5) are habits that drain the Love Bank. They fall into six categories: selfish demands, disrespectful judgments, angry outbursts, dishonesty, annoying habits, and independent behavior.

Consider This...

1. Discuss the tragic events of Jim and Karen's marriage. Are there any similarities between their marriage and yours? If you had been advising them during the first year of their marriage, what would you have suggested to them? Would that same advice have helped your marriage?

2. Try to explain the Love Bank to each other in your own words. Most couples have trouble discussing Love Bank withdrawals, because it often sounds like criticism. How could you let each other know about withdrawals that are taking place in a constructive way?

3. There are many who believe that the feeling of love cannot be sustained in marriage. What do you think? If you believe that it can be sustained, is it important enough for both of you to do whatever it takes to keep your Love Bank balances above the romantic love threshold?

4. How do Love Bank balances affect your willingness to meet each other's emotional needs? How do they affect your temptation to hurt each other? When your Love Bank balances are negative, what should you try to do for each other that you don't feel like doing? What do you feel like doing to each other that you should avoid doing?

5. What are Love Busters? Why do I emphasize habits rather than isolated behaviors?

2

WHAT IS MARITAL ABUSE?

And Why Are We Tempted to Be Abusive?

I defined a **Love Buster** in the last chapter—it's a habit that drains the Love Bank. To put it another way, it's **repeated** behavior of one spouse that causes the other spouse to be unhappy. This definition is very important because it focuses attention on habits instead of isolated, one-of-a-kind mistakes. While it's true that you make Love Bank withdrawals whenever you do anything to make your spouse unhappy, I've chosen to focus on habits because they multiply the effect of a single mistake—bad habits will drain your Love Bank much more quickly than single mistakes. If you're in the habit of doing something that hurts your spouse, you'll continue to lose love units until you change the habit or until your spouse doesn't love you anymore.

The first three Love Busters that I will introduce to you—selfish demands, disrespectful judgments, and angry outbursts—are all examples of marital abuse. They are habits that represent typical, yet very hurtful, approaches to problem-solving in marriage. If you want something from your spouse, or if you are in conflict, it's tempting to use these Love Busters to try to get your way.

> Habits multiply the effect of a single mistake.

Each one of these Love Busters illustrates the way one spouse deliberately hurts the other in a selfish effort to gain control. Instead of searching for mutually acceptable solutions to a problem, one spouse tries to impose a solution that is to the other spouse's disadvantage. And it's backed up with punishment if there is resistance.

Any one of these three Love Busters qualifies as an abusive attempt to resolve conflict, but they tend to appear in a certain escalating order. The first to appear is usually **selfish demands**—one spouse tells the other what to do. If that doesn't get the job done, **disrespectful judgments** often take their place—one spouse tries to impose his or her way of thinking on the other spouse in an effort to eventually force compliance. And if that doesn't work, **angry outbursts** are the final and most abusive step toward gaining control—punishing the other spouse until compliance is attained.

I want you to get what you need from each other because that's essential for a happy and fulfilling marriage. But these three abusive strategies will not help you. In fact, they will make getting what you need *less* likely. And if you use these Love Busters to try to resolve your conflicts, you will lose your love for each other.

One of my greatest hurdles in helping couples overcome abuse is for them to identify and understand it. When I try to persuade spouses to stop being abusive toward each other, I run into the same roadblock almost every time. The perpetrator of abuse usually does not recognize it for what it is. I often hear the shocked reaction, "I'm not being abusive—it's my spouse who's being abusive to me!" Or, "Don't I have a right to express my feelings?"

If spouses do not know when they are being abusive and why they are doing it, it's impossible to stop the abuse from taking place. So before we look specifically at the three most common forms of abuse in marriage— demands, disrespect, and anger—I will explain what abuse is and why we tend to do it to our spouses.

> Abusive strategies will make getting what you need less likely.

What Is Abuse?

I define abuse in marriage as a **deliberate** effort of one spouse to cause the other to be unhappy. Control of a spouse's behavior, attitudes, beliefs, and opinions is usually the motive, although the one doing the abusing rarely acknowledges it. The perpetrator of abuse usually knows that his or her actions cause unhappiness, but often views it as the "right" thing to do, or "for the spouse's own good." And the abuser will rarely admit that the abuse is a deliberate effort to make his or her spouse unhappy. Instead, the abuser claims the spouse's unhappiness as an unforeseen or unintentional outcome. "I didn't mean to hurt you," or "you shouldn't feel bad," is often the reaction of an abusive spouse.

Abuse
Deliberate effort of one spouse to cause the other to be unhappy.

There are, of course, many habits and activities in marriage that **unintentionally** cause the other spouse to be unhappy. These causes of unhappiness are also Love Busters because they can create massive Love Bank withdrawals, and I will be encouraging you to overcome them in the later chapters of this book. But I want to begin by helping you overcome the deliberate Love Busters, because they hurt your spouse in two ways: First, your spouse is hurt by the act itself, and second, your spouse is hurt because he or she knows it was deliberate.

Because abuse is such a tricky concept in marriage, I will devote this entire chapter to helping you see it for what it really is and why we are all tempted to be abusive. That way, you will be better able to understand and identify your own abusive instincts and habits.

If your spouse has ever accused you of being controlling, manipulative, or abusive, you owe it to your spouse, and to yourself, to read this chapter carefully so you will know what he or she is talking about. And I hope that by the time you are finished, you will make a commitment to protect your spouse from your abusive habits.

To better understand the nature of abuse, and why those who are abusive rarely see it for what it really is, let me give you a short course on the two parts of your personality. I call these two the Giver and the Taker.

Deliberate Love Busters hurt your spouse in two ways.

Basic Concept #7: The Giver and Taker

Have you ever wondered if your spouse has two personalities? One that's caring and considerate, and one that seems impossible to get along with? I'm sure you've not only noticed, but have probably been very disappointed, or even horrified, by the impossible one.

We all have them, and they make marriage much more difficult than it should be. To help you understand why you may be having so much trouble communicating and why you are tempted to be abusive when you try to resolve conflicts, I'm going to reveal these two parts of your personality to you—the Giver and the Taker.

The Giver

The part of someone's personality that is concerned only about the happiness of others.

The Giver is the part of you that is kind, generous, thoughtful, and caring. It follows this rule: **Do whatever you can to make others happy and avoid anything that makes others unhappy, even if it makes you unhappy**. In other words, the Giver encourages you to do things for others even if it means doing it in self-sacrificing ways. It's the part of you that wants to make a difference in the life of someone else. And it grows out of a basic instinct that we all share, a deep reservoir of love and concern for those around us.

But this is only half of the story. The other half is the Taker. It's the part of you that's concerned only about your own welfare and your own happiness. It follows the rule: **Do whatever you can to make yourself happy and avoid anything that makes you unhappy, even if it makes others unhappy**. It's the part of you that wants you to get as much out of life as possible. And it grows out of your basic instinct for self-preservation.

By themselves, the Giver and Taker are both shortsighted. Your Giver's concern is only for others, often at the expense of yourself, while your Taker's concern is only for yourself, often at the expense of others.

The Taker

The part of someone's personality that is concerned only about his or her own happiness.

But the Giver and the Taker don't usually work in isolation of each other. In everyday life, your Giver and Taker usually solve problems together. They recognize your need to give and take simultaneously.

For example, when you buy groceries you give money and take groceries. You don't give more money than the grocer asks for and you don't take groceries without paying for them. Instead, you strike a fair bargain where the grocer is satisfied with the money you give and you are satisfied with the groceries you purchase in return.

In marriage, however, a very strange thing happens to the way your Giver and Taker operate. They often work independently of each other. Either the Giver's in charge, encouraging you to give unconditionally to your spouse, or the Taker's in charge, encouraging you to take what you want from your spouse without consideration of your spouse's interests or feelings.

When your Giver is in charge, you're loving and considerate and you tend to make personal sacrifices to see to it that your spouse is happy and fulfilled—your Taker makes no effort to defend your personal interests. You love unconditionally when your Giver guides you, because your Giver doesn't care how you feel. Regardless of how badly you are treated, and how little you get in return, your Giver wants you to keep on giving.

> Marriage is one of the very few conditions in life that bring out the pure Giver and Taker in each of us.

But when the Taker's in charge you're tempted to be rude, demanding, and inconsiderate. All you seem to think about is yourself and what your spouse should be doing to make you happy. You expect your spouse to make sacrifices for you, because your Taker doesn't care how your spouse feels. Regardless of how badly you treat your spouse, and how little you give in return, your Taker wants you to keep on taking.

I want to emphasize that this is normal behavior in marriage. You might think you're married to a crazy person or that you're crazy. But let me assure you, marriage is one of the very few conditions in life that bring out the pure Giver and Taker in each of us. And that usually makes us seem much crazier than we really are.

It should come as no surprise to you that it isn't the Giver that ruins marriages—it's the Taker. But the Giver plays a very important role in creating the problem. When the Giver encourages us to give our spouse anything he or she wants, it sets up the Taker for its destructive acts. After you've been giving, giving, giving to your spouse and receiving very little in return—because you haven't bargained for much—your

Taker rises up to straighten out the situation. It sees the unfairness of it all and steps in to balance the books. Instead of coming to a more equitable arrangement, though, where you bargain to get something for what you give, the Taker just moves the Giver out of the picture altogether. It says "I've been giving enough, now it's time to take!"

Sound familiar? We've all been through it. But it doesn't work. All our Taker does is arouse our spouse's Taker. And the first thing you know, we're having a fight.

Since the Taker has no concern for your spouse's feelings, it encourages you to let your spouse suffer if you can gain something for yourself. *You've been suffering for your spouse's happiness,* your Taker whispers to you. *It's about time your spouse did a little suffering for your happiness.*

In fact, it will even encourage you to **cause** your spouse to suffer, if that's what it takes to get your way. And that's what abuse is really all about—deliberately hurting your spouse so that you can have what you want. If you have ever made demands of your spouse, shown disrespect, or had an angry outburst, you have yielded to your Taker's abusive way to solve problems.

Your Taker not only tries to encourage you to do whatever it takes to make you happy, it also defends you when its tactics get you into trouble. When your spouse sees your actions as selfish and abusive, your Taker gives you logical arguments to deflect criticism. It tries to make your selfish behavior seem rather thoughtful. Even when you are having a fight with your spouse, it gives you the words to justify your abuse. And when the fight is over, it helps you forget what you did, and gives you memories that make your abusive behavior seem downright compassionate. By the time you discuss the incident with your spouse, your Taker has you believing that you were Mother Teresa.

This all sounds insane, but it isn't. It is the way we all behave, which makes it normal. When I try to get to the bottom of what goes on when spouses fight, the Takers of both spouses distort the event to such an extent that you'd think they were describing completely separate incidents. How could two people remember the same event so differently? Their Takers are the culprits.

Some of the smartest people I know become idiots when faced with marital conflict. I've seen this happen in case after case. An

> A romantic relationship makes communication difficult.

intelligent man listens to his wife talking about her needs and her desires and her interests, and it's as if she's speaking a foreign language. A brilliant woman hears her husband describe his perspective and she just doesn't get it.

What makes marital communication so tough? Is it that men and women just can't communicate with each other? Or is there something about marriage that blurs their thinking?

As I already mentioned, I'm thoroughly convinced that it's marriage itself, or more specifically a romantic relationship, that makes communication so difficult. It's not the differences between men and women. The men I counsel have very little trouble resolving conflicts with women when they're not in a romantic relationship. And their wives are just as good at negotiating with men other than their husbands. It's conflicts they have with each other that seem so impossible to resolve. And that's because their Giver and Taker are working at odds with each other. Instead of striving for fairness, they are either entirely selfless or entirely selfish.

Basic Concept #8: The Three States of Mind in Marriage

Bear with me a little longer as I go on to explain how the Giver and Taker can turn you into an abusive spouse. Not only do these two influence your thinking, they also change your approach to marital negotiation. I call each approach a state of mind, and each one has its own unique negotiating rules and emotional reactions. But regardless of the state of mind, the way your Giver and Taker encourage you to negotiate is unfair and ineffective. I call these three states of mind intimacy, conflict, and withdrawal.

The State of Intimacy

The most essential prerequisite for the state of intimacy is the feeling of being in love, and being very happy with the relationship. You have that feeling when your spouse has deposited enough love units to break through the romantic love threshold.

The Giver is usually in complete control of this state of mind. So a spouse is encouraged to follow the rule of the Giver, *do whatever you can to make your spouse happy and avoid anything that makes your spouse unhappy, even if it makes you unhappy*. If both spouses follow this rule at the same time, they're both likely to have their emotional needs met and all is well. Giving to each other seems almost instinctive and they both have a great desire to make each other happy in any way possible and avoid hurting each other at all costs.

State of Intimacy

The state of mind dominated by your Giver, who encourages you to give unconditionally.

Since you are happy, the Taker has nothing to do, because its job is to make sure that you are happy. So the Taker gives the Giver full reign, and takes a nap.

In this state of mind, spouses build trust between them. They can share their deepest feelings and become emotionally vulnerable to each other because they know that they both have each other's best interests at heart. They feel so close to each other that to hurt the other person would be the same as hurting themselves.

Conversation in the state of intimacy is respectful and nonjudgmental. Couples usually express their deepest love for each other along with gratitude for the care that they're receiving. By lowering their defenses so that they can form a close emotional bond, they feel even greater pleasure when they meet each other's needs.

This is the way most people expect marriage to be—unconditionally loving and caring. When one spouse expresses a desire, the other rushes to fulfill it. There's no thought of repayment. As long as both spouses are in the same state of mind, there is actually nothing to negotiate. They give each other anything that's possible and they do it unconditionally.

Sounds good, doesn't it? But there is a serious problem with this strategy: It usually causes one spouse to gain at the other's expense. And that, in turn, can cause substantial Love Bank withdrawals for the spouse making the sacrifice. If your sacrifice becomes a habit, eventually there will be so many love units lost that your spouse's account will fall below the romantic love threshold and you will no longer be in love with your spouse. When that happens, you enter the second state of mind.

The State of Conflict

When the sacrifices you make for your spouse draw too many love units from your spouse's Love Bank account, your Taker rises from its nap and says, "Hey, what's going on? I don't like this." And as quick as you can say "bull in a china closet" out comes the Taker, along with the Taker's rule and its own emotional reactions to things. You now have an entirely new state of mind—the state of conflict. It's in this state of mind that you will be tempted to be abusive to your spouse.

Remember the Taker's rule: ***Do whatever you can do to make your-self happy and avoid anything that makes you unhappy, even if it makes your spouse unhappy***. In an effort to make you happier than you've been, the Taker prepares you for war.

In this state of mind, you demand that your spouse meet your needs. And you demand that your spouse stop doing anything that is upsetting you. You threaten your spouse with punishment until those demands are met.

State of Conflict

The state of mind dominated by your Taker, who encourages you to take unconditionally.

Your conversation tends to be very disrespectful because the Taker sees no point in respecting your spouse for his or her failure to make you happy. To justify your demands, the Taker creates disrespectful arguments that "prove" your spouse is wrong and you are right. Unconditional care is now replaced by unconditional selfishness. Your Taker no longer trusts your spouse to look after your own interests, but instead pulls out all the stops to see to it that your spouse treats you fairly. The problem, of course, is that your Taker is unwilling to treat your spouse with the same fairness. From your Taker's perspective, fairness is getting your way at all costs.

Even in the state of conflict, a couple still feels emotionally connected to each other, and that makes your Taker's selfishness even more painful to your spouse—love units can be withdrawn at a very rapid rate.

You can return to the state of intimacy from the state of conflict if, and only if, you stop hurting each other and start meeting each other's needs again. But this is extremely difficult to do once you're in the state of conflict because all of the instincts of the Taker encourage you to do the opposite. It urges you to return pain whenever you receive it.

And that's abusive. And it also encourages you to withhold meeting your spouse's needs until your needs are met.

So for most couples, the state of conflict inspires them to be short-sighted. Instead of stopping the pain they are causing each other, they create even more pain. Instead of wanting to meet each other's needs, they want their own needs met before they'll do anything. Our Takers would rather fight than try to make the other spouse happy.

The State of Withdrawal

When you're in the state of conflict, your Taker tries to make your spouse meet your needs with demands, disrespect, and anger. And if that doesn't work, your Taker will suggest a new strategy: withdrawal. In that state of mind, it tries to convince you that your spouse is not worth the effort.

Abuse is rare in this state of mind because the Taker doesn't want you to try to get anything from your spouse. Demands, disrespect, and angry outbursts are pointless because they are used only when the Taker wants something. Emotional defenses are raised, and there is no longer an emotional bond. You don't want your spouse to meet your emotional needs anymore, and you certainly don't want to meet your spouse's emotional needs.

When we're in the state of withdrawal, we raise emotional defenses so high that our spouse cannot get love units through the barrier. We don't allow ourselves to be vulnerable enough for our spouse's actions to meet our emotional needs. So even if our spouse makes an effort to do what we had demanded in the state of conflict, it deposits few if any love units.

> State of Withdrawal
>
> *The state of mind dominated by your Taker, who encourages you to emotionally withdraw from your spouse, neither giving nor taking.*

In the state of withdrawal, there's no negotiation at all. There are no discussions, bargaining, or even arguing. In the state of withdrawal we are unwilling to do anything for our spouse or to let our spouse do anything for us.

Some people think that withdrawal is a form of abuse. By refusing to discuss an issue, or even by physically walking away, it feels like a punishment. But in most cases, though withdrawal may be painful to the other spouse, it is not really punishment. Instead, it is giving up. When one spouse sees no hope in the future of the relationship, escaping into withdrawal seems the only choice possible. It's not abuse—it's escape.

States of Mind Are Contagious

These three states of mind—intimacy, conflict, and withdrawal—are not usually experienced by both spouses at the same time. But each spouse's state of mind can draw the other spouse into it.

In the state of intimacy, one spouse may inadvertently upset the other spouse enough to cause that spouse to enter the state of conflict. That's when complaints usually start. Quite frankly, if complaining would get negotiation started, the state of intimacy could be restored quickly. But when complaints don't get the job done and they turn into criticism, war is declared. As recriminations escalate for the spouse in the state of conflict, enough love units are lost to drag the other spouse from the state of intimacy into the state of conflict as well. And then both spouses behave negatively and selfishly.

> Each spouse's state of mind can draw the other spouse into it.

Typically, if they fail in their efforts to resolve their conflict, and if the unpleasant efforts of their Takers escalate, one spouse will usually escape into the state of withdrawal and raise his or her emotional barrier. The spouse that remains in the state of conflict may continue to argue for a while. Sometimes the arguing spouse can goad the withdrawn spouse back into the state of conflict, but it's more likely that the arguing spouse will simply give up and join the other spouse in the state of withdrawal. At that point, they are emotionally divorced.

The Road Back to Intimacy

Fortunately, for most couples, that's not where it ends. Someone eventually comes to his or her senses and realizes that emotional divorce is not really what they want. So they use their intelligence to dig themselves out of the hole where they find themselves. And their intelligence convinces them that they must ignore the advice of their Takers to be successful.

An apology, something the Taker would **never** want you to make, is one of the best ways to begin the trek back to intimacy. Whatever it was that each spouse did to drive the other into withdrawal should be acknowledged—usually something that was said during an argument while in the state of conflict—and a promise to avoid it in the future should be made. Furthermore, each spouse must also come to grips with what their original conflict was all about. What drove them from the state of intimacy to the state of conflict?

> An apology is one of the best ways to begin the trek back to intimacy.

In this book, I will teach you how to avoid the state of withdrawal entirely. When one of you is unhappy with the other's behavior, you will learn how to address the problem effectively, instead of arguing about it. But if you have not learned those lessons yet, and you find yourselves in the state of withdrawal, an apology is very appropriate.

The passage from intimacy through conflict to withdrawal can seem almost effortless to a couple. One day they're in a state of bliss, but before they know it, they're ready to divorce. On the other hand it takes quite a bit of work to climb back up that hill. While it's true that one of you can pull the other one back up, it's a whole lot easier when you're both working together.

Preventing the Taker from Taking Over

Whenever you feel neglected by your spouse, feel that your spouse is treating you unfairly, or feel that your spouse is being abusive, you are likely to be in the state of conflict. And that means you will instinctively follow the Taker's rule: *Do whatever you can to make yourself happy, and avoid anything that makes you unhappy, even if it makes your spouse unhappy.*

Instead of bargaining fairly with your spouse, discussing alternatives, and trying to take your spouse's feelings into account as you negotiate to fix the problem, you will try to impose *your* solution on your spouse. You will try to make your spouse do things your way,

> If you want a happy marriage, you must be able to discuss your conflicts safely and enjoyably.

whether he or she likes it or not. And it will seem like the right thing to do—after all, it's your Taker's natural instinct—but it's abusive.

Take my word for it: if you want a happy marriage, you must not do what is instinctive. Instead, you must be able to discuss your conflicts safely and enjoyably, with each other's interests in mind. The Taker's instinctive approach will prevent you from having what you need in your marriage—a loving and caring relationship.

The Taker's rule ruins *any* relationship because it is totally self-serving. But in marriage it is particularly devastating because escape from its negative consequences is so difficult. As I mentioned in the last chapter, if your spouse cannot avoid your constant withdrawal of love units, eventually he or she will hate you. Instead of seeing your spouse's loving and caring Giver every morning, you will draw out the very worst in your spouse.

"But what about me?" you may ask. "My spouse is drawing out the worst in me!"

That may be true, but the solution to the problem is not to return fire with fire. If you want to return to intimacy, you must avoid following the Taker's rule at all costs, even when you are being mistreated. It means overriding your instincts with your intelligence. And if you achieve that objective, you will have overcome abuse.

In the next three chapters I will help you avoid the Taker's favorite approaches to problem-solving—selfish demands, disrespectful judgments, and angry outbursts. Each of them follow logically from the Taker's rule, and they are each a form of marital abuse. Instead of using those flawed strategies, I will help you negotiate fairly, especially when you find yourself in the state of conflict.

Key Principles

Abuse is the deliberate effort of one spouse to cause the other to be unhappy. It hurts your spouse in two ways: by the act itself and by the knowledge that it was deliberate.

The three abusive strategies to get your way in marriage are selfish demands, disrespectful judgments, and angry outbursts.

The **Giver** and **Taker** (Basic Concept #7) are the two conflicting parts of our personality. The Giver is the part of our personality that is concerned only about the happiness of others. The Taker is the part of our personality that is concerned only about the happiness of ourselves.

Marriage is one of the very few conditions in life that bring out the pure Giver and Taker in each of us, and that makes marital negotiation very difficult because neither part of our personality knows how to negotiate.

There are Three States of Mind in Marriage (Basic Concept #8) that prevent fair negotiation. **Intimacy** is the state of mind dominated by your Giver that encourages you to give unconditionally. **Conflict** is the state of mind dominated by your Taker that encourages you to take unconditionally. Abuse tends to take place when you are in this state of mind. **Withdrawal** is the state of mind dominated by your Taker that encourages you to withdraw emotionally from your spouse, neither giving nor taking.

In marriage it is very easy to fall from intimacy to conflict to withdrawal. But it is difficult to climb back from withdrawal to conflict to intimacy. Withdrawal, however, *can* be avoided if a couple resolves their conflicts through negotiation instead of fighting.

Consider This...

1. How do I define marital abuse? The problem with my definition is that the person doing the abusing rarely acknowledges that it's **deliberate**. So when one of you does something that hurts the other, you can hide behind the excuse that it was unintentional. Has this issue ever come up in your marriage? I'll make it easier for you to understand why demands, disrespectful judgments, and angry outbursts are deliberately hurtful in the next three chapters.

2. Have you been able to identify the Giver and Taker in each of you? Some couples give each other two names when they

discover these two entirely different personalities. Have you ever done that?

3. The rules of the Giver and Taker define the way they approach conflicts in marriage. What are those rules, and how do they influence the way you try to resolve your conflicts?

4. What are the three states of mind in marriage? Can you identify them in yourself? When was the last time you were in the state of intimacy? The state of conflict? The state of withdrawal?

5. Has either of you ever felt abused by the other? Have you noticed how difficult it is to discuss the problem? If so, that's because you are usually in the state of conflict when the problem arises. The Taker's rule dominates your discussion, and your instincts discourage you from trying to stop your abuse or even acknowledge it. And you are certainly not willing to apologize. In fact, the discussion itself is likely to turn abusive. Yet, if you ever want to solve problems in your marriage, you must eliminate all abuse. If you are committed to stop being an abusive spouse once and for all, follow the advice I offer you in the next three chapters.

Part 2

The Six
LOVE BUSTERS

3

SELFISH DEMANDS

Who Wants to Live with a Dictator?

In an effort to provide for his new family, Jim spent so much time at work that he had neglected to meet Karen's emotional needs (see the illustration of Jim and Karen's marriage in chapter 1). It was an innocent mistake, but it led to her loss of love for him, which, in turn, caused her to lose interest in sex. That was a serious problem for Jim, and he didn't know how to solve it.

Karen didn't help. Instead of telling him what was bothering her, she claimed not to understand the problem herself. In response to his frustration, Jim made an almost fatal mistake—he demanded sex. As a result of this fateful course of action, his relationship with Karen took such a nosedive that it almost crashed. His demand for sex not only failed to address their underlying problems, but it eventually brought their lovemaking to a complete stop.

Jim and Karen's struggle with sex is fairly common in marriage. But you may have difficulty relating to it, because your sexual relationship may be okay. So let's look at another situation that also illustrates the inappropriateness of demands in marriage. You may have experienced something similar to this—possibly last week.

Imagine yourself cleaning up after dinner with your kitchen a mess, your kids running wild, and your husband watching TV (if you are a husband, imagine how you might feel being the wife in this situation). You are feeling very neglected and wonder how he could sit there so oblivious to your need for help. At the very least, you think, he could offer to calm the children down or dry the dishes. But instead he is just sitting there while a myriad of things need to be done.

Selfish Demands
Commanding your spouse to do things that would benefit you at your spouse's expense.

Out of utter frustration, you walk up to the TV, turn it off, point your finger at your spouse, and say, "I'm giving you a choice: you can either watch the children for me or you can clean up the kitchen, but you are *not* watching television."

If you can identify with this situation, you might consider this approach to the problem both courageous and wise. By taking control, the job will get done and the husband will be doing something that he should have volunteered to do in the first place, you might reason. But if you have ever been on the receiving end of such a demand, you can probably see the fly in this ointment.

Demands Seem Reasonable

If you're in the habit of making demands of your spouse, it's not surprising. Demands seem reasonable when we're frustrated. And most spouses make demands unless they're taught to avoid them. That's because the Taker within all of us encourages us to use demands as a way to solve a problem, especially in marriage. Remember the Taker's rule: ***Do whatever you can to make yourself happy even if it makes your spouse unhappy.*** With that rule in mind, demands make sense.

It begins when you're in the state of conflict. You are frustrated about something, and your Taker comes to the rescue. It wants you to be happy, even if it's at your spouse's expense. So it encourages you to take the direct approach—demand "cooperation." If your spouse happens to be in the state of intimacy at the time, with his or her Giver in charge, your Taker gets whatever it wants without a bit of resistance.

That's one of the main reasons that demands are so common in marriage

> Demands seem reasonable when we're frustrated.

and less common in all other relationships. In marriage your spouse is more likely to submit to demands, at least when he or she is in the state of intimacy. So demands are rewarded often enough in marriage to be commonplace. Your spouse is unintentionally encouraging you to make demands whenever he or she obeys.

Then, because you can get away with demands once in a while, you are at risk of developing the habit of making them, even when you are in the state of intimacy yourself. Your Giver usually tries to discourage demands when it is in charge. But if you make them often enough when you are in the state of conflict, they become an almost unstoppable habit.

Think for a moment how you and your spouse ask each other for favors. Do you tell each other what to do, as if one of you is a sergeant and the other a private? Do you order each other around when something needs to be done? If so, you're in the habit of making demands, even when you are feeling very close to each other and your Givers should be in charge. It's an insidious habit that, if left to run amok, can destroy your ability to solve even the simplest problems in marriage.

Demands can become a bad habit when you're in the state of intimacy. But they're an instinct when you're in the state of conflict. As soon as children begin to talk, demands become part of their vocabulary when they're frustrated. They must be taught by their parents to make requests rather than demands, regardless of how frustrated they may be. But in marriage, all of that training seems to go down the drain when the Taker is in charge. Even though you probably don't demand things of any adult other than your spouse, you assume that it's okay to do in your marriage. You don't see the damage that it does. And even if you know, deep down, that your spouse doesn't like your demands, you may not know any other way to communicate your frustration.

I've already mentioned that when demands are made to a spouse in the state of intimacy, the Giver will usually cave in without complaining. But if your spouse is in the state of conflict when you make a demand, your spouse's Taker will respond with resistance. Instead of finding a patsy to command, you find yourself battling your spouse's angry Taker, who feels it's about time that you stopped bossing him or her around. A fight ensues, and . . . well, I'm sure you've had that experience.

But fights won't stop you from making demands in the future. Your Taker keeps telling you that you have every right to make demands, even if they don't work.

Demands Are Abusive and Controlling

Remember our definition of abuse? *Deliberate effort of one spouse to cause the other to be unhappy.* That's **not** how most spouses interpret their demands. They don't think they're trying to make their spouse unhappy. They think that they're trying to make their spouse do the right thing. And a spouse shouldn't feel unhappy about doing what's right.

When Jim demanded sex of Karen, he wanted her to fulfill her responsibilities to him. But he didn't view his demand as a deliberate effort to make her unhappy. He wanted her to enjoy making love. From her perspective, however, the demand turned lovemaking into rape. She was forced to make love to him, and it definitely made her very unhappy.

To a much lesser extent, a wife's demand for help in the kitchen after dinner makes a husband unhappy. None of us wants to be bossed around, even when it means helping someone we love. A request is a different matter entirely. It assumes that the granting of the request is a special favor, and should be appreciated when it's given. There's nothing unpleasant about that. It's only when one spouse is **forced** to do something for the other that they feel abused and controlled.

And yet, it seems so unnatural to **request** help, when you feel so certain that you should **demand** it. Your frustration begins on your ride home from work. You are exhausted from a full day of preparing insurance claims, yet you face an evening of even more work caring for your husband and children.

"Why should you be responsible for all this work?" your Taker whispers in your ear. "Your husband sure has it easy. He doesn't work nearly as hard as you do and when he gets home from work he expects you to do everything. He spends a leisurely evening at home while you're working yourself to exhaustion. Is that fair?"

Upon arrival at home your Taker keeps up the chatter. "Your husband isn't even telling you when he's going to come home from work.

He expects you to have dinner ready for him. He expects the kids to be cared for and he doesn't even have the decency to call you and let you know when he's coming home."

When your husband arrives home, he says "hi" to the kids that come rushing to him at the door. And instead of acknowledging you right away, he turns on the television. Eventually he gets around to greeting you and gives you a peck on the cheek.

Your Taker responds, "Is that the only reward he can think of for all the work you've done? Hey, he's expecting you to be his slave!"

Your Giver may step in once and a while and argue on behalf of her husband. "He's had a hard day, too. He needs to relax." But no sooner does your Giver get the words out than your Taker pushes your Giver away and counters, "Are you nuts? This guy's been relaxing all day. You're the one that needs to relax, not him."

Remember what I said in the last chapter about the relative strength of the Giver and Taker. The happier you are, the stronger your Giver becomes, but the more frustrated you are, the stronger your Taker becomes. So if you were to find yourself in the situation I've been describing, your Giver would not have much of a chance to argue on behalf of your husband because it would be relatively weak. Your Taker's arguments, however, would be deafening.

I agree with the Taker that it's not fair for you to do all the work at home after a hard day at the office. Your Taker's goal, that you should be relieved of some of these responsibilities, is reasonable. But I object to the Taker's way of solving the problem. The Taker wants you to take control and demand a change. In other words, it wants to solve the problem in a controlling and abusive way, one that does not take your husband's feelings into account. That's because it doesn't care how your husband feels any more than your Giver cares about how you feel. The Taker's solution isn't any fairer than the Giver's solution that you do all the work yourself.

But wait a minute, you might be thinking. *The wife is not demanding that the husband do all the work. She is demanding that he share in the work, which is his responsibility. She will still be doing her fair share.*

I sympathize with that reasoning. But in spite of her reasonable goal, her tactics are abusive. She gives her husband no choice. Her Taker may think that her solution is fair because it works for her. But it's only fair when both of their Takers think it's fair. Her Taker is in no position to evaluate her husband's interests—they can be evaluated only by his Taker, and it has not been consulted. The alternatives that have been presented, watching the children or drying the dishes, are created by *her* Taker to relieve *her* burden. But there has been no discussion with her husband to understand his perspective. And when it comes to fairness, you can't ever trust the advice of only one of your Takers.

> A fair solution to any marital problem must take both of you into account.

A fair solution to any marital problem must take both of you into account. You must somehow solve the problem of who does what after work in a way that makes you both happy. That solution is the one that is most likely to become a habit, and once it does, it will reinforce your love for each other. The solution will help deposit love units into both of your Love Banks.

On the other hand, if your solution makes one of you unhappy, it won't work in the long run, and it will erode the love that the unhappy spouse has for the other. And even the spouse who gets his or her way by making demands will not be happy in the long run because of the effort it takes to force the other spouse to get the job done. If you want to be in love and stay in love, it makes a lot more sense to create a lifestyle that works well for both of you.

Use the Policy of Joint Agreement (Basic Concept #6) to Find Fair Solutions

To help you and your spouse make fair decisions, I encourage you to follow a policy I created with that goal in mind. I call it the **Policy of Joint Agreement**: *Never do anything without an enthusiastic agreement between you and your spouse*. Let me repeat that policy to you with emphasis. Never do **anything** without an **enthusiastic** agreement between you and your spouse. The purpose of this policy is to remind you that (1) everything you do affects each other either positively or negatively, and (2) if you want to deposit love units instead of withdrawing them, you must consider how every choice will affect both of you. Will it deposit love units or withdraw them? By waiting until you discover win-win resolutions to your conflicts, you keep your Love Banks full, and you stay in love with each other.

But the Policy of Joint Agreement does more than help keep your relationship passionate. It helps you make wise and fair decisions. By taking both of your perspectives into account, you expand your ability to do the right thing. Your joint wisdom comes together to give you added brain-power—if you respect each other's judgment. When you become skilled in using this rule, your financial decisions, career decisions, child-rearing decisions, and even decisions that affect your sexual relationship will be smarter and much more effective in helping you achieve your goals in life.

The Policy of Joint Agreement

Never do anything without an enthusiastic agreement between you and your spouse.

The Policy of Joint Agreement usually makes sense to the one on the receiving end of a selfish demand. When one spouse makes a demand without considering the feelings of the other, it's easy for that other spouse to see the problem. But the demanding spouse usually believes that he or she is doing the right thing. That's because we can't feel the effect we're having on each other in marriage. We're not plugged into each other's brains. The only thing we know for certain is how our spouse is affecting us. That's why couples need a special rule to force them to share information with each other regarding how they are being affected. The Policy of Joint Agreement is that rule.

Before you make a decision, you should ask your spouse, "How would you feel about this?" If your spouse's response is an enthusiastic "Yes!" it means that the decision you make is not only going to be good for you, it's going to be good for your spouse, too. It's a decision that will deposit love units in *both* of your Love Banks simultaneously.

In my example of the exhausted wife and the television-watching husband, there are a host of decisions that have to be made about what they do between four o'clock in the afternoon and seven o'clock in the evening. Clearly, the Policy of Joint Agreement has not been applied to this part of their day, or it would not be turning out the way it does. And as a result, neither the husband nor the wife is depositing very many love units in each other's Love Banks. The husband is making withdrawals from the wife's Love Bank because of his habit of watching TV when he comes home each evening. But the wife is also making withdrawals from the husband's Love Bank by being so upset whenever she comes home to face all the extra work. She's certainly no treat to be around at the end of the day.

The point I want to make as clearly as possible is that while this couple need to change what they do after work, demands will not lead to a mutually satisfying solution. They lead to a solution where one person tries to gain at the other's expense. From the wife's perspective, turning the TV off and getting the husband to help a little is a fair solution to the problem. But the husband's Taker doesn't see things the same way. In fact, the husband regards his wife's demands as controlling and abusive. In the actual case from which I took this example, he left the house and went back to work, with his wife in tears as he left.

After counseling thousands of couples, I don't know of a single example where demands have created the ultimate solution to a problem. Instead of leading to a solution, demands lead to resentment, and in some cases they may develop a very negative emotional reaction to the very thought of it. Psychologists call it an ***aversive reaction***. It often takes the form of a very sick feeling in the pit of the stomach whenever there are thoughts about having to do something that's been associated with pain or suffering.

That's what happened to Karen when she tried to meet Jim's demand for sex. She developed an aversion to sex, and eventually they didn't have any sex at all. Karen was not only resentful that Jim would force her to have sex with him, but she also developed an emotional reaction to sex that made it an absolute nightmare for her. Her husband's demand for sex actually made it **less** likely that Karen would meet his sexual need.

So even when a selfish demand seems to work in the short run and you get your way, it usually makes it more difficult for you to get your way in the long run. It would have been better to never make the demand in the first place, because whatever it is you're trying to get your spouse to do will now evoke a negative reaction. It will make it less likely for your spouse to do it next time.

I want you to be able to get what you need in your marriage and I want you and your spouse to be in love with each other. But you'll fail to do either of these things if you're in the habit of making demands. You won't have your needs met and you won't be in love.

Government 101

When a husband and wife first marry, and are still in love with each other, they tend to make decisions the right way by taking each other's feelings into account. The Policy of Joint Agreement tends to reign for a while, even though most couples are unaware that they are following it. Intimate conversation builds understanding and that, in turn, helps make decisions mutually advantageous.

But it doesn't take long before the pressures of life make it tempting to scrap bilateral decisions in favor of unilateral decisions. Instead of negotiating to reach mutually acceptable solutions to problems one spouse, usually the husband, decides that he must make the "final" decisions. He begins to use the Dictator Strategy. This strategy assumes that a spouse has the right, wisdom, and compassion to make decisions correctly. While the other spouse can lobby to have him take their interests into account, when a decision is made, it's final.

Selfish demands prevail when the dictator strategy is in force. If one spouse tells the other what to do, without having come to an agreement first, he or she is making a selfish demand and is using the dictator strategy which makes the loss of love almost inevitable.

Dictators haven't been known to be particularly wise or compassionate. They tend to make decisions in their own interest and at the expense of their citizens. And the same thing happens in marriage. When one spouse is given the right to make all final decisions, the other spouse usually suffers. And their love suffers.

If this strategy is left unchecked, a wife finds herself dominated by a dictator rather than a partner in a marriage. Some women settled for the dictator strategy decades ago. But few would today. And they shouldn't. The practice of a husband making unilateral decisions proves to his wife that he really doesn't care about anyone but himself.

And the problem only gets worse from there.

I have heard many young wives complain about their husband's decisions to come and go as he pleases, make his own friends, stay out late without letting her know where he is, and other thoughtless acts. All while she is obligated to stay home in the evenings with their children, cook and clean, and be available to him for sex whenever needed.

But before long the Taker in these women starts to put up a fight. "If he doesn't care about me, why should I care about him?" they reason.

So they create the Dueling Dictators Strategy. As resentment grows, the subordinate spouse decides to stage a coup, raising both spouses to dictator status.

Then guess what happens when these two spouses disagree? It's an all-out war, with each side looking after their own interests. After the dust settles, the stronger and more determined spouse wins the decision, which means that his or her solution is put into effect. But the losing dictator is already plotting more carefully for the next battle.

Unfortunately, millions of unhappy couples use the Dueling Dictators Strategy. It makes problem solving unpleasant for all involved, but at least it seems fairer than the Dictator Strategy. After all, no one loses all the time with this strategy. Now, instead of one spouse being victimized, both spouses are victimized!

At this point marriage becomes miserable. And couples that experience this often feel as if they have only two choices. They can either divorce or create a marriage of convenience. To continue in misery is simply not an option.

Those who choose a marriage of convenience begin to use what I call the Anarchy Strategy. This strategy gives up hope of resolving conflict and takes the position, "every man for himself!" A husband, wife, or sometimes both, just do whatever they want and refuse to do anything that their spouse wants. When the Dueling Dictators Strategy fails, couples grasp at anarchy as their last resort. But just like countries in anarchy, anarchic marriages become chaotic and soon fall apart. Ultimately, most of these couples eventually divorce as well.

But there is another way for couples to handle conflict—a way that doesn't destroy their love for each other and doesn't lead to divorce. It's the Democracy Strategy, where husbands and wives don't make a decision until they're both in agreement. The Democracy Strategy for marital conflict requires unanimous consent. Neither spouse can impose their will on the other.

Unlike all the other strategies we've seen, the Democracy Strategy addresses conflicts and resolves them with no victims. The outcome of every decision is in the best interest of both spouses.

So why isn't the Democracy Strategy used in all, or even most, marriages? It's because we are not born with an instinct for democracy. Instead, we're born with an instinct to get our way at any cost. That attitude puts the Dictator Strategy into play in most marriages. And once that happens, the Dueling Dictator and Anarchy Strategies are often not far behind.

The Democracy Strategy will not seem as natural to you as the others—it requires time and thought. But it's the only sensible way for you to make marital decisions. It not only provides wise solutions to your problems, but it will also draw you much closer to each other emotionally. And that's a basic requirement for every romantic relationship.

The Policy of Joint Agreement makes the Democracy Strategy possible. It gives both spouses equal power and control over the choices that are to be made. *Never do anything without an enthusiastic agreement between you and your spouse.* That simple rule forces you to find a mutually acceptable solution before any action is taken. And how do you find that solution? It's through the fine art of negotiation.

Negotiators, Take Your Places

Democracy isn't easy. And neither is marital negotiation. But for civilization and marriage alike, the rewards found in considering the interests of others are well worth the added effort. So how do you reach an enthusiastic agreement when you and your spouse face a conflict?

The most important first step that you must both take is to accept the Policy of Joint Agreement as the rule you will live by for the rest of your lives together. It helps create the question, "How do you feel about what I'd like you to do?" Without that question, you'll find yourself making unilateral decisions that will ultimately lead to a miserable marriage or divorce.

When the question is asked, and you receive a negative response, the Policy of Joint Agreement offers you two choices: Either abandon the idea or try to discover alternative ways of making it possible—with your spouse's enthusiastic agreement. That's where negotiation begins!

With practice, you and your spouse can become experts at getting what you need in ways that create mutual, enthusiastic agreement. Once you agree to this policy, fair negotiation will become a way of life for you. And you'll also be forced to abandon demands. Since they can't possibly create enthusiastic agreement from your spouse, you'll replace selfish demands with thoughtful requests.

Does this all sound impossible to you? Maybe you're so used to making unilateral decisions that you've never really considered your spouse's feelings. But trust me, if you practice following the Policy of Joint Agreement, you'll get used to asking, "How do you feel about what I'd like you to do (or what I'd like to do)?" The policy forces you to be considerate and to understand each other's concerns. And that will bring you a giant step forward in your ability to negotiate.

At first, asking the question "How would you feel?" will seem very strange to you, and even humorous. That's to be expected—because your instincts and our culture don't encourage you to think in those terms. Yet that question is at the very core of every fair negotiation in life, and you must force yourselves to ask it until it becomes a habit.

Basic Concept #10: The Four Guidelines for Successful Negotiation in Marriage

I may have convinced you that the Policy of Joint Agreement is a wise goal for marriage—if it can be achieved. But you may feel that it's not achievable in your marriage. "My spouse wouldn't agree with me about almost anything," you may be thinking. "And even if there were agreement, it certainly wouldn't be very enthusiastic."

So after I've given you this important rule, I must go one step further and give you a method to achieve it. I call this method the Four Guidelines for Successful Negotiation in Marriage. It's a step-by-step procedure used by almost all successful negotiators. And if you learn how to use it in your marriage, you'll avoid dictators and anarchy and will instead reach solutions to your problems that satisfy both of you. First, I'll describe these guidelines to you, and then I'll apply them to the problem of Selfish Demands.

Guideline 1: Set ground rules to make negotiation pleasant and safe.

Most couples view marital negotiation as a trip to the torture chamber. That's because their efforts are usually fruitless, and they come away from the experience battered and bruised. Who wants to negotiate when you have nothing but disappointment and pain to look forward to?

So before you begin to negotiate, set some basic ground rules to make sure that you both enjoy the experience. Since you should negotiate as often as conflict arises, it should always be an enjoyable and safe experience for you both. I suggest three basic ground rules:

Ground Rule 1: Try to be pleasant and cheerful throughout negotiations. It's fairly easy to start discussing an issue while in a good mood. But negotiations can open a can of worms and create negative emotional reactions. Your spouse may begin to feel uncomfortable about something you say. In fact, out of the blue, he or she may inform you that there will be no further discussion.

I know how upset and defensive couples can become when they first tell each other how they feel. So I tell them what I'm telling you—try to be as positive and cheerful as you can be, especially if your spouse says something that offends you.

Ground Rule 2: Put safety first—do not make demands, show disrespect, or become angry when you negotiate, even if your spouse does. Once the cat is out of the bag and you've told each other what you'd like to do, or what's bothering you, you've entered one of the most dangerous phases of negotiation. If your feelings have been hurt, you're tempted to retaliate. And unless you make a special effort to resist demands, disrespect, and anger, you will revert to the Dictator Strategy, and your negotiation will turn into an argument. But if you can keep each other safe, you'll be able to use your intelligence to help you make the changes you both need.

Ground Rule 3: If you reach an impasse where you do not seem to be getting anywhere, or if one of you is starting to make demands, show disrespect, or become angry, stop negotiating and come back to the issue later. Just because you can't resolve a problem at a particular point in time doesn't mean you can't find an intelligent solution in the future. Don't let an impasse prevent you from giving yourself a chance to think about the issue. Let it incubate for a while, and you'll be amazed what your mind can do.

If your negotiation turns sour, and one of you succumbs to the temptation of becoming a dictator (using demands, disrespect, or anger), end the discussion by changing the subject to something more pleasant. After a brief pause, the offending spouse may apologize and wish to return to the subject that was so upsetting. But don't go back into the minefield until it has been swept clear of mines.

Guideline 2: Identify the problem from both perspectives.

Once you've set ground rules that guarantee a safe and enjoyable discussion, you're ready to negotiate. But where do you begin? First, you must state the problem and then try to understand it from the perspectives of both you and your spouse.

Most couples go into marital negotiation without doing their homework. They don't fully understand the problem itself, nor do they understand each other's perspectives. In many cases, they aren't even sure what they really want.

Respect is the key to success in this phase of negotiation. Once the problem has been identified, and you hear each other's perspectives, it's extremely important to try to understand each other instead of trying to straighten each other out. Remember that your goal is enthusiastic agreement, and that can't happen if you reject each other's perspectives. The only way you'll reach an enthusiastic agreement is to come up with a solution that accommodates both perspectives as they are presented.

This point is so important that I will repeat it. You will not solve your problem if you are disrespectful of each other's opinions. In this second stage of negotiation, you are simply to gather information that will help you understand what it will take to solve your problem. If you reject your spouse's opinions, you will be ignoring the facts. You should not talk over your spouse, try to talk your spouse out of his or her opinion, or even use mannerisms that could be interpreted as disrespectful.

It's so much easier to negotiate the right way when your goal is enthusiastic agreement. It eliminates all the strategies that attempt to wear each other down with abuse. But when I take demands away from some couples, they are left feeling naked. They feel helpless about resolving an issue without this tool. They're so used to being dictators that they simply don't know how to find win-win solutions to problems.

Is that how you and your spouse feel? If so, remember that with practice you'll begin to feel more comfortable approaching every conflict with the goal of mutual agreement. You'll learn to ask each other questions, not to embarrass each other but to gain a fuller understanding of what it would take to make each other happy. And when you think you have the information you need to consider win-win solutions, you're ready for the next step.

> You will not solve your problem if you are disrespectful of each other's opinions.

Guideline 3: Brainstorm with abandon.

You've set the ground rules. You've identified the problem and discovered each other's perspectives. Now you're ready for the creative part—looking for mutually acceptable solutions. I know that can seem impossible if you and your spouse have drifted into incompatibility. But the climb back to compatibility has to start somewhere, and if you put your minds to it, you'll think of options that please you both.

Many well-intentioned but sadly misguided marital therapists recommend sacrifice in marriage. But a little thought should expose that approach as being terribly flawed. After all, whoever does the sacrificing would suffer, and what caring couple wants that for each other? They want mutual enjoyment with neither one suffering. It's only when we let our selfish instincts get the best of us that we expect our spouse to sacrifice for us.

You won't get very far if you allow yourself to think, "If she really loves me, she'll let me do this," or "he'll do this for me, if he cares about me." Care in marriage is not sacrificial care—it's **mutual** care. That means both spouses want the other to be happy, and neither spouse wants the other to be unhappy. If you care about your spouse, you should never expect, or even accept, sacrifice as a solution to a problem.

A subtle form of sacrifice is the "I'll do it for you this time if you do what I want you to do next time" solution. But this isn't a win-win situation: One of you ends up unhappy whenever the other is happy. And if you've ever used this strategy, you may have noticed that your spouse doesn't always follow through with his or her end of the bargain.

Win-lose solutions are common in marriage because most couples don't understand how to arrive at win-win solutions. Their concept of fairness is that both spouses should suffer equally. But isn't it better to find solutions where neither spouse suffers? With a little creativity, you can find solutions that make both of you happy.

With sacrifice and suffering out of the question, you're ready to brainstorm. And at first, quantity is often more important than quality. So let your minds run wild; go with any thought that might satisfy both of you simultaneously. The best and most creative solutions often take time to discover, so carry a PDA or pad with you so you can jot down ideas as they come to you. When you let your creative juices flow, you are more likely to find a lasting solution.

Guideline 4: Choose the solution that meets the conditions of the Policy of Joint Agreement—mutual and enthusiastic agreement.

After brainstorming, you'll have both good and bad solutions. Good solutions are those both you and your spouse consider desirable. Bad solutions, on the other hand, take the feelings of one spouse into account at the expense of the other. The best solution is the one that makes you and your spouse most enthusiastic.

Many problems are relatively easy to solve if you know you must take each other's feelings into account. That's because you become aware of what it will take to reach a mutual agreement. Instead of considering options that clearly are not in your spouse's best interest, you think of options you know would make both you and your spouse happy.

If you follow the four guidelines I've suggested, negotiation can be an enjoyable way to learn about each other. And when you reach a solution that makes you both happy, you'll make substantial deposits into each other's Love Banks. In the end, the Policy of Joint Agreement not only helps you become a great negotiator, it also protects your love for each other.

But as you've been reading my guidelines for successful negotiation, you may be wondering if you have what it takes to build a lifetime of love. It may just seem like too much to remember. That's why I'll be repeating these guidelines throughout this book. I want you to have plenty of practice. With practice, any couple can do it. And once you establish the habit of negotiating with each other, it will be easy to run through the steps whenever there is a problem to solve. It's like learning to type. At first it seems impossible, but with practice, it seems almost instinctive.

If you and your spouse have found yourselves acting more like dictators than sweethearts, it may sound overwhelming to switch to successful negotiations. But the guidelines can be implemented almost effortlessly if you practice them. Any behavior can seem automatic when repeated often enough.

So let's go through these guidelines one more time. But this time I'll apply them specifically to the task of turning the Love Buster of selfish demands into thoughtful requests.

Turning Selfish Demands into Thoughtful Requests

People feel used when you show no consideration for their feelings. And your spouse is no exception. Even when your spouse has agreed to help you, he or she can come away feeling resentful if you start ordering him or her around. So when you want your spouse to do something for you, make a request, not a demand. The difference between the two is found in your concern for your spouse's feelings and your willingness to accept "no" for an answer, at least temporarily.

You are not the boss, and your spouse is not your slave. And yet you both need to help each other in a myriad of different ways. I want you to meet each other's needs and help each other, but I want you to learn to do it in ways that are not controlling or abusive. Instead, I want you to help each other with enthusiasm. And you can learn to do that if you turn your selfish demands into thoughtful requests.

> ## Thoughtful Requests
> *Asking your spouse to do something for you, with a willingness to withdraw it if there is reluctance. The request must be preceded by "How would you feel if you were to . . ."*

Guideline 1: Make your request safe and enjoyable.

Spouses are most likely to make demands at the moment of their greatest frustration. Their Taker is fully in charge and will not take "no" for an answer. That's no time to negotiate. My advice is to cool off before discussing the issue, because you'll get nowhere if your Taker's

ACTION STEP

Make your request safe and enjoyable.

in charge. Wait until you can guarantee safety to your spouse—no demands, no disrespect, and no anger—before you tackle the issue. And have a smile on your face when you introduce the problem.

Guideline 2: Explain what you want and ask how your spouse feels about doing it.

This second step makes your problem your spouse's problem, and it makes your spouse's concerns your problem. Suddenly the focus is not just on what you want, but also on how your partner feels. That's considerate; that's thoughtful. Now your spouse doesn't feel taken for granted. You have shown that his or her feelings matter to you.

In many cases, the thoughtful request itself will make your spouse enthusiastic about doing what you've asked. Your concern for his or her feelings deposits love units, and your spouse will want to make you happy. Besides, just knowing that you care makes the task more enjoyable.

But don't bask in this bliss too long, because it isn't always that simple. If thoughtful requests produced instant agreement, most of us would have given up demands long ago. Sometimes a spouse still finds the request unpleasant to fulfill. What then?

Guideline 3: If your spouse has a problem with your request, withdraw it in its present form and brainstorm alternatives that would be mutually acceptable.

ACTION STEP

Explain what you want and ask how your spouse feels about doing it.

Thoughtfulness is more than how you ask for something. If you really care about your spouse's feelings (as your thoughtful request indicates you do), you want him or her to *enjoy* doing what you've asked. You will not take "well, all right, I guess" for an answer. If your spouse balks at helping you, withdraw the request.

This third step will not be taken by anyone who believes his or her spouse owes favors, has a duty to meet needs, or must do what he or she is told. In other words, if you are controlling or abusive, you will not follow this step. But if you are not abusive, or if you want to stop being abusive, this step is crucial.

In counseling abusive spouses, I must first convince them that they do not have the *right* to make demands. Indeed, some assume that their wedding vows gave them this right. But we have already seen how demands choke the feelings of love.

Being considerate is not just a word game. It means behaving in a way that takes other people's feelings into account. If you suspect that your spouse will find it unpleasant to meet your request, you're being thoughtless if you persist.

> **ACTION STEP**
>
> If your spouse has a problem with your request, withdraw it in its present form and brainstorm alternatives that would be mutually acceptable.

This leaves many people in a quandary. They do not want to be thoughtless, but without demands, how can their basic emotional needs be met?

The answer is brainstorming. Simple solutions can be discovered without much thought or effort, but the complex solutions needed in marriage require incubation. To find the best solutions, you must think long and hard about a problem before your brain comes up with the wisest solutions. Many of the best solutions I've witnessed have occurred to spouses after they've slept on it for a night or two.

Guideline 4: Keep brainstorming until you find a solution that meets the conditions of the Policy of Joint Agreement.

Your spouse probably wants to help you—even when he or she initially refuses your request. It isn't the helping that's being refused—it's the form the help takes. If the requested task is unpleasant, there may be another way to get the job done that is enjoyable.

For example, if Jim wants Karen to help him clean out the garage, she may object because of his timing. Suppose she's been looking forward to spending that time on another project that's more important to her. After she declines his initial request, he may ask if she would be willing to help at some other time. It may turn out that she doesn't mind helping him the following weekend.

But what if she can't imagine *ever* helping him clean the garage? What if Karen sees that as Jim's job, and his alone?

65

This is where the Policy of Joint Agreement gets a workout. Jim must not demand his way, or even demand that Karen come up with an alternative to his original request. He should approach this discussion seeking a solution, and a way to find the solution, that Karen will enthusiastically agree to.

Let's take a closer look at the exhausted wife's dilemma. If she only expects to get the help she needs when she's exhausted, it's not likely that her husband will create the habits that will help her at times of greatest need. So if she really feels that she needs help with the dishes once in a while, it makes a lot of sense to go to the trouble of creating the habit of doing the dishes together every night in a way that would be enjoyable for both of them. That way when Tuesday night rolls around and she's exhausted, his help is a done deal. She gets what she needs because it's something they've already negotiated with each other and they're doing it in a way that doesn't require sacrifice from either of them.

ACTION STEP

Keep brainstorming until you find a solution that meets the conditions of the Policy of Joint Agreement.

The husband who's sitting there watching television while his exhausted wife is slaving away at the dishes isn't a lazy husband. He's a husband who is in the habit of watching television after dinner. This man could just as easily be in the habit of helping his wife with the dishes and enjoying it just as much as watching television. The problem is, when he's already in the habit of watching television, he's going to be very upset with a wife who simply turns the television off and demands that he start washing the dishes. That isn't the way to get the job done. It creates anger and resentment and you lose a lot of love units while those dishes are being dried.

But if you explain the need in a thoughtful way and get into the right habits, the evening that this husband and wife spend together with their children could be predictably enjoyable. That's because they've created it to be enjoyable for each other. They've thought it through and decided to do things for each other that they find enjoyable. And that enjoyable routine is repeated night after night.

Later in this book, I will focus attention on how to arrive at mutually enthusiastic agreements about the five most common conflicts in marriage (chapters 9–13). And I'll have plenty of examples of how couples have discovered solutions to these problems. But for now, I want you to understand that mutually enthusiastic agreements are not only a good way to get what you need in marriage, they are also the only way that is not controlling and abusive. If you want consistent help from each other, there is no better way to get it than through an enthusiastic agreement.

Keeping Your Requests Thoughtful

Let each other know when you drift from thoughtful requests back to selfish demands. And try not to react defensively when your spouse gives you such feedback. You may be surprised the first time your spouse reminds you that you are making a selfish demand. From your perspective, you were making a request, not a demand. But if you have been in the habit of making demands, you're likely to continue making them without even thinking. And only your spouse will be able to recognize the difference between a selfish demand that's disguised as a thoughtful request, and a genuine thoughtful request.

You may complain that you didn't mean to make a selfish demand, that you meant to make a thoughtful request. But that's not the point. The point is that your spouse has interpreted what you've asked for as a demand. Until your spouse starts interpreting what you ask as requests, you're going to have to work on not only your intent, but also your wording.

And don't make the mistake that many couples make where you begin arguing about whether something was or wasn't a selfish demand. As far as I'm concerned, whoever is making the request must convince the other spouse that it's not a demand. If the spouse receiving the request is completely honest, you're going to learn quite a bit about how to adjust to his or her feelings. And in so doing you're going to be in a great position to create a lifestyle that's full of passion for both of you.

Quite frankly, your effort to convert demands into requests is a great way to communicate what you need. As you both learn to accommodate each other's needs in ways that are enjoyable to both of you, you will eventually be in the habit of getting what you need most from each other voluntarily, instead of trying to do it in ways that are controlling and abusive. Ultimately you want to receive help without even having to ask. In other words, you want your spouse to form the *habit* of helping you (as you develop the habit of helping your spouse). Demands cannot accomplish this. Demands may get the job done in the present but they sabotage the future.

Demands are the strategy of your Taker, who doesn't care at all about the feelings of your spouse. But you care about your spouse, so don't follow the instincts of your Taker. Get into the habit of doing the intelligent and caring thing for each other. If you can eliminate selfish demands from your marriage, you'll have eliminated one of the most important reasons that couples fall out of love with each other.

Key Principles

If you command your spouse to do something for you that benefits you at your spouse's expense, you are guilty of making a **selfish demand**. Demands are usually your Taker's first approach to solving a problem.

Selfish demands are abusive and controlling, but they seem reasonable to make when you are frustrated because your Taker gives you all the justification you need to make demands.

Selfish demands are more common in marriage than in other relationships partly because your spouse's Giver will tend to grant whatever you ask or demand. To overcome the habit of selfish demands, your spouse should avoid meeting your demands even when he or she is encouraged to do so by the Giver.

A **thoughtful request** is asking your spouse to do something for you, with a willingness to withdraw the request if there is reluctance and to discuss alternatives that would also be in your spouse's best interest. A request should be preceded by "How would you feel if you were to . . ."

The **Policy of Joint Agreement** (Basic Concept #6)—never do anything without an enthusiastic agreement between you and your spouse—helps couples avoid selfish demands by forbidding decisions that are not mutually beneficial.

The best way for couples to discover mutually beneficial solutions to problems is to follow the **Four Guidelines for Successful Negotiation in Marriage** (Basic Concept #10).

Thoughtful requests will help you create habits that provide the care you need from each other. Selfish demands, on the other hand, will not lead to habits if they are granted—they may lead to aversive reactions.

You should have zero tolerance for selfish demands in your marriage.

Consider This...

1. What is the difference between a selfish demand and a thoughtful request? Have you been able to identify selfish demands in your marriage? When one of you makes a selfish demand does the other spouse bring it to his or her attention? What have the consequences of such feedback been? Do you tend to punish each other for complaining about demands, or do you appreciate the feedback?

2. What is the Policy of Joint Agreement? Why is it important for you to make decisions that take each other's feelings into account? Why is an enthusiastic agreement important? It's because I want you both to benefit from each agreement you make with each other that I require enthusiastic agreement. Do you agree with me?

3. What do each of you think of the Four Guidelines for Successful Negotiation in Marriage? Are you willing to practice using them just to see if they work for you? Can you see how useful they would be if you were to eliminate selfish demands?

4. Are you both willing to eliminate selfish demands and replace them with thoughtful requests? If you are in the habit of making demands, it will take practice to avoid them. I suggest that you each make a worksheet entitled, "Selfish Demands," so that whenever one of you feels the other has made a demand, you write it on your worksheet. Be sure to avoid arguing about whether or not you have made a demand. Remember, the one who feels it was a demand defines it. It's up to the one who made the

demand to learn to rephrase it so that it is regarded as a thought-ful request.

5. Make a second worksheet entitled, "Thoughtful Requests." Write down each instance of what you considered to be a thoughtful request. And make as many requests of each other as you want. The practice will do you good. But don't be disappointed if you are denied your request in the form in which it was presented. It will give you an opportunity to consider other options so your spouse can give you what you need in ways that follow the Policy of Joint Agreement.

6. How comfortable are you in making requests of each other? When spouses are in the habit of making selfish demands, they are often reluctant to make as many requests of each other as they should. They tend to use demands as a last resort to getting what they think they deserve, and forget about asking for what they simply need from each other. By learning how to make thoughtful requests, you will probably be asking for more, and receiving more from each other, than you did when you were making demands.

4

Disrespectful Judgments

Who Wants to Live with a Critic?

Linda was raised by parents who worked long hours but never seemed to get ahead. Poor educational background was the main reason for their low income—neither parent graduated from high school. But their large family—five children—was also a contributing factor. Linda, her three brothers, one sister, and their parents shared a small house and just about everything else throughout her childhood.

After graduating from high school, Linda found a job as a receptionist, which paid enough to support her. So at eighteen, she moved away from home, rented an apartment, bought her own car, and felt on top of the world.

Tom, a new executive, found Linda very attractive. At first, he just greeted her whenever he passed her desk, but the greetings turned into conversations and before long he was regularly having lunch with her. Eventually they fell in love.

Tom was well educated, having earned advanced degrees in both law and business administration. When he met Linda's family, he was im-

71

mediately accepted and respected by them all. Her father was especially pleased that she chose to date such an intelligent man.

At first, Tom had respect for Linda and her family as well. But as their romance developed, he began making critical remarks about the decisions made by members of her family. Then, occasionally, he began to criticize Linda's decisions. Since he was so well educated, she assumed in most instances that he was correct and she was wrong. It bothered her whenever he made these critical remarks, but it happened so seldom that it did not have much effect on her love for him.

Before long they were married, and after the honeymoon Tom and Linda returned to work as husband and wife. But their relationship at work changed the very first day: Linda found herself working with her worst critic, who also happened to be her husband.

Now that they were married, Tom would bring the smallest errors to her attention and coach her on improving her posture, telephone etiquette, and other office skills. She became increasingly unhappy at work and eventually decided to quit. She used the excuse of wanting to prepare for having children, but her real reason was to escape Tom's incessant criticism. Her income, after taxes, was not enough to make much of a difference in their standard of living anyway, since Tom earned enough to support them both. Besides, she was raised to value the role of a homemaker and full-time mother.

But as soon as she quit her job, she went from the frying pan into the fire. At home Tom became even more critical than he'd been at work. He expected her to develop a high level of homemaking skills and evaluated her work each day. Her performance rarely met his standards, so she just gave up. Before long, she was spending the day watching television and sleeping.

Since his lectures on homemaking didn't seem to help, Tom turned his attention to subjects of motivation and ambition. When he came home from work, Linda had to suffer through Tom's self-improvement courses. Their discussions became so one-sided that she eventually stopped trying to explain her point of view.

Tom rationalized his efforts to straighten Linda out as his way of caring for her. He would explain that he was doing her a favor by helping her overcome weaknesses. In the end, he told Linda, she would thank him for his "coaching."

The truth was that he was being controlling and abusive. He wanted things done his way, and he didn't really care how Linda felt about it. He was trying to turn her into his personal slave. But instead of simply making demands on her, he used a more sophisticated approach to abuse—he showed disrespect in an effort to shame her into doing what he wanted. He knew that his criticism was making her unhappy, but he did nothing to protect her. His "help" was causing her to become very depressed, and his lectures made massive Love Bank withdrawals. Before long she had lost her feeling of love for him.

Linda became so depressed that Tom decided she needed professional help. First, he made an appointment to speak with me alone, to determine my competence. Then, after I passed his test, he brought her with him to the second session and wanted to be included in the interview. But I asked to speak with Linda alone while he remained in the waiting room. Within two sessions, however, I had Tom join her—for marriage counseling.

Compassion or Abuse?

Have you ever tried to straighten out your spouse? Occasionally we're all tempted to do that sort of thing. At the time, we think we're doing our spouse a big favor, to lift him or her from the darkness of confusion into the light of our "superior perspective." We think that if our spouse would only follow our advice, he or she could avoid many of life's pitfalls.

Yet our effort to keep our spouse from making mistakes usually leads to a much bigger mistake, one that destroys the feeling of love. The mistake is called *disrespectful judgments.*

A disrespectful judgment occurs whenever someone tries to *impose* his or her way of thinking or way of doing things on someone else. If you ever try to force your spouse to accept your point of view or do something the way you want it done, you're asking for trouble.

> ## Disrespectful Judgments
> *Attempts to "straighten out" your spouse's attitudes, beliefs, and behavior by trying to impose your way of thinking through lecture, ridicule, threats, or other forceful means.*

Most of us feel that our judgment is correct. When we hear others express opposing views or doing something differently than the way we are accustomed to doing it, we often feel that their opinions and behavior will get them into trouble someday. If your spouse is disagreeing with you, you don't want him or her to suffer from the pain that this mistake will create. So you try to change your spouse's opinion.

But disrespectful judgments don't really come from our Giver's compassion for others—they come from our Taker's desire to help us get what we want. The Giver doesn't try to impose anything on people—it tries to accommodate people's opinions and behavior. It's the Taker that's unaccommodating and rigid, trying to get what's best for us at the expense of others. It tries to fool us (and our spouse) into thinking we're being compassionate when we try to straighten out our spouse. But disrespectful judgments are not compassionate at all—they're abusive.

Disrespectful Judgments—the Second Stage of Abuse and Control

When you want your spouse to do something for you, your Taker's first approach to the problem is to demand change. That's the first stage of abuse and control. Then, when demands don't work, disrespectful judgments are not far behind. It's a more sophisticated form of control, because it *seems* to be motivated by care rather than selfishness. With disrespectful judgments, the Taker tries to fool both you and your spouse into thinking that you're doing your spouse a favor.

If Tom had understood his true motives for trying to straighten out Linda, he would have known that he was trying to get his way at her expense. He wanted her to do things his way at work, and then when she quit, he wanted her to do things his way at home. The ruse of care was used to hide his Taker's controlling and abusive ways. Linda knew that whatever he was doing hurt her terribly, but she was duped into thinking it was somehow good for her.

Many spouses will see though the deception of the Taker, and when their spouse makes disrespectful judgments they know it's based on selfishness. For them, the Love Buster is exposed for what it is. But even if, like Linda, a spouse *is* deceived into thinking that disrespect is motivated by care, the result is the same—it destroys the feeling of love. That's because disrespect always hurts. Even though Linda believed that Tom was doing the right thing by trying to straighten her out, his disrespectful judgments still destroyed her love for him.

Ridicule Hurts, Too

Tom's efforts to straighten Linda out were not her only problem. Whenever she expressed an opinion, Tom tended to make fun of her. He thought her ideas were so stupid that they were funny, and told her so whenever she tried to express herself.

While disrespectful judgments are usually an effort to try to show that you're right and your spouse is wrong, sometimes in marriage the sole purpose of disrespect is entertainment. For some, whenever they ridicule their spouse, they're not trying to change his or her opinions or behavior, but rather using the situation as something to laugh at— something that they find funny.

When it comes right down to it, almost all humor is ridicule of one form or another. Most jokes are designed to point out the foolishness of people's thinking or behavior. But in marriage, making your spouse the butt of ridicule is extremely dangerous. Not only is it very hurtful to the one being ridiculed, but if you're not careful, the tables can be turned and the ridiculed spouse can return ridicule in a way that doubles the pain. Some spouses raise ridicule to an art form where they use every opportunity to make fun of each other. But it's not fun for the person being ridiculed. In fact, it usually makes massive Love Bank withdrawals.

> Almost all humor is ridicule of one form or another.

In marriage you have an opportunity to know each other's deepest secrets and greatest weaknesses. You know some of each other's most embarrassing moments, which leave both of you very vulnerable to each other's ridicule. It's extremely important for you to know each other so well that you thoroughly understand your weaknesses. But that creates a vulnerability and responsibility that's almost unprecedented in life. The price of learning each other's deepest secrets should be a guarantee never to use that information to hurt or try to make fun of each other.

I hope you're beginning to see what disrespectful judgments really are: an instinctive way to make your spouse feel miserable. Since you make Love Bank withdrawals whenever you offend your spouse, disrespect is a real Love Buster.

Disrespectful Judgments Don't Get the Job Done

Tom would have preferred using demands to get his way with Linda because it's the simplest way to control a spouse. But he found that after a while she resisted his demands. So he took the next step in trying to force her to do his bidding. When he told her to do something for him, and she questioned his reasons and motives, he gave her an explanation to try to convince her that he was right and she was wrong. And he did it in a disrespectful way.

When Tom told Linda that she was not cleaning their house to his standards, she would sometimes argue back that if he didn't like the way the house looked, he could try cleaning it himself for a while. So Tom's demands had to be reinforced—the Taker's way. He would explain that if she didn't keep the house clean to his standards, she was shirking her responsibility as a wife and mother. In other words, he tried to make her feel guilty about the way she performed her housekeeping duties.

Since this approach to marital problem solving is so common, and so instinctive, I want you to clearly recognize this fact—while disrespectful judgments may seem sensible at the time, they hurt the other person. And because they hurt, they're abusive.

But they're not only abusive, they're also stupid. They don't get the job done. At first, Linda tried a little harder to meet Tom's housekeeping standards, but she eventually gave up almost entirely. She didn't keep the house cleaner after Tom scolded her—she simply became depressed.

And yet, it's what every couple usually does when they have a fight. They make demands, and then back up the demands with disrespectful judgments. It's so instinctive that it may be difficult for you to understand the point I'm trying to make. But just think about your own fights for a moment. Have they gotten you anywhere? No. Are you happier after you rake each other over the coals? No.

And that's the point. Disrespectful judgments are abusive because they cause pain, they are controlling because they try to force your spouse into your way of thinking, and they're stupid because they don't work.

So, how should you get the job done? There is a way to get everything you need from each other. But first, you must completely eliminate your disrespectful judgments.

The Road to Recovery

When Linda became depressed, Tom assumed that she had not learned the lessons he tried to teach her, so he pressed them with even greater diligence. But the harder he pressed, the more depressed she became. He was so convinced he was right that he was oblivious to both the pain he was inflicting on her and the failure of his method.

The first time I spoke with Linda, she explained how unpleasant her life had become since she married Tom. She used to enjoy housework, and looked forward to raising children. But now that Tom expected her to become a professional home economist, a whole lifetime of failure loomed before her. Raising children no longer appealed to her, because it would only increase the ways that Tom could criticize her. She felt useless and trapped. And if that wasn't bad enough, her sexual attraction to Tom had disappeared entirely. Everything he expected of her, including lovemaking, had become repulsive.

In my session with Tom, I explained to him that, in his effort to help his wife, he'd overlooked her emotional reactions. Perhaps there was some value in his goals for her—we all want to improve—but his failure to consider her feelings made his advice useless. Instead of encouraging change, he caused her to become depressed.

Since there was a part of Tom's personality that cared a great deal for Linda and wanted her to be healthy and happy (his Giver), he was willing to test my theory. If she recovered from her depression, he was willing to make the changes permanent. By this time, even his Taker was looking for a new approach, because her depression was making Tom unhappy. Anything he could do to make her more cheerful would be in his best interest.

I focused attention on the way Tom and Linda made decisions. Until they came to my office, Tom tried to make many of Linda's decisions for her. And he rarely consulted her about her feelings on those issues. Linda had very little confidence in her own judgment, and the longer she'd been married, the more convinced she became that Tom was smarter— so she let him make decisions for her. But even if he were smarter, he was in no position to make decisions for her if her feelings and interests were not considered. And even then, if their problems were to be solved the right way, she would have to make her own decisions.

The more you understand your spouse's feelings and interests, the more you'll understand and appreciate why your spouse thinks and behaves the way he or she does. And the less likely it is that you'll be disrespectful in your efforts to change those attitudes and behavior.

If you show respect for your spouse's opinions and ways of doing things, you are in a position to motivate change. But the change must be seen as beneficial to your spouse. And it must be with your spouse's enthusiastic agreement. Sound familiar? It's the Policy of Joint Agreement as applied to changes in attitude and opinions. When enthusiastic agreement becomes your objective, disrespectful judgments turn into *respectful persuasion*.

Respectful Persuasion
Changing beliefs and opinions in ways that result in enthusiastic agreement.

In marriage, a husband and wife's differing perspectives and value systems can bring benefit to both. Each partner brings both wisdom and foolishness to the marriage. By respectfully discussing each person's beliefs and values, the couple has an opportunity to create a superior system. But the task must be approached with mutual respect if it is to work. Without that respect, the husband and wife cannot improve their values and behavior—and they will lose their love for each other.

Using the Policy of Joint Agreement to Create Respectful Persuasion

If Tom was to overcome disrespectful judgments, Linda had to become an equal partner in their decision making. He needed to understand and respect her perspective on each issue they faced, and give her equal power in coming to final decisions. They needed the Democracy Strategy in resolving their conflicts. So I offered Tom a plan that would help him respect Linda's opinions.

The plan began with the Policy of Joint Agreement: Never do anything without an enthusiastic agreement between you and your spouse.

This rule gave Tom and Linda a new perspective on their goal for making decisions. From then on, Tom could never force his way of thinking on her, because that would not result in her enthusiastic agreement. He could not shame her; he could not talk over her; he could not ridicule her. Those tactics might lead to a reluctant agreement, but not to an enthusiastic agreement. If he wanted to change her mind or behavior, he had to *respectfully persuade* her, because that's the only method that had any hope of leading to an enthusiastic change of mind.

Up to the day Tom was introduced to the Policy of Joint Agreement, he rarely discussed his plans with Linda and didn't feel he needed her approval. He believed he was being thoughtful when he merely told her what he was doing, and when he bothered to get Linda's reluctant agreement to his plans, he felt he was going the extra mile.

But from that day forward, everything Tom did had to meet with Linda's *enthusiastic* agreement. I knew he'd find the rule incredibly difficult to follow at first, and I expected him to make many mistakes. But it would set him on a course that would eventually lead Linda out of her depression and would ultimately save their marriage.

After Tom and Linda agreed to follow the Policy of Joint Agreement, we focused attention on the details of their joint decision-making. To get an enthusiastic agreement with Linda, Tom had to learn to treat her opinions and behavior with respect. At the same time, Linda needed help in developing a higher regard for her own perspective and feelings.

Four Guidelines to Respectful Persuasion

After Tom and Linda had agreed on their goal, enthusiastic agreement, they were ready to learn the procedure that would achieve that goal: **The Four Guidelines to Respectful Persuasion.** You'll notice that these guidelines mirror the Four Guidelines to Successful Negotiation that I introduced in the last chapter.

Guideline 1: Make your discussion safe and enjoyable.

If you want your spouse to be open to new ideas, the last thing you want is defensiveness on his or her part. And the best way to overcome defensiveness is to eliminate any reason to be defensive. In the past,

ACTION STEP

Make your discussion safe and enjoyable.

Linda had experienced demands, disrespectful judgments, and occasional angry outbursts whenever Tom had tried to change her opinions. So it would take her a while to fully trust him to make their conversations safe. My advice to her was that if she felt any pressure from him to agree, or if he did anything to make their conversation unpleasant, then she had the right to end the discussion at that point. Tom made every effort to make Linda feel comfortable when they talked to each other so that she would not feel pressured by him.

Guideline 2: Express your conflicting opinions to each other with respect and understanding.

When you have a conflict of opinion, can you clearly explain *your spouse's* opinion as well as you can explain your own? Many needless arguments arise because spouses misunderstand each other.

Unless you can state your spouse's opinion clearly and succinctly, your spouse will either keep trying to explain it to you, or give up. So you should make it clear that you understand and respect each other's opinion. If you don't achieve that objective, there's no point in continuing your discussion, because you will fail in coming to an enthusiastic agreement.

ACTION STEP

Express your conflicting opinions to each other with respect and understanding.

But how can you respect an opinion you don't agree with? you might ask. The answer to that question is at the crux of understanding the skill of persuasion. There's a huge difference between respect for an opposing opinion, and acceptance of that opinion. It's not only possible, but it's essential to respect an opinion that you wish to change. Disrespecting an opposing opinion gives the impression that you don't understand it and don't *want to* understand it. In contrast, if you demonstrate that you do see the value of that opinion in certain situations but still see the need for change, your conflicting opinion will carry more weight.

Being able to state *your own* position clearly is also crucial in helping your spouse understand your motives and true objectives. For example, if I want my wife to wear her seat belt, I might tell her that I care about her safety and it makes me nervous when she drives without being buckled up. This type of explanation helps her understand the emotional reasons behind my opinion.

In response to my concern for her welfare, she may explain to me that she doesn't wear a seat belt because it makes her feel confined and wrinkles her clothes. Explaining her position in emotional terms takes the issue away from a philosophical debate. It turns out that she is not opposed to people wearing seat belts. In fact she believes it is a good idea to wear them. She just doesn't feel it's necessary for *her.*

In this example, we are not in disagreement over the principle itself. We merely disagree over the application of the principle to my wife's behavior.

In fact most arguments are like this—not rooted in different beliefs but in differing *emotional reactions* to the application of beliefs. If Joyce *feels* uncomfortable when she wears seat belts, she will tend not to wear them.

If I tell her to wear seat belts I lose love units because she doesn't like to be told what to do. Then, if I tell her that she is wrong to avoid wearing them, I lose more love units. Instead of appreciating the fact that I care about her safety, she thinks I'm being disrespectful.

If I want to avoid losing love units, *she* must believe that my opinion is in her best interest. And she must learn to wear seat belts in a way that is comfortable for her. I try to achieve those objectives in the third step.

Guideline 3: Explain how your opinion might be in your spouse's best interest and brainstorm ways to test the value of your opinion.

In the second step, you are to explain your opinions to each other with respect. But the third step will take special effort if you are to remain respectful. That's because this step is your first effort at trying to change your spouse's mind. How can you do that with respect?

I suggest you begin by expressing your respect for the opinion of your spouse, even though your goal is to try to change it. You might say, "Even though I don't agree with you, I know you have good reasons for your opinion. But I would like to suggest some other reasons that may change your mind."

Some people have great difficulty making the above statement because they don't believe their spouse has any good reasons for his or her opinions. This attitude reveals an underlying misunderstanding. As I mentioned earlier, the more you understand people, the more reasonable their opinions are.

ACTION STEP

Explain how your opinion might be in your spouse's best interest, and brainstorm ways to apply your opinion to your spouse in an acceptable form.

As I have said repeatedly, respect is crucial in persuasion, but it isn't something that your Taker would ever encourage you to do. Remember your Taker isn't interested in how other people feel or how other people will benefit. Your Taker is only interested in how you feel. So your Taker's strategy for persuasion is to try to force your spouse into your way of thinking without looking after your spouse's interests. Your Taker wants to make your spouse accept your point of view because it's good for you. If he or she doesn't go along with it, your Taker will then try to punish your spouse. So respect is completely unintuitive to your Taker. And if your persuasive efforts have been guided by your Taker lately, respect will be unintuitive to you as well. But let me assure you if you want to persuade your spouse to your point of view in a respectful way, you must demonstrate convincingly that it's in your spouse's best interest.

Using our seat belt example, I would be foolish to shout at Joyce, "Can't you see how stupid you are when you don't wear your seat belt?" That would not only be an ineffective and antagonizing statement, it would also reflect my own ignorance of her reasons for not wearing them. Instead, I might explain how unpleasant her life could become if she were thrown through the windshield. I might also point out her risk of being fined if the police stop her. On a more positive note, I could suggest that, once she adjusts to a seat belt, she will have greater control over her car and may feel more secure in her seat. I could even suggest wearing clothes that don't wrinkle when she drives, or leaving her jacket in the backseat.

Respectful persuasion never involves an attack on your spouse's defenses. Joyce may disagree with me, saying that some people have been killed because they use seat belts—sometimes they are unable to unlock the strap to escape a burning automobile. I should accept the reasonableness of her defense. Remember, her initial problem was that seat belts made her feel confined. It's reasonable for her to fear being locked in a burning automobile, unable to escape.

Thus far in our discussion, I have tried to explain how my position is in Joyce's best interest, and she has explained that she doesn't agree with me. If I were to attack her explanation, it would probably get me nowhere. Instead, it's more prudent to take another approach: Simply ask her to test my opinion for a brief period of time to see if she likes it.

People often make a big mistake in marital "discussions" when they try to force each other to make a committed change rather than a temporary one. Joyce is not convinced that my opinion is correct for her, so expecting her to make a commitment to my position is ridiculous! But her curiosity about my opinion and her respect for me may encourage her to risk a test of my opinion.

I might suggest to Joyce that she try to wear her seat belt each day for a week and see how she feels about it at the end of the week. In advance of the test, I would explain that habits take time to develop, so if she is comfortable with the first week's test, she may need to extend the test for a few more weeks so that she will develop a habit of seat belt wearing.

In some situations, a test is not possible. For example, investing all your retirement savings into a new business pretty well commits you to the program once you make the decision. But most examples of disrespectful judgments that I have encountered as a marriage counselor could have been reformulated to accommodate a test.

Guideline 4: If your spouse agrees enthusiastically with your opinion, based on the results of a test, you have achieved respectful persuasion. If the test fails to persuade, either go back to brainstorming or drop the subject.

Clearly understand the bargain: If your spouse is not comfortable with your position after the test, you may ask for yet another test. But if your spouse feels the first test was sufficient, you should agree to drop the subject. At this point in respectful persuasion many spouses make a mistake. They focus more attention on *persuasion* than on being *respectful*. If your test is ineffective in persuading your spouse, you may have another opportunity someday, but at this point you may have to back off, unless your spouse is enthusiastically willing to continue brainstorming.

> **ACTION**
> **STEP**
>
> If your spouse agrees enthusiastically with your opinion, based on the results of a test, you have achieved respectful persuasion. If the test fails to persuade, either go back to brainstorming or drop the subject.

If on the other hand your test is successful, resist the temptation to force a commitment to your position. If your spouse finds that your opinion works, it's likely to be incorporated into his or her judgment.

If Joyce were to try wearing her seat belt each day for a week and by the end of the week she were to find the experience reasonably comfortable, she would probably be willing to extend the test for a few more weeks, as we had originally agreed. The problem would take care of itself without further intervention on my part.

But if Joyce did not find that my test worked for her, I would be in no position to insist on another test or, worse yet, try to force my position on her. I may discuss the outcome of the test with her, trying to understand what went wrong, and I can ask if she would be willing to try another one. But if she refuses, I should thank her for her willingness to try my first test and leave the subject alone, at least for a while.

Remember, the goals of respectful persuasion are: (1) to avoid making Love Bank withdrawals, and (2) to resolve conflicts—in that order. That way you will have many opportunities to resolve conflict because the process will always be painless. But as soon as you do anything that your spouse finds unpleasant, it's no longer respectful persuasion, and it's unlikely to be repeated very often. The entire process must be safe and enjoyable or your spouse will try to avoid it entirely. If you feel you must persuade your spouse at all costs, the cost will be love units, and you will be far less likely to persuade. Even if I force my wife to say she agrees with me and even force her to do what I want, I cannot force her to love me. Only the process of respectful persuasion can protect my account in her Love Bank as we try to resolve our conflicts.

Some Unresolved Conflict of Opinion Is Inevitable

Now at this point you may be feeling that if you drop the subject you'll be very unhappy with the outcome. But I want you to be aware of a very important fact—you do not have to change each other's minds about something to create behavior that makes each other happy. Remember, it's what you do for each other that will make you happy, or what you do to each other that will make you unhappy. So in your efforts to create a more passionate marriage, one where you'll find each other absolutely irresistible, your attention should be focused on each other's habits and not necessarily on each other's beliefs, opinions, and attitudes.

My mother was a social and fiscal liberal and my father was a social and fiscal conservative. They had many discussions about their differences, but it never led to a resolution. Yet throughout their lives they respected each other's opinions, and were in love with each other. You don't have to agree on everything to have a great marriage.

And remember that respectful persuasion is a two-way street. Joyce has the right to try to influence my judgment just as much as I have the right to try to influence hers. Technically she has every right to try to convince me that wearing seat belts is a *bad* idea. Since most of us are convinced we should make a habit of wearing them, it's not a very reasonable illustration. Still, none of us has a corner on truth and we all can improve our judgments. Being open to the possibility that our loved one may be right about anything is a critical step toward respectful persuasion.

If I want to persuade my wife, I must respect her opinion enough to be willing to let her persuade me. I must be open to the possibility that she could be right and I could be wrong about any issue we discuss. And I should be willing to test her opinion, just as she is willing to test mine.

Disrespectful Judge or Respectful Persuader?

How can you know if you're a perpetrator of disrespectful judgments? Ask your spouse. You may not realize how you come across. In most cases I've seen, I've found disrespect to be "in the eye of the beholder." In other words, it's a very subjective call. Disrespect is usually whatever the offended spouse thinks it is.

85

But there are a few questions I've written that will help clarify the issue if there's any doubt. Ask your spouse to answer these questions honestly. If your spouse's answers identify you as one who makes disrespectful judgments, you'll probably be tempted to make yet another disrespectful judgment and claim that he or she is wrong! Resist that temptation because you have just discovered a leak in your Love Bank account. Fix it, don't deny it's there.

If you feel terribly uncomfortable having your spouse complete the questionnaire, or if your spouse would prefer not to, then do your best to answer the questions *as you think your spouse would.*

Each statement should be answered with a number between 1 and 7. A 1 indicates, "not at all," and a 7 indicates, "all the time." The numbers 2 through 6 indicate varying degrees of acceptance or rejection of the statement.

The scoring of this questionnaire is simple. Unless all your spouse's answers are 1, you're probably engaging in disrespectful judgments. Almost all of us are guilty of this from time to time, so don't be alarmed if you get some 2s or 3s. But if your spouse gives you any 4s, 5s, 6s, or 7s, you should get to work ridding your marriage of this Love Buster.

Don't make the mistake of winning the battle only to lose the war. An important part of romantic relationships is the support and encouragement lovers show each other. Disrespectful judgments do the opposite. If they have crept into your marriage, make an effort today to eliminate their destructive influence.

Disrespectful Judgments Questionnaire

1. Does your spouse ever try to straighten you out?
2. Does your spouse ever lecture you instead of respectfully discussing issues?
3. Does your spouse seem to feel that his or her opinion is superior to yours?
4. When you and your spouse discuss an issue, does he or she interrupt you or talk so much it prevents you from having a chance to explain your position?
5. Are you afraid to discuss your point of view with your spouse?
6. Does your spouse ever ridicule your point of view?

I encourage you to adopt a policy of zero tolerance when it comes to disrespectful judgments. Take my word for it, if you're in the habit of being disrespectful to each other, whatever hope you might have of changing each other's minds about crucial issues is a sheer fantasy. People don't change their minds after being shown disrespect. Instead, they go into a defensive mode, making them far less likely to be persuaded. On the other hand, it's very important for both of you to gain from each other's wisdom. Both of you will benefit greatly if you can change each other's minds in a respectful way.

> Adopt a policy of zero tolerance when it comes to disrespectful judgments.

I want you to be able to influence each other. But I want you to do it effectively and in a way that doesn't destroy your love for each other. Each of you has quite a bit of wisdom to offer the other if you are respectful toward each other.

When I discussed demands with you in the last chapter, I pointed out the fact that the expression of your needs to each other was so important that it was absolutely essential for you to learn to do it effectively. Demands are a very ineffective way to get your needs met. And so I encouraged you to use the more effective thoughtful requests.

We have the same situation here. I think it's extremely important for you and your spouse to influence each other's thinking. And the primitive instinct of your Taker, disrespectful judgments, just won't get the job done. Instead I'd like you to break the habit that your Taker has taught you and replace it with the intelligent new habit of respectful persuasion, so that whenever you have a disagreement about a belief or a value or an attitude or a behavior, you'll be able to resolve that conflict in a way that will take each other's feelings into account. It's a far more effective way to resolve conflicts, and it helps build your love for each other.

Key Principles

Disrespectful judgments are attempts to "straighten out" your spouse's attitudes, beliefs, and behavior by trying to impose your way of thinking through lecture, ridicule, threats, or other forceful means.

When selfish demands fail to get you what you need from your spouse, your Taker's next approach is to use disrespectful judgments.

Disrespectful judgments are abusive and controlling, but your Taker tries to disguise them as a way to care for your spouse.

Respectful persuasion requires respect for your spouse's opposing opinion, and a test of the value of your opinion to your spouse.

Failure to reach agreement on attitudes and beliefs will not destroy your love for each other, as long as you follow the Policy of Joint Agreement whenever you make decisions. But being disrespectful about your differing views will not only fail to change those views, it may destroy your love for each other.

You should have zero tolerance for disrespectful judgments.

Consider This...

1. What is the difference between disrespectful judgments and respectful persuasion? Have you been able to identify disrespectful judgments in your marriage? When one spouse makes a disrespectful judgment does the other spouse bring it to his or her attention? What have the consequences of such feedback been? Do you tend to punish each other for complaining about disrespect, or do you appreciate the feedback?

2. Review the Policy of Joint Agreement with each other. What is it? Why is it important for you to make decisions that take each other's feelings into account? Why is an enthusiastic agreement important?

3. Are you both willing to eliminate disrespectful judgments and replace them with respectful persuasion? If you are in the habit of being disrespectful, it will take practice to avoid it. I suggest that you each make a worksheet entitled, "Disrespectful Judgments," so that whenever one of you feels the other has been disrespectful, you write it on your worksheet. Be sure to avoid arguing about whether or not you have been disrespectful. Remember, the one who feels you have been disrespectful has an important point to make and you should try to understand it.

It's up to you to change your approach so that it is interpreted by your spouse as respectful persuasion.

4. Make a second worksheet entitled, "Respectful Persuasion." Write down each instance of what you considered to be an instance of respectful persuasion. And try to persuade each other as much as you want. The practice will do you good. But don't be disappointed if you are not persuasive. It will give you opportunities to understand what your spouse considers convincing and what doesn't work.

5. How skilled are you in trying to persuade each other? When spouses are in the habit of being disrespectful, they are often reluctant to try to change each other's minds as often as they should. They tend to use disrespect as a last resort to getting what they think they deserve, and forget about trying to persuade each other to get what they need. Follow the Four Guidelines to Respectful Persuasion in trying to change each other's opinions. By learning how to respectfully persuade, you will probably be challenging each other's opinions and behavior more often, and receiving more wisdom from each other than you did when you were being disrespectful.

5

Angry Outbursts

Who Wants to Live with a Time Bomb?

Jill's father was kind and generous 99 percent of the time. But during that other 1 percent, he terrorized the entire household with his anger. So even though Jill's boyfriend, Sam, lost his temper once in a while, she considered him well-mannered compared to her father's outrageous behavior. Sam didn't hit anyone, he didn't break furniture, and he was never arrested for disorderly conduct—he was a real gentleman!

Before they married, Sam directed his anger away from Jill. He'd curse other drivers on the road, he'd fume over his boss's foolish decisions, and he'd become irate when salespeople failed to wait on him quickly. Jill did many of the same things, so she just chalked this up to human nature.

One morning soon after they were married, both Sam and Jill overslept and were running late. As they scurried about, getting dressed, Sam suddenly had a problem.

"Jill, I'm out of clean shirts," he shouted.

She didn't quite know how to respond. Since they both worked, Jill and Sam usually "shared" the washing and ironing of clothes, but they had come to no formal understanding about who did what.

Like most people with anger problems, Sam was a very generous person. He would go out of his way to help others, especially Jill. So most of the time, "sharing" meant that he would do all of the washing and ironing. He wasn't happy about it, but didn't say anything until that fateful morning.

Jill tried to lighten up the situation. "I don't think any of mine will fit you," she joked.

"Was that supposed to be funny?" Sam shot back.

"Wear the one you wore yesterday," Jill suggested, trying to be helpful.

But Sam had already decided that she was at fault. "You had to notice that I was out of shirts last night," he bellowed.

"Me, notice your shirts? Please, get serious." With that she turned to finish getting ready herself.

"I'm not done talking to you. You knew I was out of shirts, didn't you?"

"No," she said, "I didn't know you were out of shirts. But even if I did, it's your problem, not mine."

With that, Sam flew into a rage, complete with recriminations, condemnations, and obscenities.

Jill started to cry. This was the first time Sam had directed his anger toward her. Although he was not being physically violent, it hurt her deeply. Sam left the room, and nothing more was said about the incident.

This angry outburst was the first of many Jill would endure during the first year of their marriage. The pattern would always be the same: Sam would have a problem, assume that Jill should have done something to solve it, and when she did not, he would lose his temper. Then she would cry, and he would back off. As time passed, however, the frequency and intensity of these outbursts increased.

They were planning to have children, but Jill wisely chose to see a marriage counselor first. She was afraid Sam's anger would eventually turn into the mayhem she had witnessed as a child.

Jill was wise to see a marriage counselor for another reason. Sam's angry outbursts had punched a hole in her Love Bank—it had sprung a leak. After one year of marriage, she was losing her feeling of love for Sam.

Every time Sam lost his temper, he was punishing Jill. This was doubly painful for Jill—she not only suffered from his punishing anger but also from the shocking realization that he was *trying* to hurt her. The man who had committed himself to her protection had become her greatest threat.

Why do couples destroy the love they have for each other with angry outbursts? In most cases, the problem begins with the false assumption that their spouse should do this or that for them. And when they don't face up to their responsibilities, they should be forced to do the right thing.

Angry Outbursts

Deliberate attempts to hurt your spouse because of anger, usually in the form of verbal or physical attacks.

Control is ultimately behind every angry outburst. And when a spouse does not do what is expected (selfish demands), recriminations usually follow.

Sam accused Jill of being an uncaring person because she didn't wash and iron his shirts. That's a disrespectful judgment. Then, when she didn't respond properly to his accusations, his angry outburst was justified as punishment for her attitude.

An angry outburst is usually an effort to teach a lesson—the one partner feels hurt and angrily tries to show the other how that feels. But in most cases, the angry spouse does not expect this punishment to ruin their love—after all, they promised to love each other forever.

They may have made the promise, but it was one they couldn't keep. People's feelings for each other are determined not by promises but by the Love Bank. When couples deliberately try to hurt each other, they deplete their Love Bank accounts. Romantic love becomes the victim of their anger.

Escalating Abuse

So far in this book I've talked with you about two types of Love Busters, selfish demands and disrespectful judgments. I have warned you not to tolerate either of them. Now I will try to help you understand and overcome a third Love Buster: angry outbursts.

I've taken these first three Love Busters in sequence because they represent an escalation of control and abuse in marriage. Remember, control is making your spouse do what you want, and abuse is hurting your spouse intentionally. Neither of these should be tolerated in marriage.

Selfish demands are usually where abuse begins, because they are attempts to force your spouse to do something for you that he or she is reluctant to do. In other words, you're trying to gain at your spouse's expense. You're willing to let your spouse suffer to get what you want.

> These first three Love Busters represent an escalation of control and abuse in marriage.

The next level of abuse in most marriages is disrespectful judgments. In fact, they usually come on the heels of a failed selfish demand. If you can't force your spouse to do what you want with a demand, then your Taker will encourage you to escalate the abuse with disrespectful judgments.

If you stop to analyze the fights between you and your spouse, I think you'll see what I mean. You'll find that they often begin with demands, and from there disrespectful judgments quickly follow. And if you don't have the sense to stop arguing, this next Love Buster, angry outbursts, is sure to rear its ugly head. It's usually the final stage in the escalation of abuse, where couples consciously and deliberately do all they can to hurt each other in a fit of rage.

Anger: A Threat to Your Spouse's Safety

I've listened patiently to husbands who have sworn never to hit their wife again, but by the next time I see them, they've inflicted even more bruises. One man I counseled, who claimed to be "cured" of his violent tendencies in a religious service, tried to kill his wife a short time later. Another man attempted to kill his wife three times before she finally divorced him. After each attempt on his wife's life, including the last, it was determined by counselors that it was safe for his wife to return to him.

I have witnessed many cases of murdered and permanently injured men and women who gave their spouse one chance too many. That's why my approach to domestic violence is extremely cautious, and often requires separation while an angry spouse is learning to control his or her temper.

Your anger is the greatest threat to your spouse's safety. Even if you've never been physically violent, and have limited your angry outbursts to verbal tirades, emotional abuse can be extremely damaging. And there's no assurance that you will not resort to physical violence during one of your fights. But you risk more than physical or emotional harm during an angry outburst: You risk losing your spouse's love for you. Without a doubt it's a Love Buster.

When you're angry, hurting others seems reasonable. They caused you to be unhappy, and they'll keep upsetting you until they're punished. They can't be reasoned with; the only thing they understand is pain and personal loss. Once you inflict that punishment, they'll think twice about making you unhappy again!

Anger's solution to a problem is to punish the troublemaker. This emotion overrides intelligence, which knows that punishment usually doesn't solve problems (at least for adults); it only makes the people you punish angry, which causes them to inflict punishment on you.

Most of the people that I've counseled who are perpetrators of angry outbursts don't see their anger as a serious problem in their marriage. As far as they're concerned, the real problem is their spouse's behavior that they think triggers their angry outbursts. "If she'd just stop being so annoying, I wouldn't get angry." "If he'd be a little more thoughtful and considerate I wouldn't lose my temper." In other words, most of the people who have angry outbursts feel that the other person made them do it.

That's the way the Taker thinks. Your Taker wants you to be happy and wants your spouse to make you happy, or at least to stop making you unhappy. And it will use any tactics necessary to accomplish that objective. Of course, angry outbursts don't really accomplish it very well, but the Taker thinks it's worth a try. The fact that your angry outburst is destroying your spouse's love for you is of no consequence to your Taker. It's not interested in your relationship; it's interested in getting your way. And it mistakenly thinks that your anger will somehow get your spouse to do what you want. But you don't get what you want, and you become your spouse's greatest threat in life.

Generosity Can Lead to Angry Outbursts

Angry people tend to feel that their spouse just isn't treating them fairly. But some of their feeling of injustice comes from the fact that they don't really negotiate to get what they need. As I already mentioned, Sam was a generous man. But his generosity helped cause his resentment. He was under the illusion that caring spouses give sacrificially to each other. If he cared for Jill, he would give sacrificially to her, and if she cared for him, she would give sacrificially to him. She would notice that his shirt inventory was down, drop whatever she was doing, and get right to work washing and ironing shirts. Sam felt that he would do the same for Jill if the roles were reversed—because he cared about her.

Don't get me wrong. I care enough about Joyce to sacrifice my own interests for hers. And she feels the same about me. But we care enough about each other to refuse that offer. We don't want the other person to suffer for our personal benefit. That's why we try to find solutions to problems that make us both happy.

Sacrifice on the part of either spouse for the sake of the other means that someone is being uncaring. Why would a caring spouse want the other to suffer for his or her benefit? The one accepting the sacrifice would have to be uncaring at that moment. That's why a couple who cares about each other would meet each other's needs in ways that do not require sacrifice.

But Sam's Giver and Taker did not understand that reality. His Giver encouraged him to make sacrifices for Jill, and his Taker expected Jill to make a few sacrifices for him just to be fair. When Jill wanted something from him, he gave it to her regardless of how unpleasant it might be to do it. So he felt it was only fair for her to do the same.

When our own sacrifices in marriage are not reciprocated, it usually makes us feel very resentful. We think we have a right to feel angry, because an obligation was not fulfilled. But the very nature of generosity doesn't create an obligation at all—it does not require reciprocity. In fact, when we do something for our spouse out of generosity, it should be assumed that he or she doesn't have to do anything in return for our sacrifice.

Our Giver understands that reality, and encourages us to give unconditionally. But the Taker does not see our generosity in the same way as our Giver sees it. It wants something for our effort, and encourages us to have an angry outburst when nothing is forthcoming. It wants justice. Your Giver wants you to give unconditionally, but your Taker is never in on that bargain. And it is likely to respond with resentment whenever you try to be generous and your spouse doesn't reciprocate. It wants your spouse to give you something in return for your generosity.

I think you can see the problem that Sam and Jill faced. Unspoken expectations and a failure to negotiate a mutual enthusiastic agreement led to Sam's resentment and that, in turn, convinced him that his angry outburst was justified. There's a sense in which Sam's generosity ultimately created the seeds for the destruction of their relationship. By being generous, he failed to negotiate what he needed with Jill, and that failure could have ended their marriage.

Angry Outbursts Should Never Be Tolerated

There are reasons for angry outbursts, but there are no excuses. Whatever causes one spouse to feel justified in blasting away at the other, its outcome is always the same: It causes pain and suffering to the very person that you promised to love and cherish. Instead of evening the score, or solving the problem, it withdraws love units. Your angry outburst causes your spouse to love you less. And anger is so unpredictable and so dangerous that you shouldn't even live with your spouse until you can guarantee his or her protection.

I've recommended separation for many of the spouses that I've seen for angry outbursts when they cannot control their temper. When you're angry, you are not simply upset—you're insane. You are not reasoning correctly because your brain is flooded with adrenaline. You think the way paranoid people think—that your spouse is your worst enemy and is deliberately trying to hurt you. Any effort that your spouse makes to reason with you is rebuffed. You are dangerous.

Even therapy that is ultimately successful does not suddenly end abusive acts. It brings about only a gradual decrease. This can sometimes be tolerated if we were dealing with, say, name-calling. An occasional slipup like that during the therapeutic process will not usually threaten the safety of a spouse. But it's quite another matter when the occasional failure takes the form of a violent act, even if it's not physical.

I offer a plan to overcome angry outbursts in this chapter. And in most cases, the plan can be followed without the need for separation. But if the arsenal of weapons you use during an angry outburst puts your spouse in physical danger, I strongly suggest following the plan while separated, because you will most certainly have failures from time to time as you overcome this abusive habit. Only when your spouse's physical and emotional safety can be guaranteed should you live with each other again. You should adopt a zero-tolerance policy toward angry outbursts.

I hope you agree with me that an angry outburst in any form leaves your spouse unprotected. No one should have to put up with your angry outbursts, especially your spouse. So if you've decided to end your verbal or physical attacks on your spouse once and for all, you're a good candidate for my plan to completely eliminate angry outbursts.

A Plan to Overcome Angry Outbursts

Sam was not so sure he had a problem with angry outbursts. That's a common perspective of those who can't seem to control their temper.

Anger is deceitful: It lets you forget what really happened and offers you a distortion of the truth. When Jill described one of Sam's angry outbursts to me, he shook his head in disbelief. "It just didn't happen that way," he said in all sincerity. "I don't understand why you would tell Dr. Harley such a thing."

Of course, I wasn't at the scene, but experience has taught me to give the benefit of the doubt to the victim. When couples have tape-recorded their fights, the one having the outburst is usually surprised at what he or she said.

As I mentioned earlier, I view an angry outburst as a form of temporary insanity. What is said and done is often about as irrational as a psychotic episode, and when it is recorded, the one having the angry outburst usually agrees with my assessment once he hears and sees himself in action.

The fact that the details of the angry outburst are often forgotten or remembered falsely is also typical of a psychotic episode. Insane behavior usually takes a detour around our intelligence and has us behave in very primitive and irrational ways. Then it either fails to give us any memory of what we did or gives us an inaccurate memory that makes the outburst seem more rational than it was.

Anger is deceitful and it is also cunning: It tries to convince you that an angry outburst is caused by someone else's behavior. Sam felt that Jill "made him" angry. If she had been more considerate, he would not have lost his temper. So it was her fault.

Many of my violent clients, both men and women, have told me that they had no choice but to lose their temper. Besides, their spouses had it coming to them. They deserved the angry reaction.

How do you go about stripping anger's deceit and cunning from outbursts so that anger can be seen for what it is? It's an ugly monster. How do you remove the screen that it hides behind?

Step 1: Acknowledge the fact that you, and you only, determine if you will have an angry outburst. No one "makes" you angry.

What a place to begin. Sam was thoroughly convinced that Jill made him angry, and that there was little he could do to avoid his angry outbursts. *If Jill would be more thoughtful,* he reasoned, *I would be less angry.* How could I convince Sam that he could completely overcome angry outbursts without Jill making any change in her behavior? And to go one step further, how could I convince him that unless he took full responsibility for his angry outbursts, he could not learn to control them?

ACTION STEP

Acknowledge the fact that you, and you only, determine if you will have an angry outburst.

I think that I'm a good counselor for those with anger problems, because I have had a history of angry outbursts myself. When I was growing up, I lived with parents who had serious anger issues, and I suffered many beatings, especially at the hands of my mother. I expressed my own frustration with anger, and was in many physical fights with my peers.

But, like Sam, I never lost my temper with Joyce while I was dating her. I knew I was on thin ice, and she would certainly not put up with anger. So I was able to keep it under control—when I was with her.

One day I had an epiphany. I was replacing a transmission in r and it slipped out of my grasp and fell on top of me. I promptly lc temper, and tried to destroy just about everything in sight, incluuing the transmission. I was actually thinking that the transmission had fallen on me just to upset me. And everything else was somehow also involved. By the time I had a chance to calm down, I had put quite a few dents in the car, but the transmission itself was as good as new. It's hard to wreck a transmission with your bare hands.

As I looked at what I had done, and the reason that I did it, I realized that I had become temporarily insane. The transmission couldn't possibly have decided to drop on me. I let it slip. It was my fault. And yet, I blamed the transmission.

It was at that moment that I came to realize that I was insane whenever I lost my temper. And when I became angry with a person, I was dangerous. The transmission had nothing to fear, but I could hurt another person. And if that person were Joyce, I would be making the mistake of a lifetime.

So I made a decision that very day that I would not lose my temper again. At first, it took quite a bit of effort to avoid being angry. But eventually, I didn't even have to think about it. When I found myself in a frustrating situation, I rarely felt angry, and I never lost my temper. And that's the way I feel today.

How did I do it? The first step was realizing that only I was responsible for my angry outbursts, and that I could avoid them if I chose.

Over my lifetime, I've counseled scores of men with very serious problems with angry outbursts. Many of these men spent time in prison due to violent acts committed while they were angry. And I always begin their plan of recovery with their acknowledgement that no one "makes" them angry—that they are completely responsible for their angry outbursts.

On a related subject, many anger management therapists today agree that we are all responsible for our anger. But many feel that our anger is caused by our poor self-esteem. If we were to feel better about ourselves, we would not feel as angry. I want to warn you in the strongest terms to reject that reasoning for two reasons.

First, the angriest people I've ever counseled have high self-esteem, not low self-esteem. They feel entitled to whatever they want, and get angry with those who don't give it to them. There is considerable research on this subject that points to improved self-esteem as increasing angry outbursts, not decreasing them.

Second, as soon as you give yourself any excuses for your angry outbursts—other people, the way you were raised, or even your poor self-esteem—you will not overcome your angry outbursts. That's because any excuse will sidetrack you from the best way to learn to control your temper, and that begins with accepting full responsibility for your actions. The following steps I recommend will help you completely eliminate this Love Buster regardless of whom you're with, how you were raised, or any problems you may have with self-esteem.

Step 2: Identify instances of your angry outbursts and their effects.

After I was able to convince Sam that he, and only he, could control his temper, we had another problem to face: Did he have a problem with anger or didn't he? That may seem like a strange second step in my plan for recovery, but I know firsthand how deceitful anger can be. For the one losing his temper, it can seem like a simple expression of frustration. For the one on the receiving end, however, it can be a frightening display of insanity.

ACTION
STEP

Identify instances of your angry outbursts and their effects.

So I had to help Sam see his anger for what it really was—a monster. And the person in the best position to describe the effect of his anger was his wife, Jill.

I asked Jill to answer the following questions:

1. On a scale from 0 to 6, with 0 indicating no unhappiness and 6 extreme unhappiness, what number most accurately reflects how much unhappiness you experience when your spouse attacks you with an angry outburst?
2. How often does your spouse tend to attack you with an angry outburst?
3. When your spouse attacks you with an angry outburst, what does he or she typically do? List the ways you are attacked.
4. Which of the ways you are attacked cause you the greatest unhappiness?
5. When did your spouse first attack you with an angry outburst?

6. Have your spouse's angry outbursts increased or decreased in intensity and/or frequency since they first began?
7. How do recent angry outbursts compare with those of the past?

I've counseled many who, after reading their spouse's answers to these questions, simply laugh. They are amazed that their spouse would write down what they believe are lies about their behavior. The deceit and cunning of their anger blind them to the truth. In some cases, they even lose their tempers as they are reading the answers.

If your spouse completes this questionnaire and you are tempted to view it as sheer fantasy, remember what I said about anger's deceit and cunning. Your spouse is in a much better position to record what you do when you are angry, so accept his or her word for it at this stage of the program. You must see anger for what it is: a threat to the safety and security of your spouse—and your marriage.

Jill's answers to these questions defined the problem and made it clear that Sam was making her unhappy with his angry outbursts. That was reason enough to do something about it. As Sam and I looked over Jill's answers, tears came to his eyes.

Sam saw that Jill had rated her unhappiness a 6, "extremely unhappy." He didn't want her to be unhappy and certainly didn't want to be the cause of her unhappiness.

What he had seen as an honest expression of his frustration she interpreted as an ambush, a painful attack. His method of communicating his feelings had turned him into her worst enemy.

Sam's vicious attacks on Jill's character and judgment (disrespectful judgments) were weaved into his angry outbursts. He would tell her how selfish she was, how he was doing everything for her and she was doing nothing for him. He also would berate her abilities, charging that her only value was in her figure, not in her head.

His rantings simply weren't true. She did many things to prove her care for him and she was a highly skilled legal secretary, in great demand because of her knowledge and clerical ability. Sam's angry outbursts were filled with irrational statements made to hurt her, not to solve his problem.

Jill described the shirt incident as the first time she felt attacked by his angry outbursts. She had been a witness to his anger prior to

ACTION
STEP

Understand why
your angry outbursts
take place.

that incident but until then it had not been directed toward her. She went on to describe his recent attacks and how they had become more frequent and more abusive. Jill also said that she was unwilling to raise children in an environment overshadowed by the threat of violence.

After Sam finished reading Jill's answers to the questions, he agreed to stop losing his temper. He made no excuses and, for once, agreed with her interpretation of the problem. We were ready to go to the next step.

Step 3: Understand why your angry outbursts take place.

Now it was Sam's turn to answer a few questions. Why did he lose his temper? I gave him the following questions to answer before our next appointment.

1. What are the most important reasons that you use angry outbursts to punish your spouse?
2. When you use angry outbursts to punish your spouse, what do you typically do?
3. When you use angry outbursts to punish your spouse, what hurts your spouse the most?
4. After you use angry outbursts to punish your spouse, do you usually feel better about the situation than before you used them? Why or why not?
5. Do you feel that punishment evens the score, and that without it your spouse wins and you lose? Explain.
6. Do you ever try to control or avoid using angry outbursts to punish your spouse? If so, why do you do it? How do you do it?
7. If you were to decide never to use angry outbursts to punish your spouse again, would you be able to stop? Why or why not?
8. Are you willing to stop using angry outbursts to punish your spouse? Why or why not?

There is something about all of these questions that should jump out at you. Do you see it? Each question assumes that angry outbursts are *intended* to be a punishment. As it turns out, one of the ways people deceive themselves about anger is to interpret it as something other than punishment. One of my clients called it an expression of his creativity; another viewed anger as a cry for help. I probably haven't heard them all but I've heard hundreds of ways that perpetrators of violence have downplayed what anger really is. It's punishment, pure and simple.

The purpose of angry outbursts is to inflict pain and suffering on the target. Any other interpretation is part of anger's deception. When the deception is removed and you see it for what it is—punishment—it's much easier to ask the question *why?*

Sam understood that he was punishing Jill whenever she was the target of his anger. As he answered the questions in the privacy of his home, he began to uncover the reasons. After they were married, he had a growing feeling that she was more important to him than he was to her. He was very generous with her, but he did not see the same generosity returned by her. He made sacrifices for her regularly, but she did not make the same sacrifices for him.

And her career seemed to be the most important thing in her life. His feelings were hurt whenever she made her work a higher priority than his interests. So whenever he lost his temper, he usually attacked her career, which he felt was coming between them. But he also attacked Jill.

As we went through his answers, he realized that he was using anger to even the score, to make her feel some of the pain he felt. He admitted that after an outburst he felt a little better. At least he had expressed his frustration instead of keeping it bottled inside of him.

After Sam made the commitment to control his temper, he didn't think it would be difficult to achieve. He would just have to make the decision to stop and that would be that. Most people with angry outbursts feel that way. Some are right, but time would tell if Sam was being realistic.

He had seen the error of his ways and he had decided to change. But was that enough?

Step 4: Try to avoid the conditions that make angry outbursts difficult to control.

Before Sam left my office, I gave him a few more questions to answer for our next session. They concerned the angry outbursts we had been discussing in the assignment he had just completed:

1. In the instances of angry outbursts that you identified earlier, describe the conditions that seem to make angry outbursts difficult to control. Include your physical condition (amount of sleep, physical health, etc.), setting, people present, behavior of those people, your mental state, and any other relevant information.
2. What changes in any of those conditions or efforts to avoid those conditions might help you avoid angry outbursts in the future?
3. What changes identified in question 2 can be made with your spouse's enthusiastic agreement?
4. Describe your plan, which can be made with your spouse's enthusiastic agreement, to change or avoid the conditions. Include a deadline that also meets with his or her enthusiastic agreement.

Almost all of the conditions that tend to make angry outbursts more difficult to control usually begin with two very serious mistakes. The first mistake is to assume that caring people make sacrifices for each other. Remember the Policy of Joint Agreement? *Don't do anything without an enthusiastic agreement between you and your spouse.* That means if you're doing something for your spouse that you regard as a sacrifice, you're not following the Policy. Caring couples consider how they both feel simultaneously, and neither spouse expects or wants the other to suffer for them. It's only the uncaring side of us that expects our spouse to make sacrifices on our behalf.

ACTION STEP

Try to avoid the conditions that make angry outbursts difficult to control.

But the problem goes beyond making sacrifices. It's also a misunderstanding regarding agreements. The person prone to angry outbursts often feels that there's an unspoken understanding—if I do this for you, you'll do this for me. But when that agreement isn't made clear and isn't understood by the other spouse, disappointment is sure to follow. So one of the lessons Sam learned was that he should not only avoid making sacrifices for Jill, but he should also be sure that agreements were clearly understood by both of them.

Another lesson Sam learned was that his angry outburst often came at the end of an argument that should never have taken place. The argument would begin with a demand—telling Jill what to do. When she was unwilling to comply with the demand, he would say something disrespectful, and if that didn't work, out came his arsenal of weapons.

He also learned that he could lose his temper if Jill demanded something of him, followed by disparaging remarks if he didn't comply. It can seem reasonable to respond with an angry outburst when your spouse threatens you for failing to deliver on his or her demand.

So an angry outburst can be a reaction to your spouse's failure to meet your demand or your reaction to your spouse's demand of you. In either case the demand itself is the first error. And by eliminating demands altogether you'll be getting rid of a very important condition that makes angry outbursts seem reasonable.

The same thing can be said for disrespectful judgments. If you say anything that your spouse interprets as being disrespectful, your spouse will not only be hurt by your comment, but may also feel justified in responding with an angry outburst. And the same is true if your spouse says something disrespectful about you. By overcoming disrespectful judgments in your marriage, again, you eliminate one of the important conditions that make it more difficult to avoid an angry outburst.

Another condition that may challenge your ability to control your temper is your physical state of mind. You may find, for example, that when you wake up in the morning you tend to become frustrated with very little provocation. A glass of orange juice may be all it takes for you to pull yourself together and gain control of yourself. If that's the case, your first item of business every morning should be to go to the refrigerator and drink a glass of orange juice.

Physical surroundings may also affect your temptation to lose your temper. For example, battling traffic on your way home from work may put you in such a foul mood that nobody would want to have dinner with you, especially your spouse. So either changing your work schedule or changing the route you take to get home might make a world of difference in the attitude that you have most evenings.

You'll find that if you create a lifestyle around the Policy of Joint Agreement, where the events of your day are compatible with both your sensitivities and the sensitivities of your spouse, you'll greatly reduce the conditions that tend to frustrate you.

When a husband and wife come to an agreement, I want it to be an *enthusiastic* one. Halfhearted, self-sacrificing arrangements generally fall apart the first time they're tested. So any changes that would help Sam control his temper had to be agreed to enthusiastically by Jill.

Sam felt that mornings were worst for him and that he tended to wake up irritable. Little things that Jill would do or say bothered him terribly at that time of the day. Later in the day, he seemed to have a completely different outlook on life and he could handle irritations much better.

Jill's job was Sam's greatest source of frustration. Whenever she talked about it, particularly when she talked about her boss, it drove him nuts. He saw her job in general and her boss in particular as great threats to their future. Sam was fearful that Jill would eventually have an affair with her boss.

It is quite common for jealous husbands or wives to be angry with their spouse. The threat of something or someone coming between them makes them furious. Their anger, of course, doesn't begin to solve the problem. In fact it tends to drive their spouse into the arms of anyone who will save him or her from their terror experienced in marriage. Whether or not Sam had anything to fear from Jill's boss, his anger greatly increased the risk of an affair.

Angry outbursts make the solution to marital problems much more difficult to find. The conflict that Sam had with Jill over her work and her relationship with her boss could be resolved, but not with the threat of an angry outburst.

So I encouraged Sam to resolve his conflict with Jill *after* he had learned to control his temper, rather than making it a *condition* to control his temper. It's like negotiating with terrorists. Whatever they demand, you cannot let them have it. They must remove the threat to innocent citizens before you discuss a resolution. Otherwise they will use that threat every time they want something.

Sam's early-morning irritability was another matter entirely. Jill was perfectly willing to avoid discussing conflicts with him in the morning, and Sam also agreed. So they decided that their morning conversation would be limited to "please pass the orange juice," avoiding any unpleasant topics. And he followed my advice to have that glass of orange juice as soon as possible in the morning.

Step 5: Train yourself to control your temper when you cannot avoid frustrating situations.

It may seem to you that in Step 4 I'm backtracking on what I said in Step 1. In other words, it may seem that I don't really think that angry outbursts are completely within our control, because I focus on outside conditions in Step 4. But Step 5 should straighten out that misconception. While the first line of defense against angry outbursts should be to try to avoid conditions that are frustrating, I am a witness to the fact that even when these conditions cannot be avoided, you should control your temper. If your spouse seems uncooperative, or if he or she refuses to stop making demands, being disrespectful, or having angry outbursts, or if he or she continues to do the things that irritate you most, you can control your temper even under those conditions. I've found that when a person simply can't avoid frustrating situations, the best way to keep their cabinet of weapons locked up is to relax.

ACTION STEP

Train yourself to control your temper when you cannot avoid frustrating situations.

For someone with a history of angry outbursts, that solution sounds really stupid at first. How can you relax when you are faced with a spouse who keeps badgering you, ridiculing you, and has their own problems with anger? I've had many spouses tell me that they try to avoid a fight by leaving, and their spouse blocks the door, preventing their escape. One person I've counseled was chased by his spouse all around the yard before he finally pushed her to the ground. The police charged him with domestic violence, and he spent a week in jail. I told him that it was the best thing that could have happened to him because now he understood why he had to learn to control his temper under the most irritating conditions—he would spend even more time in jail the next time he failed.

Relaxation in the face of terribly irritating conditions reverses the physiological cause of an angry outburst—adrenaline. When you are faced with a threat, adrenaline is secreted, and it builds up in your blood, affecting the way your brain operates. It switches your neural pathways so that irrational thoughts are triggered, and you are motivated to behave with vengeance. If you don't calm down when faced with adversity, you cannot think rationally when you need your intelligence the most. Your intuitive response is to lash out at the one causing your frustration. And when that person is your spouse, you can't let that happen.

So I trained Sam to relax when in frustrating situations. While using biofeedback equipment to measure his emotional reactions, we discussed some of the most annoying experiences he had ever faced. After measurements indicated that he was agitated, I asked him to relax all of his muscles, going from the top of his head to the bottom of his feet. As he learned to voluntarily relax his muscles when he began feeling tense, he was able to reduce the time it would take to calm himself down. I sent him home with a device that gave him feedback regarding his emotional state, so he could practice relaxing throughout the week.

You can practice relaxing under adversity without using biofeedback equipment. All that's needed is your ability to imagine something your spouse does that frustrates you, and then relaxing after you think about it. Instead of feeling increasingly resentful about the situation, you find yourself feeling more objective. You are able to think about solutions to the problem without becoming angry.

Quite frankly, anger management training takes time, because it's not just the adrenaline you are learning to reduce. It's also the neural pathways that you are changing. By responding to adversity with relaxation, you are training your brain to think rationally when faced with frustrating situations, instead of responding to them with anger. The more you practice calming down when frustrated, the more your brain changes the way it handles those situations. After a while, you don't even feel angry when annoyed. Instead, you think about the problem in an intelligent and rational way.

Years ago, some therapists felt that the way to deal with anger was to express it openly. Punching bags were given to clients to vent their frustrations. Based on my own analysis of the problem, you would expect that these methods would have made matters worse—and they did. By venting your anger, you are reinforcing the neural pathways that cause you to respond to frustration with an angry outburst. Today, there are very few who use that technique because it doesn't work. On the other hand, most specialists in anger management have come to recognize the value of relaxation techniques in helping people eliminate angry outbursts. And they also notice that the longer these people apply these techniques, the less angry they feel. Their brains are actually changing to make them wise when they feel that they're under attack.

Angry outbursts in marriage should be avoided at all costs, because they represent an extreme form of abuse. And mistakes made by the other spouse should never be viewed as an excuse. This means that when you feel irritated, instead of venting your anger, you walk away. If you can't walk away, you learn how to relax. In some cases, you may need to separate from your spouse to avoid being abused yourself. But under no circumstances should you ever allow yourself to become the abuser.

The goal of an effective program of anger management is to avoid an angry outburst when you're irritated the most, when people seem the most insensitive. If you can't achieve that objective on your own by following my plan to overcome angry outbursts, find a therapist who has a proven record in helping spouses avoid domestic violence. The therapist you choose should not only teach spouses to avoid angry outbursts, but he or she should also be able to keep the marriage together during therapy. Be careful to avoid therapists who try to solve your anger problem by encouraging you to end your marriage.

Step 6: Measure your progress.

Before Sam left my office, I invited Jill to join us and handed her a form with these instructions:

Please list all instances of your spouse's angry outbursts and acts that you consider punishment for something you did. These include verbal and physical acts of anger and threatened acts of anger toward you, cursing you, and making disrespectful or belittling comments about you. Include the day, date, time, and circumstances, along with a description of each angry outburst.

I asked Jill to keep a record of how well Sam kept his commitment to control his temper. Measuring progress is the most critical step in this plan to overcome angry outbursts, and the victim is usually the best one to do the measuring. Jill, more than anyone else, would know when Sam slipped up. As I mentioned earlier, the Taker tries to make us forget what we did when we're angry, so those who have difficulty

ACTION STEP

Measure your progress.

controlling their anger are not good at measuring their own progress. Furthermore, Jill's documentation would be a big help in understanding precisely what it was that bothered her so much.

Before they left my office, I told Sam that he would have to accept as truth whatever Jill wrote down. He was not to argue with her about her interpretation of his behavior, but just try to avoid doing it in the future. I warned him that there would be some surprises the first week.

Sure enough, when they had their next appointment, only three days later, she had already written down two instances of angry outbursts—and one of them was in the parking lot on the way out of my office.

"Why is she doing this to me?" Sam complained. "I didn't lose my temper. All I did was tell her that I didn't think we needed to go through all of this. Can't I express my feelings anymore?"

I explained that this was one of the surprises I had warned Sam about. It was important for him to understand exactly how Jill interpreted his "expression of feelings." To her it was punishment. I suggested that he should not express his frustration to her until he felt very relaxed.

Two days later, I talked to him again on the telephone, and he proudly announced that Jill had no new entries since my last appointment with him. For the very first time he realized that his expression of frustration when agitated threatened Jill and made her unhappy. He would need to learn how to talk to her when he was relaxed, so that she would feel safe.

When I saw Jill and Sam for their next appointment, I talked with Jill first and read the entries in her progress report. She explained how difficult it had been to be truthful, because she was afraid that the report itself would cause Sam to lose his temper. It's true. Some of my clients have reacted to the report with angry outbursts. One man actually tore it up when he read it because he did not agree with his wife's report.

Whenever that happens, it brings into focus the seriousness of the spouse's problem. In some cases a more intense plan of action must be created to address the fact that the anger is out of control. And, as I already mentioned, I have encouraged many couples to separate until a spouse can prove enough control to guarantee the other spouse's safety.

If you are trying to overcome angry outbursts, ask your spouse to measure your progress, just as Jill measured Sam's progress. As was also the case with selfish demands and disrespectful judgments, your spouse is the best judge of your behavior.

A raising of the voice is often interpreted as an angry outburst. When that happens, I encourage the spouse to avoid arguing about definitions, and simply stop raising his or her voice when having a discussion. Your spouse may be very sensitive to your anger and may be greatly affected by even the slightest hint of your becoming angry.

Don't quibble about whether you've had an angry outburst or not. The point is that whatever it is your spouse considers an angry outburst is causing your spouse to suffer, and it's a habit that you can eliminate.

At this point you might ask the question, how long should my spouse go on documenting any instances of my angry outbursts? My answer: For the rest of your life. Of course if you're successful there won't be any instances to document. But if you ever do something in the future that your spouse interprets as an angry outburst, he or she should have the right to bring it to your attention and you should have the responsibility of acknowledging it, apologizing for it, and analyzing what went wrong. Did you follow the plan? Is there a new condition that makes it particularly difficult to control your temper? Whenever you have an angry outburst, you should address the issue immediately so that you can avoid it in the future.

When Sam completely eliminated his verbal abuse and feelings of anger toward Jill, he explained some of the changes in his thinking to me.

"I know what makes me feel angry. It is thinking that Jill doesn't really care about me and all she cares about is herself. But if I relax, I stop thinking those thoughts, and I tell myself that we will be able to work out our problems."

Jill really did care about Sam and wanted to have a family with him someday. She was definitely on his side and wanted him to succeed in controlling his anger. Within a few weeks, they were engaged in serious negotiations about the way her work affected him, and she made some very important changes to accommodate his feelings, particularly about the way she talked to him about her boss. She also made a point of avoiding any contact with her boss that was not purely business-related.

Sam's anger had driven her away from him, and now that he had proved he could protect her from it, she was drawn back to him, something he had wanted all along.

They also came to some very important agreements regarding child-rearing techniques. I warned them that Sam's tendency toward anger could easily be resurrected once the children arrived, and that would also withdraw love units from Jill's Love Bank. So they both agreed that any discipline would be mutually and *enthusiastically* agreed to, or it wouldn't happen. And if he was ever angry toward their children, he would do nothing to punish them. Instead, he would relax.

People with a predisposition to anger are predisposed to bad marriages and, ultimately, divorce. But if you can recognize anger for what it really is, a Love Buster, and learn how to protect your spouse from it, you not only save your marriage, but you also save yourself from a life of endless searching for someone who will put up with it.

Despite what some "therapists" have thought in the past, controlling your anger does not cause you to build resentment, and does not lead to serious emotional problems. I've counseled hundreds of people who have been successful in protecting their spouse from their angry outbursts, and none of them became more resentful or went crazy. Instead, they felt a lot better about themselves, and their spouses felt downright emancipated. It made solutions to their problems inevitable.

As I've said over and over, anger has no place in marriage. While it is a normal human reaction, it is also a destructive reaction, and you must protect your spouse from it if your spouse is to be happy and secure living with you.

Selfish demands, disrespectful judgments, and angry outbursts very often blend into each other. Sometimes it's a little difficult to know what is a selfish demand, what is a disrespectful judgment, and what is an angry outburst, because in many arguments you have them all at once. When a spouse is making a demand he might also be disrespectful and angry at the same time. That's one of the reasons that I put these three Love Busters on a continuum of abuse. All three of them represent ways that your Taker tries to get what you need by taking advantage of your spouse.

These three strategies are all very instinctive and can be seen in most of us when we're just a year old. Demands, disrespect, and anger are strategies that we're all born with to get our way. But just as they're inappropriate for children and we try to teach children to avoid them, they're certainly inappropriate in marriage. If your parents didn't do a very good job teaching you to avoid demands, disrespect, and anger, for the sake of your marriage and your spouse you need to learn to avoid them now. And you can learn to avoid them.

I've seen many marriages turn completely around because spouses have decided not to tolerate their own anger, disrespect, and demands. And when that happens, it gives them the opportunity to negotiate effectively. That's how you and your spouse really get what you need from each other. I want you to have what you need in your marriage. But anger, disrespect, and demands simply won't get it for you.

In chapters 9–15, I spend more time on the topic of marital negotiation with the Policy of Joint Agreement. It's only when you and your spouse make decisions that are in your mutual best inter-

> Your love and passion for each other are more important than whether or not you resolve your conflicts.

ests that you'll both be depositing love units into each other's Love Banks simultaneously. You'll not only resolve your conflicts, but you'll resolve them in a way that builds your passion for each other.

It's very important to remember that your love and passion for each other are more important than whether or not you resolve your conflicts. If you're in love with each other, you'll have what you really want the most in your marriage. On the other hand, if all your conflicts are resolved and you're not in love with each other, you'll feel cheated. So remember this very important principle: how you treat each other will determine how you feel about each other. If you believe that, you should take my advice and completely eliminate from your marriage demands, disrespect, and anger.

Key Principles

An **angry outburst** is a deliberate attempt to hurt your spouse because of anger, usually in the form of verbal or physical attacks.

When selfish demands and disrespectful judgments fail to get you what you need from your spouse, your Taker's next approach is to use angry outbursts. It is the third and final escalation of abuse as a strategy for getting your way.

Angry outbursts are abusive and controlling, but your Taker justifies them by trying to convince you that your spouse makes you lose your temper.

An angry outburst is temporary insanity, and the direction it takes is unpredictable. Permanent physical damage and even murder can occur during an angry outburst where the risk had not been apparent prior to the episode. This is an important reason why couples should have no tolerance for angry outbursts.

My plan to help you overcome angry outbursts consists of six steps:

Step 1: Acknowledge the fact that you, and only you, determine if you will have an angry outburst. No one "makes" you angry.

Step 2: Identify instances of your angry outbursts and their effects.

Step 3: Understand why your angry outbursts take place.

Step 4: Try to avoid the conditions that make angry outbursts difficult to control.

Step 5: Train yourself to control your temper when you cannot avoid frustrating situations.

Step 6: Measure your progress.

If my plan to help you overcome your outbursts doesn't work when you try it on your own, seek professional help to guarantee your spouse's safety. You should have zero tolerance for your angry outbursts.

Consider This...

1. What is an angry outburst? Have you been able to identify angry outbursts in your marriage? Does the one having the angry outburst see it for what it really is, an abusive and controlling habit?

2. When one of you has an angry outburst, does the other spouse bring it to his or her attention? What have the consequences of such feedback been? Do you tend to punish each other for complaining about angry outbursts, or do you appreciate the feedback?

3. Describe your arsenal of weapons. What do you tend to do when you have an angry outburst? Which weapons are the most offensive to your spouse?

4. Do you take full responsibility for your angry outbursts, or do you blame them on your spouse? Remember, you will not be able to overcome your angry outbursts until you realize that you, and only you, can control them.

5. Do you understand the conditions that tend to trigger your angry outbursts? How do selfish demands and disrespectful judgments tend to trigger them? You will notice that when your spouse makes a selfish demand or disrespectful judgment about you, it can make you feel angry. And when you make a selfish demand or disrespectful judgment without getting what you want from your spouse, it can also make you feel angry. But feeling angry and having an angry outburst are not the same. No one can avoid feeling angry once in a while, but we can all avoid angry outbursts. What is the difference between the two?

6. If you are in the habit of having angry outbursts when you have a conflict, it will take practice to avoid them. Agree with each other that if either of you feel angry during a discussion, you will break off your conversation and relax. Let adrenaline dissipate from your system before you return to the topic.

7. I suggest that you each make a worksheet entitled, "Angry Outbursts," so that whenever one of you feels the other has had one, you write it on your worksheet. Be sure to avoid arguing about whether or not it has taken place. Remember, the one who feels you have had an angry outburst has an important point to make and you should try to understand it. It's up to you to change your approach so that what you do and say is not interpreted by your spouse as an angry outburst.

8. If either of you cannot seem to gain control over your angry outbursts, I suggest you find professional help. Most hospitals and mental health clinics offer anger management therapy that has proven to be effective. But not all therapy is equal, so be certain that the therapist you select is recommended by doctors or social service agencies who have witnessed firsthand their effectiveness in treating this serious problem. And also be certain that they follow the six steps in my plan to overcome angry outbursts.

6

DISHONESTY

Who Wants to Live with a Liar?

The first time Jennifer was dishonest with Ed about her feelings was during their honeymoon. They were having dinner together in a restaurant that was on the beach. The evening was beautiful and from where they were seated, they could watch the waves crashing onto the sand.

Then Ed's cellular phone rang, and the mood suddenly changed. Ed had given his number to some of his best customers and one of them wanted help with a problem.

Ed excused himself to talk to his customer, leaving Jennifer to enjoy the scenery and her dinner—alone. Half an hour later Ed returned, with apologies for the interruption.

Though Jennifer was deeply offended by the way Ed had treated her, she did not tell him how bad she felt. Instead, she told him how much she was enjoying the scenery.

That call at dinner was not the only one that interrupted their honeymoon. Ed received several calls, even one while he and Jennifer were about to make love. Jennifer was hurt that Ed was trying to conduct business during their honeymoon, but she never let him know. She wanted him to be successful in his business and felt she had to learn to adjust.

While they had been dating, Jennifer found it easy to be honest with Ed about her feelings. He was a great guy, always trying to make her happy, so her accolades far outweighed her complaints. On the few occasions when he did something that upset her, she mentioned it briefly, and he quickly made accommodations. But after they were married, she didn't feel that it was appropriate for her to let him know when she was offended, because it was almost always job-related. For example, he left her home alone three nights each week, which bothered her. But she let him think she was happy with the arrangement. She knew how important his demanding job was for both of them.

By the time they had children, both Ed and Jennifer had become increasingly preoccupied with the ever-escalating responsibilities of life. Their marriage suffered because they neglected each other's emotional needs, but neither Ed nor Jennifer thought it right to complain. In fact, they had read a marriage book that warned them to avoid complaining. Their dishonesty was now mutual and growing.

Ed felt unfulfilled with their sexual relationship, but he understood the pressure Jennifer was under. After a long day of childcare, he knew she'd be tired when he came home from work late at night. He felt that it would be unfair to expect her to meet his sexual needs whenever he felt amorous. So he didn't tell her about his increasing sexual frustration.

Jennifer was also growing increasingly frustrated with Ed's neglect of her. Once in a great while, when he came home after another late night at the office, she'd admit, "I'm feeling lonely."

Ed would react with a sigh of resignation, "It took me longer than I thought to close the sale. I'll try to be home earlier next time, but you can't hurry these things along."

"Yeah, I guess you're right." Jennifer would drop the subject and Ed would think she was satisfied with his answer. But she wasn't. She had told him how she felt, and he didn't seem to care.

And Ed even told Jennifer how he felt about their sexual relationship—once. When Jennifer explained that the children made her feel too tired at night, he said he understood. And he did, but the problem still bothered him.

Meanwhile, both Ed and Jennifer were innocently creating incompatibility. Slowly but surely they were growing apart because neither one said anything when his or her emotional needs were not met. Eventually, they were no longer in love with each other.

Basic Concept #6: The Policy of Radical Honesty

Ed and Jennifer's problems were a result of their failure to follow one of my basic concepts—**The Policy of Radical Honesty:** *Reveal to your spouse as much information about yourself as you know—your thoughts, feelings, habits, likes, dislikes, past history, daily activities, and future plans.* There are three very important reasons why radical honesty is essential in marriage.

> ### Policy of Radical Honesty
> *Reveal to your spouse as much information about yourself as you know—your thoughts, feelings, habits, likes, dislikes, past history, daily activities, and future plans.*

First, radical honesty provides a clear road map for marital adjustment. A husband and wife who are honest with each other can identify their problems very quickly and, if they know how to negotiate with each other, dispose of them very quickly. Sometimes dishonesty covers up both the problems themselves and the solutions to those problems.

If you are honest, you reveal the facts about how you feel, what you've done, what you're doing, and what you plan to do. The more facts you have, the better you'll understand each other. The more you understand each other, the more likely it is that you'll come up with solutions to your problems. Ed and Jennifer drifted into a loveless marriage because they failed to reveal crucial facts that would have helped them both understand the problems that they faced.

The second reason that radical honesty is essential in marriage is that it meets an important emotional need. For many, honesty deposits so many love units that they fall in love with the person who's radically honest with them. In other words, for those people to be in love, there must be a clear and unobstructed view into each other's minds.

But there's also a third reason for radical honesty in marriage, and that's the reason I will showcase in this chapter. Dishonesty is a Love Buster. When one spouse lies to the other spouse or tries to cover the truth in some way, the other spouse is almost invariably offended. And that offense causes massive Love Bank withdrawals.

Radical honesty provides a clear road map for marital adjustment.

At the point we left Ed and Jennifer, dishonesty had prevented them from making adjustments to each other's emotional needs because they failed to introduce their problems. And the honesty that could have helped them bond with each other was missing. But there was more dishonesty that had yet to be revealed. In fact, the scope of their dishonesty was so great that it almost ended their marriage. This happened in several ways.

Types of Dishonesty

There are four types of dishonesty in marriage: (1) protection, (2) looking good, (3) avoiding trouble, and (4) compulsion. While the motives and excuses are very different for each type, the results are the same—the marriage suffers.

Protector Liars

In my opening illustration, Jennifer and Ed were practicing a very common type of dishonesty when they failed to reveal their negative reactions: Protection. They were trying to protect each other from unpleasant information. In most marriages, people tend to keep a certain amount of negative feedback from each other because they don't want to appear to be nagging or complaining too much. Almost everybody can think of times when they have withheld their true feelings or unpleasant information to avoid upsetting their spouse. But whenever that happens, they become "protector liars."

It seems quite innocent, doesn't it? But the problem with protective lying is that it does not protect—it *denies* a spouse crucial information. As Ed and Jennifer "protected" each other from the truth about their feelings, they were both allowing huge withdrawals of love units to continue unabated. Ed's work schedule was siphoning love units out of Jennifer's Love Bank, but she didn't let him know how it was affecting her. Each time Jennifer turned down Ed's sexual advances, she was making withdrawals in Ed's Love Bank, but he pretended that there was nothing wrong.

How would you feel if your bank stopped giving you monthly statements on your checking account but continued to deduct fees for overdrafts without informing you? You'd be outraged. "When our customers run out of money in their accounts," the bank manager might say, "we try to protect them from that unpleasant information." That's crazy! You need accurate information the most when you're overdrawn, so you can deposit enough to avoid bouncing checks.

> Protective lying *denies* a spouse crucial information.

The same is true in marriage. If Jennifer and Ed had known how often they were making Love Bank withdrawals, they could have made adjustments to prevent further losses. But without that information, they were blindly drifting out of love.

Trying-to-Look-Good Liars

It would have been bad enough if lying to protect was the only type of dishonesty to infect Jennifer and Ed's marriage. But dishonesty in marriage can take several forms, and Ed also suffered from a second type of dishonesty—lying to look good.

Some people need admiration and approval so much that they try to make themselves look better than they really are. To leave a favorable impression, these "trying-to-look-good" liars fabricate achievements and abilities so that others will have higher regard for them. Most of us want to put our best foot forward, but this type of liar misrepresents the facts. For some, it's just an embellishment of something that actually took place, but for others, the entire event is a lie.

Ed was a trying-to-look-good liar. It started when he first dated Jennifer. He knew that she had done well in school, so he made up stories about his school achievements. As far as she knew, he was among the top in his class. But the truth was that he was an underachiever. Granted, he had the ability to get good grades, but he never really gave it much effort. Those A's and B's that he told her he earned were actually C's and D's. He hardly made it through high school, but who ever checks school records?

Then, during their marriage, Ed continued to exaggerate his achievements, especially those at work. When Jennifer asked him how his day went, he often made up stories about sales he made and commendations he received from his supervisor. She would tell him how proud she was of him, and to keep up the good work.

His stories were so convincing that he believed some of them himself. On one occasion when he was asking for a raise, he reminded his supervisor of an outstanding sale he had recently made, only to remember halfway through the conversation that it was merely one of the stories he had told his wife. It was embarrassing when he had to admit it never happened, but he got out of the situation by blaming his poor memory and dropping his request for a raise.

But Ed knew it was not really a memory problem—it was an honesty problem. He had developed the habit of lying to make himself look better than he really was. He thought he could keep up the deception throughout his marriage, but lies have a way of tripping us up eventually.

Avoid-Trouble Liars

Dishonesty can spread like a virus. One lie can lead to another, and one type of lying can lead to another type of lying. Ed's lying to look good created problems for him that led to yet a third type of dishonesty—lying to avoid trouble. It arises from the threat of being caught doing something wrong.

What is right and wrong, of course, is often in the eyes of the beholder, so "avoid-trouble liars" often feel that their own shady actions are appropriate but they suspect that others will judge them harshly if they were to know about them. In marriage, these people do things that their spouse would disapprove of, but to avoid their spouse's judgment, they lie.

> Lies have a way of tripping us up eventually.

Jennifer suspected that Ed was embellishing his sales record, and so one day she mustered up the courage to call his supervisor to get the facts. What she heard was devastating. He had not only been lying to her about having an outstanding sales record, but had been fired six weeks earlier for poor performance. Ed's supervisor had warned him several times that if his sales did not improve they could not continue to employ him, and they finally had let him go.

For six weeks, Ed left the house each day pretending to go to work. But instead of going to his old job he was looking for a new one. He had hoped to find something quickly and tell Jennifer that he quit the old job for a better offer, so that she would be none the wiser.

Was Ed's lie to protect Jennifer, to make himself look good, or to avoid trouble? Sometimes a lie has many motives, and in this case, there could be an argument made for a little of all three. But when Ed pretended to go to work, he was definitely avoiding trouble. If he were to tell Jennifer he had been fired, his lies about his sales would unravel and he would be seen as the underachiever he really was.

Another couple I counseled also suffered from the ravages of avoid-trouble lying. Always short of cash, Sally hated begging Steve for money. So she opened her own bank account by forging her husband's signature on a ten-thousand-dollar loan application. She planned to make the payments with the money she earned working part-time. Steve suspected that something was going on, because she seemed to have an expensive new outfit just about every week. But she claimed that she was simply finding incredible bargains.

Sally's plan might have gone undetected if she hadn't lost her part-time job, and then missed a payment on the loan. When Steve got a call from the bank, the cat was out of the bag.

"None of this would have happened if Steve hadn't been so cheap" was Sally's excuse. According to her, she had a right to spend more money than Steve gave her, and so she took matters into her own hands. She justified her dishonesty as necessary for her survival.

People who have affairs often feel the same way about their behavior. With their spouse unwilling to meet their needs, they are "forced," they claim, to find another who is willing. Most people caught in affairs are more upset about the fact that they were caught than they are about the pain they've caused their spouse and children. They are outraged by their spouse's snooping—invading their privacy. While admitting that they hurt their spouse, remarkably few actually feel guilty about it. They tend to believe that if their spouse had met their needs in the first place, they would not have had to go to the trouble of finding someone else.

Lying is bad enough, but trying to shift blame to the offended spouse is adding insult to injury. A humble and contrite apology is the only appropriate response to an uncovered lie. But most liars make matters worse by trying to defend their indefensible act.

Born Liars

When Jennifer first learned about all of Ed's dishonesty, she thought that she had married a compulsive liar—the fourth type of dishonesty. But, thankfully, that was not Ed's problem. Compulsive lying is very different than those we have discussed so far, and is fairly easy to identify.

I call those who lie about anything and everything, whether they have a good reason to lie or not, "born liars" because they don't seem to be able to control it, nor do they know why they do it. These people often lie about trivial experiences and don't seem to know what is true and what is a lie. Even solid evidence to the contrary does not always dissuade them.

Born liars sometimes live double lives. Occasionally you'll read a news story about a con artist who has finally been caught after passing himself off as a doctor or lawyer or marrying two or more people. These people are usually born liars. When caught red-handed in a crime, they sincerely deny any involvement and can even pass lie detector tests. Such liars are fascinating to psychologists such as myself, but for obvious reasons they're impossible as marriage partners. Since honesty is essential in marriage, and these individuals simply cannot tell the truth, their marriages are usually very short-lived.

> Born liars are dishonest about trivial experiences, and don't seem to know what is true and what is a lie.

This fourth category, compulsive lying, is obviously the most extreme form of dishonesty, and thankfully, very few of the spouses I counsel are born liars. I've found that it's almost impossible to treat this kind of dishonesty because the person doing the lying rarely sees it as a problem, and may be incapable of doing anything to overcome it.

Since this form of lying should be quite obvious to anyone with an inquisitive mind from the first date on, compulsive liars usually do not get very far in romantic relationships. Those who end up marrying such people have little or no interest in their personal lives. It's rare for anyone to be that disinterested.

If you and your spouse struggle with dishonesty, chances are that it falls into the categories of lying to protect, to look good, or to avoid trouble. Fortunately, these three types of dishonesty *can* be overcome.

Can Honesty Be a Love Buster?

As you contemplate what your marriage might be like if you practice radical honesty, you may be wondering if honesty, in some cases, is a Love Buster itself. Are there times when a couple can be *too* honest with each other, and when it would be better to avoid conflict by keeping a spouse in the dark?

That's what Ed and Jennifer believed. They assumed their relationship would suffer harm if they expressed their true feelings. And on the surface, this argument seems to make sense. Love Busters are habits that make your spouse unhappy; so if your expression of honesty troubles your spouse, it must be a Love Buster, right?

> Dishonesty usually only postpones your spouse's discovery of the truth.

But if you take a closer look, you find that the Love Buster usually isn't the honesty itself, but the behavior that honesty reveals. Confessing to an affair will certainly upset your spouse, but it isn't the confession that's upsetting. It's the affair! In fact, lying about it makes it even more upsetting.

Dishonesty usually only postpones your spouse's discovery of the truth, and once it's revealed, your spouse will be upset by both your thoughtless behavior and your dishonesty. And of the two, your dishonesty will usually hurt your spouse more than whatever it was you were trying to conceal. Dishonesty in marriage, once discovered, causes incredible pain. That's why it's dishonesty—not honesty—that is a Love Buster.

Don't Wrap Your Honesty in Love Busters

While we are on the subject of how the disclosure of truth can be painful, couples often make it much more painful than it needs to be. That's because disclosure of truth can be accompanied by Love Busters.

In reaction to Ed's failure to be home with Jennifer in the evenings, suppose she had greeted him at the door with, "You never have time for me anymore, you selfish jerk! I don't know why I ever married you!" She gets points for honesty, but her disrespectful judgment and angry outburst ruin it all. Ed would not hear her complaint about his neglect because he'd be running for cover.

Or suppose that Ed were to decide to take the same approach to his sexual frustration as Jim did in my opening illustration—by demanding sex. That's one way to get your feelings out on the table, but it's honesty wrapped in demands. And it would communicate brutal selfishness to Jennifer, not an unmet emotional need.

Many people wrap their honest feelings in the poison of Love Busters. When Takers respond and havoc results, they go back to bottling up their feelings. They think, *I tried being honest and look where it got me.*

It's not easy to express honest feelings without being demanding, disrespectful, or angry, but if you don't avoid those Love Busters, you will fail to communicate your needs to each other effectively. Here are a few examples of how to be honest without being abusive:

"I'm the least important person in your life; you'd rather be with anyone else but me," is a disrespectful judgment because you are making a sweeping generalization about your spouse's priorities and opinions. A less judgmental statement might be, "I know that you're uncomfortable being with me right now." But even that's a bad idea, since you are *telling* your spouse how he or she feels.

In contrast, "I become upset when I'm left alone at night" is an honest expression with no Love Busters in sight, because you are merely explaining to your spouse how *you* feel.

"If you don't start spending more time with me soon, I'll find someone else to join me in the evenings," is a selfish demand. It comes with a threat of punishment if you don't obey.

"I'd like to spend more time with you" is an honest way to communicate your feelings without using Love Busters.

In conquering the Love Buster of dishonesty, you must do more than reveal the truth. You must make sure you express it in a way that informs without needlessly causing harm.

How Honest Should You Be?

You may agree with me that spouses should be honest with each other but you may wonder how far honesty should go. So to eliminate any confusion, I'll explain how honest I encourage couples to be by focusing attention on each of the four parts of the Policy of Radical Honesty:

1. *Emotional Honesty:* Reveal your thoughts, feelings, likes and dislikes. In other words, reveal your emotional reactions—both positive and negative—to the events of your life, particularly to your spouse's behavior.
2. *Historical Honesty:* Reveal information about your personal history, particularly events that demonstrate personal weakness or failure.
3. *Current Honesty:* Reveal information about the events of your day. Provide your spouse with a calendar of your activities, with special emphasis on those that may affect your spouse.
4. *Future Honesty:* Reveal your thoughts and plans regarding future activities and objectives.

Emotional Honesty

Most couples do their best to make each other happy, at least at first. But their efforts, however sincere, are often misdirected. They aim at the wrong target.

> ### Emotional Honesty
> *Reveal your emotional reactions—both positive and negative—to the events of your life, particularly your spouse's behavior.*

Imagine a man who buys his wife flowers every night on the way home from work. What a wonderful thing to do—except that his wife is allergic to them. Because she appreciates the gesture, though, she never mentions her allergies but just sniffles in silence. Soon, however, she begins to dread the thought of her husband coming home with those terrible flowers. Meanwhile, he's getting bored with the marriage because she is always feeling lousy and never has energy to do anything. But of course he won't tell her that.

This couple's marriage is in trouble, not because of any lack of effort, but because of their ignorance—ignorance caused by dishonesty. He thinks he's doing a good thing by bringing home flowers, but he doesn't realize that's the cause of their malaise. Let's say that, in his effort to show even more love for her, he brings home more and more flowers. Ultimately she's collapsed on the couch, gasping for breath, surrounded by flowers, while he wonders what went wrong.

Of course, this is a preposterous story, but it portrays the way many couples misfire in their attempts to please each other. Their lack of honesty keeps them from correcting their real problems.

Some people find it difficult to express their emotional reactions, particularly the negative ones. But negative feelings serve a valuable purpose in a marriage. They are a signal that something is wrong. If you successfully steer clear of angry outbursts, disrespectful judgments, and selfish demands, your expression of negative feelings can alert both you and your spouse to an adjustment that must be made.

> You need accurate information from each other.

Honesty enables a couple to make appropriate adjustments to each other. And adjustment is what a good marriage is all about. Both of you are growing and changing almost daily and you must constantly adjust to each other's changes if you are to remain compatible. But how can you know how to adjust if you're not receiving accurate information about these changes? You'd be flying blind, like a pilot whose instrument panel has shorted out.

You need accurate information from each other. Without this, unhappy situations can go on and on—like the flowers piling up in the allergic woman's home. But if you communicate your feelings to each other, you can correct what you're doing wrong before it becomes a habit.

If Jennifer had told Ed how his behavior was affecting her on their honeymoon, for instance, he could have made an adjustment to accommodate her. If he had told her he was becoming dissatisfied with their sexual relationship, she could have adjusted for him. Instead, their dissatisfaction continued and grew, putting their marriage in jeopardy.

In addition to expressing negative emotions honestly, don't overlook the expression of positive feelings. These are generally easier to communicate, yet many couples have not learned to communicate them well. And by this failure, they miss an important opportunity to *deposit* love units. Whenever your spouse makes *you* feel good,

> Without honest
> communication,
> failure is *guaranteed.*

if you express those feelings clearly and enthusiastically, you'll make *your spouse* feel good, knowing that his or her care is appreciated.

The mere communication of feelings does not assure that all the necessary adjustments will be made. There is still work to do. But without honest communication, failure is *guaranteed.*

Historical Honesty

Should your skeletons stay in the closet?

Some say yes: Lock the door, hide the key, and leave well enough alone. Communicate your past misdeeds only on a need-to-know basis.

But I say your spouse always needs to know. Whatever embarrassing experiences or serious mistakes are in your past, you should come clean with your spouse in the present.

Ed made a serious mistake when he lied to Jennifer about his academic achievements. He told her that he had earned high marks in school, when in fact the opposite was true. Granted, she may have chosen not to marry him if he had told her the truth about his past while they were dating. But she had a right to that information.

Historical Honesty
Reveal information about your personal history, particularly events that demonstrate personal weakness or failure.

Ed deliberately misled Jennifer into thinking that he had been an achiever when in fact he had serious problems motivating himself to fulfill responsibilities. His tendency toward underachievement in his teen years followed him as an adult to his sales job, where he could not motivate himself to make the sales calls that were required of him. But by keeping his history a secret, he was unable to adequately confront his problem and find solutions that would accommodate his predispositions.

Your personal history holds significant information about you—information about your strengths and weaknesses. Your spouse needs to understand both your good and bad points if appropriate adjustments are to be made. When can you be relied upon? When do you need help?

A man who has had an affair in the past is particularly vulnerable to another one. If a woman has been chemically dependent in the past, she'll be susceptible to drug or alcohol abuse in the future. If you express your past mistakes openly, your spouse can understand your weaknesses, and together you can avoid conditions that tend to create problems for you.

No area of your life should be kept secret. All questions asked by your spouse should be answered fully and completely. Periods of poor adjustment in your past should be given special attention, because problems of the past are commonly problems of the future.

Not only should *you* explain your past to your spouse, but you should also encourage your spouse to gather information from those who knew you before you met. I encourage couples who are considering marriage to talk with several significant people from each other's past. It's often an eye-opener!

> No area of your life should be kept secret.

I also encourage you to reveal to each other all romantic relationships you've had in the past. Names should be included along with a description of what happened.

"But if I tell my wife what I've done, she'll never trust me again."

"If my husband finds out about my past, he'll be crushed. It will ruin his whole image of me."

I have heard these protests from various clients trying to hide their past. *Why dig it all up?* they ask. *Let that old affair stay buried in ancient history. Why not just leave that little demon alone?* I answer that it's not a little demon but an extremely important part of their personal story that says something about their habits and character.

But what if you haven't strayed since it happened? What if you've seen a pastor regularly to hold you accountable? Why put your spouse through the agony of a revelation that could ruin your relationship forever?

If that's your argument, I'd say you don't give your spouse much credit. Honesty doesn't drive a spouse away—*dishonesty* does. When you hold something back, your spouse tries to guess what it is. If he or she is correct, then you must continually lie to cover your tracks. If incorrect, your spouse develops a false understanding of you and your predispositions.

Maybe you don't really want to be known for who you are. That's sad, isn't it? You'd rather keep your secret than experience one of life's greatest joys—to be loved and accepted in spite of known weaknesses.

While revealing your past will strengthen your marriage, it's not necessarily painless. Some spouses have difficulty adjusting to revelations that have been kept secret for years—the saints they thought they married turn out to be mere mortals. To control the emotional damage of particularly shocking revelations, it may be helpful to express them to your spouse in the presence of a professional counselor. Some spouses may need some personal support to help them adjust to the reality of their spouse's past.

In cases I've witnessed, however, spouses tend to react more negatively to the long-term deception than to the concealed event. The thoughtless act might be accepted and forgiven, but the cover-up is often harder to understand. If you reveal it instead of waiting for your spouse to discover it, though, it's proof that you are taking honesty in your marriage seriously and will be making an effort in the future to avoid the Love Buster of dishonesty.

You may find historical honesty to be frightening, and that's understandable. But let me assure you that I've never seen a marriage destroyed by truth. When truth is revealed, there are often negative reactions and some shaky times, but ultimately the truth makes marriages stronger. On the other hand, dishonesty destroys intimacy, romantic love, and marriages.

Current Honesty

In good marriages couples become so interdependent that sharing a daily schedule is essential to their coordination of activities. But in weak marriages they are reluctant to reveal their schedules because they often engage in activities that they want to keep from their spouse. They hide the details of their day, telling themselves, "What he doesn't know won't hurt him," or "She's happier not knowing everything."

Even when activities are innocent, it's extremely important for your spouse to understand what you do with your time. Make sure you're easy to find in an emergency or when your spouse just wants to say hello during the day. Keep your cell phones close by so that you can contact each other 24/7. Almost everything you do will affect each other, so it's important to know what each of you is doing.

If Jennifer and Ed had established a habit of exchanging daily information early in their marriage, his six-week deception would have been almost impossible to arrange. They would have called each other throughout the day to keep each other informed regarding any changes in their schedules, and she would have called his office on the very first day he was absent to discover he was no longer employed. But then, if they had practiced the Policy of Radical Honesty, his motivational problem probably would have been resolved years earlier. Instead of taking on a career in sales, which requires incredible self-motivation, he would have chosen a career where less motivation is acceptable.

Current Honesty

Reveal information about the events of your day. Provide your spouse with a calendar of your activities, with special emphasis on those that may affect your spouse.

Honesty is a terrific way to protect your spouse from potentially damaging predispositions and inappropriate activities. When you know that you'll be telling your spouse what you've been up to, you're far less likely to do anything that would get you into trouble.

Future Honesty

After I've made such a big issue of revealing past indiscretions, you can imagine how I feel about revealing future plans. They're *much* easier to discuss with your spouse, yet many couples make plans independently of each other. Why?

Some people believe that communicating future plans just gives a spouse the opportunity to quash them. They have their sights set on a certain goal and they don't want anything to stand in their way. You may be trying to avoid trouble in the present, but eventually the future will arrive and your plans will be revealed. At that point your spouse will be hurt that you didn't consider their feelings when you made your plans. And that will withdraw love units.

The Policy of Joint Agreement—*Never do anything without an enthusiastic*

It's extremely important for your spouse to understand what you do with your time.

131

agreement between you and your spouse—is certainly relevant in discussions of your future plans.

Future Honesty
Reveal your thoughts and plans regarding future activities and objectives.

"If I wait for my wife to agree," a husband might say, "we'll never accomplish anything. She's so conservative, she never wants to take any risks, and so we miss every opportunity that comes along." But isn't that approach, in essence, a disrespectful judgment, forcing the husband's perspective onto the wife? If he genuinely cares about her, he will want to include her interests and feelings in every decision.

"Oh, but the plans I make are best for both of us," a wife might say. "He may not understand my decision now but once he sees how things turn out, he'll thank me for going ahead with it." That's disrespectful. Even if your plans work out, your spouse will still feel offended about not being included in the planning.

Encouraging Honesty

You may want your spouse to be honest, but do your own values encourage it? Do your reactions discourage your spouse from revealing the truth, even if it's pleasant? To see how you rate, answer these questions:

1. If the truth is terribly upsetting to you, do you want your spouse to be honest only at a time when you are emotionally prepared?
2. Do you keep some aspects of your life secret and do you encourage your spouse to respect your privacy in those areas?
3. Do you have well-defined boundaries that you encourage your spouse not to cross?
4. Do you like to create a certain mystery between you and your spouse?
5. Are there subjects or situations where you would want to avoid radical honesty?
6. Do you ever make selfish demands when your spouse is honest with you?

7. Do you ever make disrespectful judgments when your spouse is honest with you?
8. Do you ever have angry outbursts when your spouse is honest with you?

If you answer "yes" to any of the first five questions, you tend to compromise on the value of honesty. Apparently you feel your marriage is better off with dishonesty in certain situations. That little crack is all dishonesty needs to slip into your marriage and run amok. You see, there are always "reasons" to be dishonest. As soon as you allow one to sneak in, it will invite all its friends, and before you know it, you have a dishonest relationship.

If you answered "yes" to questions 6, 7, or 8, you are punishing honesty and encouraging dishonesty. The way to help your spouse learn to be truthful is to minimize the negative consequences of his or her truthful revelations. If your spouse is faced with a fight whenever truth is revealed, you invite dishonesty. Your spouse will learn to say anything to avoid arguing—and then do what he or she pleases. But what if there are no fights? No judgments? No demands? If you can eliminate these Love Busters, you'll make it much easier for your spouse to be honest with you.

Overcoming Dishonesty

There are many psychotherapists and even clergy who are not convinced that honesty is the best policy. Some go so far as to encourage dishonesty in some circumstances because of their misguided view that what one spouse doesn't know about the other spouse won't hurt him or her. So it should be no surprise to you that many, if not most, marriage counselors do not know how to help couples overcome dishonesty.

But because I have found radical honesty to be so important in marriage, it should also be no surprise to you that I've created a tried and proven plan to help overcome dishonesty in your marriage. If you follow these steps, you will not only eliminate the Love Buster, dishonesty, but you will also create a love builder by meeting the emotional need for honesty and openness.

Step 1: Identify what type of liar you are (protector, try to look good, or avoid trouble) and what parts of honesty you have difficulty achieving (emotional, historical, current, and future).

ACTION
STEP

Identify what type of liar you are and what parts of honesty you have difficulty achieving.

If dishonesty has crept into your marriage, your spouse may not be entirely aware of it. If you have an angry outburst, your spouse can identify the offense as soon as it happens. But in the case of dishonesty, your spouse may not know that it's occurred until months later when he or she has the evidence for dishonesty firmly in hand. So the first step in overcoming this Love Buster is to reveal it as the monster that it is. If you really want to become honest, you must first reveal the *fact* that you've been dishonest. And you must reveal the *way* in which you tend to be dishonest.

Are you a protector liar, a trying-to-look-good liar, an avoid-trouble liar, or all three? And do you tend to lie about your emotional reactions, your past history, your present activities, your future plans, or all four? By revealing the fact that you have been dishonest, and the ways you've been dishonest, you take the first and extremely important step that requires radical honesty. It's only as you reveal dishonesty that you're able to usher it out the door.

Step 2: Understand why you have been dishonest.

After you have admitted your dishonesty, the next step is to understand what motivates you to be dishonest, and why dishonesty has established itself in your marriage. I suggest that you answer the

ACTION
STEP

Understand why you have been dishonest.

following questions to help you discover some of the causes of your dishonesty. If both you and your spouse have a problem with honesty, you should both answer these questions. The purpose of this questionnaire is to try to get at the root of why you're dishonest and what you think you might do to overcome your dishonesty.

Before you answer these questions, though, reflect on the four parts of honesty (emotional, historical, present, and future). You may wish to answer the questions differently for each of the four. If that's the case, make four copies of the questions on separate sheets of paper.

1. What are the most important reasons that you are dishonest with your spouse?
2. How does your dishonesty hurt your spouse (ask your spouse to answer this question)?
3. If you have tried to overcome dishonesty in the past, how did you try to do it? What were the results?
4. If you were to decide that you would be radically honest with your spouse, and would never again be dishonest, could you do it? Why or why not?
5. Are you willing to be radically honest with your spouse? Why or why not?
6. Add any further information that might help you avoid dishonesty with your spouse in the future.

One of the subjects that comes up when people complete this questionnaire is the alleged need for privacy. As a marital therapist, I have never been an advocate for privacy in marriage. As a matter of fact, privacy does the opposite of what I want to see couples achieve—an integration of their wisdom in making decisions together. I want them to know each other thoroughly and respond appropriately to each other's needs. So the kind of partnership that I try to create for couples does not allow for privacy, and it certainly doesn't allow for a secret second life where spouses are engaged in potentially offensive behavior behind each other's backs. An affair, probably the most hurtful thing that one spouse could do to another, is almost impossible without a secret second life. And a secret second life is impossible if a couple agrees to radical honesty.

Of course, if you're going to be radically honest, you should also eliminate any offensive behavior. If your spouse doesn't like something you're doing, stop doing it. That prospect, of course, might be a serious roadblock in your path to becoming radically honest. Your Taker will not like it one single bit. But then, if you leave decisions up to your Taker, your marriage can't possibly survive.

Step 3: Create a strategy to overcome dishonesty.

After you know what you want to achieve, the next step is to create a plan to achieve it. To help you arrive at that strategy, answer the following questions:

1. Describe your dishonesty. Include a description of your feelings, your thoughts, your attitudes, and the way you are dishonest (emotional, historical, present, future).
2. Describe the conditions that seem to trigger your dishonesty. Include physical setting, people present, behavior of those people, and any other relevant conditions.
3. What changes in those conditions would help you avoid dishonesty?
4. Which changes can be made with your spouse's enthusiastic support and agreement?
5. Describe your plans to change these conditions. Include a deadline to make the change complete. Be certain that your spouse has your enthusiastic agreement.
6. Which of the changes described in the third question cannot be made with your spouse's enthusiastic agreement, or cannot be made at all?
7. Describe your plan to overcome dishonesty when those conditions exist. Include a deadline for successful completion of the plan. Be certain that the plan has your spouse's enthusiastic agreement.
8. How will you measure the success of your plan to overcome dishonesty? Does this measure of success have your spouse's enthusiastic agreement?
9. If your plan does not succeed within your designated time limit, will you make a commitment to your spouse to seek professional help in designing and executing an effective plan to overcome dishonesty? How will you go about finding that help?

As I've already mentioned, one of the ways to overcome a bad habit is to simply get rid of the conditions that seem to trigger that habit. You may notice, for example, that there are certain people in your life that tend to encourage you to be dishonest with your spouse. Perhaps with those people you find yourself engaging in certain behavior that offends your spouse. And then when your spouse asks about what you've been doing, you lie about it. By simply eliminating these people as friends you may find you've eliminated your dishonesty as well.

ACTION STEP

Create a strategy to overcome dishonesty.

You'll probably find that your inquiry into the conditions that trigger your dishonesty tends to focus quite a bit of attention on what I've called a *secret second life*. Of course, I encourage you to completely eliminate a secret second life and by doing so you may find that this is the solution to your problem with dishonesty. If you're simply not doing things that would offend your spouse, you're not going to be as tempted to be dishonest.

But you may find that the conditions that seem to trigger your dishonesty can't be changed. For example, financial pressures may tempt you to be dishonest. When you can't pay your bills you are tempted to keep that fact from your spouse. And you simply can't change the condition of your financial pressure.

In that situation you should create a strategy where, under those very conditions that tempt you to be dishonest, you deliberately practice being honest. You explain to your spouse how difficult it is to reveal the fact that you can't pay your bills and involve him or her in all financial decisions. To make it easier to be honest, you could deposit all the money you earn into a checking account that your spouse can clearly see. All the bills that you pay are paid only after there is a mutual and enthusiastic agreement. Any unpaid bills would be known and their disposition would be agreed to by your spouse.

If you and your spouse become partners in decision-making, where all the decisions that you make follow the Policy of Joint Agreement, and you don't allow yourself a secret second life, it's much easier to be honest.

Step 4: Document your progress.

When you're ready to put your strategy to overcome dishonesty into action, I encourage you to document your progress. Title a sheet of paper "Dishonesty Worksheet" and use it to list all instances of dishonesty.

ACTION STEP

Document your progress.

Most of my plans to overcome Love Busters require that the offended spouse complete the worksheet to document progress. But in this case, you and your spouse should complete it together, since there may be instances of your dishonesty that your spouse would not know of if you did not tell him or her.

Indicate the day, date, time, description, type of dishonesty, and circumstances whenever you document an instance of dishonesty. If your strategy to overcome dishonesty is successful, you'll find yourself listing fewer and fewer instances of dishonesty. This plan will eventually lead you into the habit of being completely honest with your spouse and your spouse will be in the habit of encouraging that honesty by avoiding demands, disrespect, or anger when you are honest.

Once you've been able to overcome this Love Buster, dishonesty, you'll find your relationship improving in many different ways. You'll have not only eliminated this great offense to your spouse, but by being honest you'll have learned to meet a very important emotional need. Your honesty will also open the door to effective ways to meet other emotional needs, and you'll be in love with each other as a result.

You will also have a much easier time resolving conflicts because you'll have a much clearer understanding of both the conflict itself and how each of you will react to possible resolutions. By having the facts on the table, it will be much easier to find solutions that make you happy simultaneously. Without the barrier of unspoken feelings, you'll be able to cut to the chase, understand each other quickly, protect each other's feelings, and create solutions to your conflicts that will help you build a deeper love for each other. And that's my ultimate goal for your marriage. I want you to be in love. And the way for you to be in love is to make each other happy by meeting each other's important emotional needs, and avoid making each other unhappy by eliminating Love Busters such as dishonesty.

Key Principles

The Policy of Radical Honesty (Basic Concept #6): Reveal to your spouse as much information about yourself as you know: your thoughts, feelings, habits, likes, dislikes, personal history, daily activities, and plans for the future.

Radical honesty is essential in marriage because (1) it provides a clear road map for marital adjustment, (2) it meets an important emotional need, and (3) dishonesty is a Love Buster—it causes massive Love Bank withdrawals.

There are four types of dishonesty in marriage: (1) protection, (2) looking good, (3) avoiding trouble, and (4) compulsion.

Honesty is not a Love Buster. When thoughtless behavior is revealed, it's the thoughtless behavior, not the honesty, that causes unhappiness.

Avoid wrapping honesty in the Love Busters of selfish demands, disrespectful judgments, or angry outbursts.

Encourage your spouse to be honest by valuing honesty, and by avoiding its punishment.

Consider This . . .

1. What are the four types of liars? We are all dishonest once in a while. Where are you the most vulnerable? If you were to classify yourself as one of the four types of liars, which would come closest to describing you?

2. What is the Policy of Radical Honesty and what are the four parts of the policy? Do you agree that you should both follow this policy? If so, why? If not, why not? You will probably find that you are likely to want your spouse to be honest with you more than you want to be honest with your spouse.

3. If the truth is terribly upsetting to you, do you want your spouse to be honest only at a time when you are emotionally prepared?

4. Do you keep some aspects of your life secret and do you encourage your spouse to respect your privacy in those areas?

5. Are there conditions under which you would not want honesty at all costs between you and your spouse?

6. Do you encourage honesty, or do you punish it? Repeat the questions I raised earlier (see pages 132–33) to measure negative reactions to honesty.

7. Do you ever have angry outbursts, make disrespectful judgments, or make selfish demands when your spouse is honest with you?

8. If dishonesty has claimed some of the love you could be having toward each other, how do you to plan to get rid of it once and for all? Do you think you can follow my four steps to overcoming dishonesty on your own? Or will you need someone to help motivate you and hold you accountable?

9. Try following my four steps to overcoming dishonesty on your own as a test of your ability to motivate each other. But if you can't seem to get it off the ground, or it stalls, get help from a counselor with experience helping couples overcome dishonesty and a proven record of success.

7

ANNOYING HABITS
Who Wants to Live with a Dripping Faucet?

Long before she married Mike, Sharon knew that some of his habits irritated her. For instance, she didn't like the way he sat in a chair. She admired men who sat straight and tall, giving the impression that they were alert and attentive. When a man slouched in his chair, it reminded her of some of her fat and lazy relatives.

But slouching was Mike's specialty—especially when he came home after work and parked in front of the TV.

"Mike, it really bothers me when you sit like that," she told him when they were newlyweds. "Please sit up in the chair."

Mike straightened up and continued watching television with a better posture, but a few minutes later he slumped back into the same position.

When Sharon returned to the room, she was always very disappointed. "Why do you sit like that, when you know it bothers me?"

Mike would quickly straighten up and say, "Oh, I'm sorry."

"You can't possibly be sorry. You just don't care how I feel."

"Look, Sharon," he'd answer, getting a little irritated. "I've had a hard day at work. Just don't look at me, and you'll feel much better."

Sharon would sometimes leave the room in tears, but Mike would be too absorbed in TV to notice. At first, her tears reflected her anger toward Mike, but after a while she began to doubt herself.

It's such a small thing, she thought. *He needs to relax after work, and I'm just being selfish to expect him to sit in his chair a certain way.*

So she decided to keep her feelings to herself. Whenever she saw Mike slumped in his chair, it still annoyed her but she didn't say anything. While the marriage seemed peaceful, Mike was losing love units with each slouch.

He never knew what was happening to his Love Bank account, and Sharon may not have been fully aware of it either. She didn't want to nag him about it because she felt he had a right to sit any way he chose, but still it bothered her. As time went on, Mike developed other annoying habits, such as chewing ice and spitting it back into his glass, but as with his sitting posture, Sharon felt she had no right to change him.

When they came to see me for counseling, Sharon was in withdrawal and wanted a separation. She wouldn't tell Mike what was bothering her—she simply told him that they weren't right for each other.

Mike's poor posture had become only one example of many habits that made him an almost constant irritant to Sharon. She could hardly tolerate being with him for more than a few minutes at a time, because that's how long it took before another one of his annoying habits appeared. Though she didn't believe in divorce, she just had to get away from Mike and his bad habits.

Yet Mike's "bad" habits were all essentially innocent. They all fell into the same category as his sitting posture. His eating habits, his tone of voice when he disciplined the children, phrases he overused, and the mess he left around the house were simply mannerisms—the ways that he did things. None of these habits were "evil" or intentionally offensive, and Sharon knew this. Another woman might not react the same way, and would be delighted to have him for a husband. But his behavior drove Sharon up a wall. Though she felt guilty about her reaction, it had become so strong and negative that she was sure she'd go crazy unless they split up.

Why Are We So Annoying?

When was the last time your spouse did something that annoyed you? Last week? Yesterday? An hour ago? If you're male, the answer is probably "last week," if at all. But if you're female, it's more likely to be "this very minute."

For some reason, women seem to find men more annoying than men find women. But, male or female, our annoying habits draw love units out of our spouse's Love Bank every time.

As a marriage counselor, I tell couples that eliminating annoying habits will improve their marriages. This is not rocket science. It only makes sense that you'll get along better if you stop doing things that drive each other to distraction. But you'd be amazed how many couples just don't get it.

"If Sharon just accepted me for who I am," Mike suggested, "she wouldn't mind it when I pick my teeth after a meal."

"Picking his teeth with his finger," Sharon adds. "And by the time he really gets into it, he's got his whole fist in his mouth."

Annoying Habits
Behaviors repeated without much thought that bother the other spouse.

Couples often sit in my office and try to convince me that they should be able to do whatever they please—that the objecting spouse should adjust to the annoying habits.

Of course, when *we're* annoyed, we usually think others are being inconsiderate, particularly when we've explained how it bothers us and they continue to do it. But when our behavior annoys *others*, we feel we have a right to persist, demanding that others adjust to us.

I often wish I could swap spouses' minds: Mike becomes Sharon for a day and feels what Sharon feels when he picks his teeth. If he could only know *how* annoying his habits are, surely he would try to become more considerate. He might argue that it wouldn't bother him if Sharon picked her teeth, but that's not the point. If he could feel what Sharon feels, he would understand why she wants him to change.

So one reason we are annoying is that we don't feel what our spouse feels. As a counselor, I try to help couples become more empathetic— see situations through each other's eyes. Sometimes that helps motivate spouses to overcome annoying habits.

But there is another reason that we are annoying—we often don't care how our spouse feels.

Viewed from the perspective of our Giver, we should be trying to eliminate anything that our spouse finds annoying. After all, the rule of the Giver is: *Do whatever you can to make your spouse happy and avoid anything that makes your spouse unhappy, even if it makes you unhappy.* If your spouse doesn't like something you're doing, you should simply stop doing it even if it would require great sacrifice.

> One reason we are annoying is that we don't feel what our spouse feels.

Our problem, of course, is that our Taker doesn't quite see it the same way. Remember the Taker's rule: *Do whatever you can to make yourself happy and avoid anything that makes you unhappy, even if it means making others unhappy.* That rule encourages you to continue any annoying habit that you happen to have. If your spouse says that he or she doesn't like what you're doing, you ask yourself, "Do I like it?" If the answer is, "yes," you keep right on doing it.

Remember, the Taker is not concerned about how your spouse feels. It's only concerned about how you feel. *Besides*, your Taker would argue, *I'm not trying to make my spouse feel bad. I'm just being myself. It's up to my spouse to accept me as I am. If he or she expects me to change, it must mean that my spouse doesn't really care about me.*

Of course this is a very familiar argument to me, because I've heard it time and time again by the couples that I counsel. When I explain to them that their annoying habits are ruining the love that they could have for each other, I often hear the argument that they want to be loved for who they are, not what they do, especially when what they do is innocent—when it's mannerisms that just come naturally to them.

Quite frankly, all of us are changing habits on a regular basis. Sometimes we do it by design, and sometimes circumstances simply change our habits for us. But we don't change our identity whenever we change a habit. I'm the same person regardless of how I sit in a chair or how I eat. So if I can convince you that your habits are not sacred, that they don't represent characteristics of your identity that will be forever lost if you change them, I can then help you avoid needless loss of love units by simply changing some of your habits: those that your spouse finds annoying.

Habits That Bother Your Spouse Unintentionally Withdraw Love Units

The bottom line is that a couple who want to stay in love must pay close attention to the way they affect each other. A marriage just doesn't work if either spouse ignores that reality. Whether they're intentional or not, habits affect the love they have for each other. So if one spouse finds some of the other's habits annoying, they simply have to go. Otherwise their marriage won't be what either one wants it to be.

Because annoying habits usually have this element of innocence, couples generally don't view them with the same seriousness as, say, angry outbursts, which are an intentional effort to hurt the other spouse. And I would agree with that analysis. Angry outbursts are a show-stopper. You simply cannot solve your problems as long as they exist.

> Whether they're intentional or not, habits affect the love spouses have for each other.

But if you're to consider the total number of love units lost, it can be argued that annoying habits might actually withdraw more love units than angry outbursts. While angry outbursts might occur only once every six months, annoying habits are unrelenting, day after day, week after week, month after month. Your annoying habits and the annoying habits of your spouse slowly but surely drain your Love Bank. If you and your spouse don't consider them seriously, your Love Bank is going to be like a sieve. Regardless of how fast you keep pouring love units into that Love Bank, they may drain out even faster unless annoying habits are eliminated.

Overcoming Annoying Habits

Most of our behavior is habitual. We may think we act spontaneously and creatively, but on closer analysis, we tend to be very predictable. We do have the power to change, however. We can turn annoying habits into pleasing ones if we have a good reason to do so. The following steps will help any couple get rid of the annoying habits that keep them from experiencing the best marriage has to offer.

145

Step 1: Identify each other's annoying habits.

The first step in solving most problems is to identify the problem, and that is certainly true when it comes to overcoming annoying habits. Both of you should make a list of as many as occur to you. In creating that list, you will be able to think of some of them almost immediately. But other habits will only occur to you when your spouse actually does them. So get out a pad of paper or PDA and keep it close by, so you can add to your list when inspiration strikes. Take a few days to complete your inventory.

Beside each annoying habit you list, enter a number between 1 and 10, indicating how intensely you are annoyed (1 = mildly annoying, 10 = extremely annoying). The numbers help identify the behavior that is withdrawing the most love units.

ACTION STEP

Identify each other's annoying habits.

When I ask a couple to list each other's annoying habits, the wife's list is almost always longer than the husband's list. In fact for many couples I counsel, the husbands have no entries at all, but it's not uncommon for a woman to list more than fifty habits and activities she finds annoying. One wife I counseled completed twenty-four single-spaced pages containing her husband's annoying habits.

I assure husbands that a long list of irritating behaviors should not lead them to conclude that they are incurably incompatible and that there is no hope. In fact, making the list is the first step toward improving compatibility—resolving problems that have been swept under a rug. They must uncover the dirt before they can vacuum it up.

And yet, this exercise has a high risk for hurt feelings. It's easy for your Taker to convince you that your spouse's long list is an act of disrespect. But it's nothing of the kind. It's simply an honest reaction to habits that you can, and should, change.

But if you are not careful, you may actually be disrespectful when you make your lists. Go easy in the way you describe the annoying habits. Remember, most annoying habits are innocent—you happen to find them annoying. The reason you want your spouse to change his or her habits is not necessarily because there is something wrong with the habits themselves. It's because they may prevent you from being in love.

I asked Sharon to let me see her list before she showed it to Mike. That's because I wanted to be sure that it did not contain any disrespectful comments. I wanted her descriptions of annoying habits to be simple and nonjudgmental. But she did not heed my advice. Her list still contained many comments such as "you should stop eating like a pig," and "stop being so lazy and learn to pick up after yourself." After we weeded out her disrespectful judgments, the list described Mike's most annoying behavior respectfully.

> Most annoying habits are innocent.

I'm not there to help you weed disrespectful judgments out of your lists, so check your lists very carefully before you show them to each other. Don't make the same mistakes that Sharon made when she made her first list. Instead, describe your spouse's annoying behavior as simply as possible, without making any value judgments about it. It annoys you, and that's all you need to explain. This was Sharon's list.

Intensity Rating	Annoying Habits
10	Slouching in the living room chair
7	Tone of voice when disciplining the children
8	Overusing certain phrases, such as, "you don't say."
9	Leaving toothpaste, toothbrush, shaver, and towel on the bathroom sink
8	Leaving clothes on the bedroom floor after getting ready for bed
9	Stuffing chips into mouth before swallowing the ones already there
7	Chewing ice and spitting it back into the glass
8	Licking the knife at the dinner table

Step 2: Eliminate the easy ones first.

A list of annoying habits usually includes a few habits that can be easily overcome with a simple decision to stop doing them. These are new habits that have not had time to become hard-wired into your brain, or habits that do not provide much gratification.

But the one who is annoyed thinks all bad habits should be easily overcome. Sharon thought that if she told Mike that the way he sat in

ACTION STEP

Eliminate the easy ones first.

the chair annoyed her, he could either stop doing it because he cared about her feelings, or he could keep doing it because he didn't care. It didn't occur to her that there was a third alternative—he cared about her feelings, but sat in an annoying way anyway because he was in the habit of doing so.

Sharon, like most people, did not understand the control habits have over us. She was under the illusion that we make a deliberate decision to do each thing we do. Truth is, most of what we do is automatic and effortless. One habit follows another and we really don't give much thought to what we do throughout the day.

Mike did not understand the control habits have over us either. He thought he could stop doing everything that Sharon listed with a simple decision to stop. But after we discussed each one with an eye to how long he had been doing it, and how much pleasure each gave him, we decided that knife-licking might be Mike's easiest habit to overcome.

It turned out that we were right. He had not been licking his knife long, and it also gave him very little pleasure. So from that day on, Sharon never saw him do it again. But he knew that if she ever did, it would be re-entered onto her list.

If you can check off one or more annoying habits that you know will be easy to overcome, it will shorten the time it takes to eventually check them all off the list. But most habits take some time to change, so don't make the mistake of assuming that a simple decision to change is all it takes. And most annoying habits are not easy to change, so don't tackle too many annoying habits at once. That's why, in the next step, I asked Sharon to select the ones that bothered her most.

Most of what we do is automatic and effortless.

Step 3: Select the three most annoying habits to overcome.

You can eventually eliminate most of each other's annoying habits, but to be successful you'll have to focus on only a few at a time. I suggest three at a time. Select the three behaviors that are the most annoying and eliminate those first.

Sharon had a fairly short list of annoying habits. So, after eliminating knife-licking, it would have been tempting to work on all seven of the remaining habits to keep those Love Busters from doing any more damage.

ACTION STEP

Select the three most annoying habits to overcome.

But I did not recommend that to Sharon and Mike. Instead, I suggested that they focus on the three habits that got her highest intensity ratings. If more than three have the same high rating, I would have had Sharon select the three that she wanted to see overcome first.

On the list above, there was only one "10"—the way he sat on the chair in the living room. The next most annoying habits, "9s," were chip-stuffing and bathroom-messing. If there had been more 9s, Sharon would have picked the two that she wanted Mike to overcome first.

Step 4: Determine why the annoying habit exists.

After three annoying habits have been selected, we're ready for the next step. We need to know why each habit formed and what's keeping it there. I use the following questionnaire to help a couple investigate the background of each habit.

1. When did this habit begin?
2. What are the most important reasons you began this habit?
3. What are the most important reasons you have this habit now?
4. When you engage in this habit, how do you feel?
5. When you engage in this habit, how does your spouse feel?
6. Have you ever tried to avoid this habit? If so, how did you do it?
7. Why didn't it work?
8. What would make the elimination of this habit more likely?

ACTION STEP

Determine why the annoying habit exists.

The purpose of each question is fairly self-explanatory. Not only do I want a couple to understand the background of the behavior, but I want them to think it through as well. Most spouses engage in annoying behavior for trivial reasons. They may give a more philosophical explanation, but deep down they may know that it's there simply because it was repeated often enough to become a habit. And when it comes right down to it, they can get used to doing it another way.

At this point you may find my approach to helping you overcome annoying habits a bit tedious. Making lists and filling out worksheets may seem very foreign to you and unnecessarily burdensome. You may take the position that if you simply decide to overcome this annoying habit you should be able to do it. Why all the paperwork?

ACTION STEP

Create a plan to overcome the annoying habit.

Well, the reason that I encourage you to go to all this trouble is because if you don't actually write down the annoying habits that you want to eliminate, you'll forget what it is you're trying to do. And if you don't document your reasons for engaging in an annoying habit, you will have difficulty creating a plan to overcome it. In other words, these worksheets that I'm encouraging you to use will make your success far more likely. So please bear with me as you're filling out these forms. They may seem unnecessary to you right now, but after you start seeing success, I think you'll agree with me that they're essential.

There are only two more forms to go, so hang on just a little longer.

Step 5: Create a plan to overcome the annoying habit.

Whenever you create a plan to overcome a habit, remember that the habit is something you do almost unconsciously. The way you eat your cereal during breakfast, take a shower in the morning, and get into your car are instances of automatic, almost effortless habits. Over 95 percent of all you do is in the form of habits, because you really don't think about them, you simply do them. That's why some people think that habits should not be changed. They don't know quite how they got their habits and assume they're there for a good reason. But as it turns out, many of your habits are there for trivial reasons. It's the way you happened to do something at one point in time and you have just continued doing it that way ever since.

Habits are formed by simply repeating the new behavior often enough. Eventually you do it without giving it much thought. But if your spouse finds one of your habits to be annoying, it can be overcome by repeating another behavior in its place. It's a simple strategy that will work every time you try it.

There are two approaches that I recommend to overcoming an annoying habit. One is to change the conditions that trigger the habit, and learn a new habit under new triggering conditions; and the other is to learn a new habit under the same conditions that trigger the old habit. Of these two approaches, the first, eliminating the conditions that trigger an annoying habit, is much easier to implement than changing the behavior under the influence of the triggering conditions.

I'll give you an illustration of how that works. Sharon was annoyed by the way Mike sat in the living room chair while watching television. For Mike, the conditions of coming home from work and the placement of the chair and television were triggering conditions. His brain was wired to drive home after work, get out of his car, walk into the house, go straight to his favorite chair, grab the remote control, slouch, and then start watching TV.

My plan to help Mike overcome his annoying habit began by breaking up his homecoming routine. I suggested that when Mike came home from work each day, instead of going straight to the remote control, he spend about ten minutes sitting down with Sharon and a cup of coffee. They were to talk about how the day went and how they were planning to spend their evening. It helped break up his routine, which also changed the triggering conditions of his annoying behavior. And that made it easier to develop a new habit of how he would sit while he watched TV.

> Habits are formed by simply repeating the new behavior often enough.

Just that one change made all the difference in the world. It turned out that much of Sharon's irritability about how he sat in the chair had quite a bit to do with his finding the TV more interesting than her. Now, instead of slouching in his chair, Mike was sitting across from Sharon talking to her about their day. He not only eliminated a habit that caused anger and resentment, but he replaced it with a habit that met one of Sharon's important emotional needs, intimate conversation. Mike had a lot of love units to deposit, and talking to Sharon every day after work was a great way to start.

When it came time to watch TV, Mike sat in a different chair with the TV in a different location. That made it easier for him to form a new habit. The first day, he asked Sharon how she would like him to sit in the chair. She wanted him to sit up straight, but that made him feel uncomfortable. He tried various positions, but nothing except slouching seemed comfortable to him.

Part of his discomfort was due to the fact that *any* new behavior can be uncomfortable at first. Whenever a new behavior is introduced to your brain, it must form new neural pathways before it feels natural to you. The more you repeat the new behavior, the more complete the new neural pathways become. Eventually, the pathways are completed, and you have a new habit—automatic and almost effortless.

I knew that Mike sat up straight in his chair at work and it didn't bother him, so he wasn't having a physical problem sitting that way. I suggested that he practice sitting the way Sharon wanted him to sit for just one week, to see how he would feel after doing it a few times.

> *Any* new behavior can be uncomfortable at first.

For a few days Mike was uncomfortable coming home and finding that he could not sit in his chair and watch television right away. And he found that sitting down with his wife, talking about his day was somewhat uncomfortable as well. But after talking to Sharon after work and sitting the way Sharon wanted him to sit for just a few days, Mike agreed that it became much more natural and comfortable for him.

The longer Mike practiced his new after-work routine, the more effortless it became. In fact, he eventually got to a point where he experienced quite a loss when Sharon was not there to greet him when he arrived home. That's the way our habits work. When we're in the habit of doing something, we miss it if we're prevented from doing it.

The example I just used was based on the assumption that you can change the triggering conditions of the original annoying habit. We got rid of the chair and moved the television. That change provided the opportunity for a new habit to be formed. But what if you can't get rid of the triggering conditions?

Suppose the chair and the television are just going to stay where they are. And suppose that Sharon was not able to talk to Mike after work to break up his old habit of watching TV right away. How would you go about changing the behavior then? As it turns out, it's much more difficult to do, but it can also be done.

It takes a great deal more practice to change a habit when the conditions that trigger it can't be changed. It might have taken Mike weeks of sitting up straight if he had been faced with the same conditions. He would have had to deliberately practice his new sitting habit every night, and it might have been uncomfortable for a much longer period of time. That's why I encourage most couples to try to eliminate triggering conditions if at all possible. But if the status quo causes an unrelenting loss of love units, it's worth the effort to overcome annoying habits when triggering conditions cannot be changed.

Step 6: Measure your progress.

Whether a plan is easy or difficult to implement, it helps to document your progress. I encourage the couples I counsel to keep track of how things are going by writing any instance of the annoying habit on a sheet of paper. Of course, each record represents a failure to follow the plan. The date, time, and circumstances should also be documented. The spouse who finds the habit annoying should keep the record.

In completing this report, honesty is essential. An annoyed spouse might be tempted to go easy on their mate and under-report annoying incidents. Of course, this can undermine the entire process, and lead to no change in the habit. Even occasional failures can prevent a new habit from forming.

ACTION STEP

Measure your progress.

If a plan is followed perfectly, there is nothing to document. There are no failures. But if an annoying habit persists, I suggest changing the plan to completely eliminate it.

I don't consider a habit overcome until at least three months have passed with no failure. A phenomenon called "spontaneous recovery" can sometimes cause the habit to mysteriously reappear months or even years after it seemed to end. But in such recurrences, the habit is no longer well formed and can usually be overcome quickly by going right back to the original plan for its removal. Instead of months of practice, only days are required to resume the new habit.

Step 7: Overcome the next three annoying habits on the list.

After you succeed at eliminating the three most annoying habits with a plan for each, you're ready to overcome the next three that are on the list. And you'll find that the next three will be much easier to overcome, because you now know the system for changing bad habits into good habits.

But at this point you may ask the question, *won't this turn out to be an endless task? Just as soon as I've eliminated all the annoying habits on the list, won't more come along? Am I going to be working on this the rest of my life?*

If you're following the Policy of Joint Agreement, where whatever you do is with the mutual enthusiastic agreement of you and your spouse, any new annoying habits simply won't ever be formed. They'll never get off the ground. You may do something once or twice before you realize that it doesn't have your spouse's enthusiastic agreement, but that's not nearly enough repetitions for it to become a habit. And it's very easy for you to overcome something that's not yet become a habit.

ACTION STEP

Overcome the next three annoying habits on the list.

Almost everything you do affects each other, so take your annoying habits very seriously. When you learn to overcome them, you will have eliminated one of the most insidious ways that spouses lose their love for each other. After you go to the trouble of changing a few habits, it will be just as easy to make your spouse happy as it was to make your spouse miserable.

Your annoying habits are not essential to your identity, and are certainly not inevitable. They are there for trivial reasons, and can be changed to make it just as effortless to deposit love units as it's been to withdraw them. You'll be far more attractive to your spouse after those annoying habits have been eliminated.

Key Principles

Annoying habits are behaviors repeated without much thought that bother your spouse.

We engage in annoying habits because we don't feel what our spouse feels or we don't care how our spouse feels when we do them.

Whether it's intentional or not, a couple's behavior will affect the love they have for each other.

Habits are formed by simply repeating the new behavior often enough.

Any new behavior is often uncomfortable at first. Whenever a new behavior is introduced to your brain, it must form new neural pathways before it feels natural to you. But the more a new behavior is repeated, the stronger the new neural pathways become. Eventually, the pathways are completed, and a new habit is formed—automatic and almost effortless behavior.

Consider This…

1. What is an annoying habit? I'm sure you have already overcome a few in your marriage. Can you think of things you've done in the past that were annoying to each other that are no longer an issue? How did you go about ridding yourselves of those Love Busters?

2. How have your Giver and Taker tried to influence you regarding annoying habits? Remember, the Giver will try to encourage you to accept the other's annoying habits, while your Taker will try to convince you that yours should be accepted as a part of your identity. Why do both arguments lead to the loss of love in marriage?

3. Most annoying habits are innocent—you don't do them to upset each other, it just turns out that way. Why can this make annoying habits more difficult to overcome than the other Love Busters we've discussed so far?

4. Does my plan to help you overcome annoying habits seem unnecessarily tedious? If it seems too overwhelming and prevents you from getting started, modify it enough that you will be willing to follow it for a while. But if you fail to eliminate annoying habits with your plan, agree to return to my plan, because my plan works whenever it's tried.

5. Remember my warning that habits are much more difficult to change than most people think. On the other hand, all habits can be changed. If you repeat a new behavior often enough, and by doing that succeed in eliminating just one annoying habit, you will have learned what most behavioral psychologists like myself have already learned—how to change human behavior. When an annoying habit is overcome, your personal identity remains the same, but you become a much more attractive person.

6. How does the Policy of Joint Agreement prevent the creation of new annoying habits?

8

INDEPENDENT BEHAVIOR
Who Wants to Live with an Inconsiderate Jerk?

Brian came to my office with his wife Kay, wanting to know why she wouldn't make love to him. In my interview with Kay, she admitted that the spark was gone, and that she had lost her feeling of attraction for her husband. It wasn't that Brian lacked skill in lovemaking—he certainly knew how to be a good lover. Kay's problem was that she no longer felt emotionally connected to him.

In the early years of their marriage, Kay had tried to become a part of Brian's life. But he insisted on having his own friends, hobbies, leisure activities, and, in general, ways of living that were independent of her. He would not integrate her into his life, and she was not consulted in the decisions he made. So she finally gave up and learned to be just as independent as he was. She lived her life without considering his feelings, just as he had not considered her feelings.

What's Wrong with Independence?

At first glance, independent behavior in marriage might seem not only desirable but also essential for a healthy and happy marriage. After all, who wants to be clingy and dependent? And who wants a spouse who is clingy and dependent—unable to do anything by themselves or make any decisions of their own?

But independent behavior is not the only alternative to unhealthy dependency. Another far superior alternative is what I call **interdependency**, which is behaving in ways that take each other's feelings into account.

_____

Independent Behavior

Activities of a spouse that are conceived and executed as if the other spouse did not exist.

_____

It all goes back to what I have been repeating throughout this book—almost everything you do in marriage will affect each other either positively or negatively, whether or not you intended to do so. If you want a marriage that makes both of you happy, you must pay close attention to the ways your behavior affects each other. And then you must learn to behave in ways that make each other happy, and avoid making each other unhappy.

For purposes of this discussion, let me give you my definition of independent behavior in marriage—it's the activities of a spouse that are conceived and executed as if the other spouse did not even exist. It's independent in that it neglects the interests and feelings of the other spouse.

Interdependent behavior, on the other hand, is the activities of a spouse that are conceived and executed with the interests of both spouses in mind. It recognizes that, in marriage, activities must be mutually acceptable to guarantee the protection of each spouse's interests and feelings.

_____

Interdependent Behavior

Activities of a spouse that are conceived and executed with the interests of both spouses in mind.

_____

It's the difference between a sole proprietorship and a partnership. If you own 100 percent of a business, you have the right to make your own business decisions. But if you have a partner who owns an equal share of the business, you should come to an agreement before making decisions. Otherwise the business relationship will suffer, and the business itself will suffer. Marriage is definitely a partnership, and if decisions are not mutually agreeable, they will hurt the relationship and the productivity of the marriage.

The Rooms of Brian's House

I used an imaginary house to help Brian understand how his lifestyle affected Kay. Each room in this house represented one of the roles he played in life. There was a career room, a leisure activity room, a family room, a religious practices room, and, yes, a marriage room.

Brian's career room was filled with furniture and projects designed to make him a successful production manager. His leisure activity room contained golf equipment and immediate access to friends who enjoy playing golf with him. The family room contained video games and a television set that he used when he spent time with his children. His religious practices room had been made into an Episcopal chapel. And right in the middle of his marriage room was a big bed.

As he made his way through an average day, Brian would visit the rooms representing the roles he played. When in any one room, he would keep the doors to the other rooms closed so that he could focus his undivided attention on the role he played in that room. He found that he did his best when he avoided the distractions of other roles he played in life.

Since Brian regarded Kay and her interests as a distraction, he relegated her to only one room in his house—the marriage room—and that made her feel neglected and resentful. While it was true that Brian gave Kay his undivided attention when he met her in the marriage room and made a special effort to meet her needs, she felt totally neglected the rest of the time. She wanted him to invite her into every room, so that she would be fully integrated into his life, but he refused. Instead, he wanted her to create a house of her own with a marriage room where he could join her.

So that's what Kay did. In her house, she also had a career room, but it was outfitted with furniture and projects designed to make her a successful accountant. Her leisure activity room was full of gardening books and supplies. Her family activity room contained bicycles and sporting equipment used when she took her children to their after-school sporting events. Her religious practices room was a Baptist chapel. And in her marriage room, there was . . . nothing. She had emotionally bailed out of the marriage and excluded Brian from all of her rooms. And to make her point perfectly clear, she refused to sleep with him. In their real house, she slept in a separate room.

Of course, the problems between Brian and Kay were about much more than sex. Kay's refusal to make love may have been the first symptom of a bad marriage that got Brian's attention. But there had been plenty of other warning signs before that. She had begged him to spend weekends with her, instead of golfing with his friends. She cried when he refused to participate in their children's school projects and activities. And she felt like a widow taking her children to church each week without their father. His entire lifestyle made her unhappy and caused massive Love Bank withdrawals. And if his independent behavior had continued much longer, he would have risked divorce.

Why Is Independent Behavior So Tempting?

Unfortunately, Brian and Kay aren't very different from many married couples today when it comes to independent behavior. And this Love Buster threatens to tear many of them apart. But of all the Love Busters we've discussed so far, this one usually sneaks in under the radar. For many couples, they don't see how destructive their independent behavior is to the health of their marriage.

Those on the receiving end of independent behavior are usually aware of how destructive it can be to a marriage, but those who engage in it usually think that it actually strengthens a marriage. Without it, they would feel trapped and suffocated. Who they choose as friends, what they do on the job, where they spend their spare time, and even how they pay their bills—these are choices that they believe no one, not even their spouse, should interfere with. They view any attempt to take away their "freedom of choice" as controlling and manipulative, a marriage-wrecker for sure.

Independent behavior also feeds on the mistaken belief of some that it actually makes spouses more attractive to each other. If clingy dependency is viewed as the only alternative to independent behavior, they're probably right. But they ignore the fact that neither of those options creates a happy marriage. Only interdependent beh[...] achieve long-term marital satisfaction.

Another reason that independent behavior is tempting is spouses believe they should be blindly trusted in the decisions they make. If their spouse challenges their decisions, they consider it to be disrespectful. In fact, many of my clients have tried to misapply the Love Buster category of disrespectful judgments to their spouse's complaints regarding their independent behavior. "If you respected me, you wouldn't challenge my decisions," is a common defense.

> Only interdependent behavior helps achieve long-term marital satisfaction.

But the most important reason independent behavior is tempting in marriage is that it's instinctive. Your Taker wants you to be happy at all costs, ignoring the interests of others. So you are born with a predisposition to make decisions that are good for you regardless of how it affects your spouse, at least when your Taker is in charge.

And when your Taker encourages you to behave independently of your spouse, it will easily justify your thoughtlessness. After all, your Taker is your defense attorney, and it is always prepared to explain why everything you do on your own behalf is reasonable. It will try to convince you that you have the right to make independent decisions, that those decisions will make you more attractive to your spouse, and that when your spouse challenges your decisions, he or she is being disrespectful. But the bottom line is that whenever you ignore your spouse's interests and feelings, you are eroding the love he or she has for you, and you are destroying your emotional bond.

> Whenever you ignore your spouse's interests and feelings, you are destroying your emotional bond.

Brian felt that what he did in the rooms of his imaginary house should not have any impact on Kay, because the doors were closed and she was not invited to participate. But present or not, everything he did, even in the privacy of his rooms, affected her one way or another. When he went golfing with his friends, he withdrew love units from her Love Bank. His working schedule also upset her, as did the way he chose to interact with their children. Even his religious practices bothered her. Keeping her in the hallways of his house did not prevent her from feeling the impact of each independent behavior.

Slowly but surely Kay was finding Brian's lifestyle increasingly intolerable. Eventually she woke up to the realization that they had nothing but their children to keep them together.

In most marriages, independent behavior is the primary cause of fights. When you behave as if your spouse doesn't exist, your spouse's Taker won't tolerate it, and will encourage him or her to go to war with you. But Brian and Kay didn't fight. They made very few demands of each other, were rarely disrespectful, and never had an angry outburst. Instead of fighting, Kay simply let Brian's independent behavior drain her Love Bank, and that was the reason she started thinking about divorce—she had lost her love for him.

To some extent, Kay felt that Brian had the right to make independent decisions. So she could see no solution to their problem. While in theory she wanted to become emotionally reconnected to Brian, she couldn't see herself joining him in each room of his house. By this time, she was even unwilling to invite him into her rooms—she wasn't attracted to him anymore. And yet, if she was to become emotionally bonded to him again, they had to become integrated into every aspect of each other's lives.

I told Brian that if he wanted a happy marriage, Kay's feelings and interests had to be considered in every decision he made. As equal partners, they should create a completely integrated lifestyle, enjoyable for both of them. That, in turn, would lead to the emotional bonding Kay needed to restore the sexual relationship they had once enjoyed. And, more importantly, it would turn a divorce in the making into the partnership that they should have had all along.

Two Policies That Can Help Create Interdependence

To help Brian and Kay create an integrated lifestyle, two steps were required. First, they had to invite each other into all of the rooms of their imaginary houses, and then they had to come to an agreement as to how each room should be decorated.

The first step required them to apply a rule that I introduced to you earlier in this book, in the chapter on dishonesty. I call it the Policy of

Radical Honesty: *Reveal to your spouse as much information about yourself as you know, your thoughts, feelings, habits, likes, dislikes, personal history, daily activities, and plans for the future.* This rule helps couples invite each other into the rooms of their imaginary houses. It gives them a clear and accurate description of each other's thoughts and activities.

Policy of Radical Honesty

Reveal to your spouse as much information about yourself as you know: your thoughts, feelings, habits, likes, dislikes, personal history, daily activities, and plans for the future.

At first, Kay was more reluctant than Brian to become radically honest. But he kept her completely informed of all his daily activities and plans for future activities. He even gave her a schedule of where he would be, and a telephone number where he could be reached in an emergency. His willingness to invite her into his rooms eventually encouraged her to invite him into her rooms as well. By providing information to each other about their daily activities and plans for the future, they were swept into the inner recesses of the lives that had previously been hidden from each other.

But they needed to complete a second step before their lives could be integrated and they could become equal partners together. They had to agree on how the rooms would be decorated. That second step required them to follow another rule that should be very familiar to you by now—the Policy of Joint Agreement: *Never do anything without an enthusiastic agreement between you and your spouse.*

The word "anything" in the Policy of Joint Agreement means that all rooms of a house and everything in each room are subject to scrutiny and possible replacement. So if Brian were to follow the policy, he had to think about Kay's reaction to *everything* he did, not just what went on in the "marriage room," or even just a few of the other rooms. She had to be consulted about what went on in every room. And Kay had to do the same after inviting Brian into her rooms. In other words, did they approve of each other's activities? If either of them were not enthusiastic, they would have to be changed. All of the rooms had to eventually contain activities that they would both enthusiastically accept.

It's common for spouses to view the prospect of redecoration with horror. "I have my rooms furnished just the way I like them," would be a common reaction. "When my spouse starts throwing things out and bringing things in, it will not be the comfortable room I carefully created."

The Policy of Joint Agreement addresses that issue by requiring all changes to be **mutually** agreeable. In other words, Kay could not create a new lifestyle unless Brian was as sold on it as she was, and vice versa. Neither had the right to force each other into a room that was uncomfortable. Instead, they had to create a lifestyle that was comfortable for both of them.

The Policy of Joint Agreement
Never do anything without an enthusiastic agreement between you and your spouse.

Brian wanted to know why I insisted on an "enthusiastic" agreement. He felt that a simple agreement would be a big step in the right direction—why insist on enthusiasm?

I explained that marital agreements are often coerced or self-sacrificing. I didn't want either of them to think that they had to agree just to get along, and I didn't want either spouse to sacrifice his or her interests so that the other could have what he or she wanted. Kay was not simply a guest in Brian's rooms and Brian was not a guest in Kay's rooms. They were equal partners with the right to rearrange them to make them mutually comfortable.

The Policy of Joint Agreement prevents abuse and control in marriage. It makes absolutely no sense to try to force a spouse to do something when enthusiastic agreement is the objective. No one is expected to suffer. Both are expected to thrive because only win-win outcomes should be tolerated. It isn't just Kay's enthusiastic agreement that is required before a decision is made. Brian's enthusiastic agreement is required as well. There is to be no furniture or activities in any of his rooms that he does not also enthusiastically support. The goal of marriage is to become united in purpose and spirit, not to overpower or control each other.

> The goal of marriage is to become united in purpose and spirit.

How Easy Is It?

Couples who already have an interdependent lifestyle have little or no trouble following the Policy of Radical Honesty and the Policy of Joint Agreement because they have learned how to behave in sensitive and caring ways regardless of the roles they play.

> The Policy of Joint Agreement and the Policy of Radical Honesty help create understanding, emotional bonding, intimacy, and romantic love.

But couples like Brian and Kay with independent lifestyles have great difficulty following these policies—at first. They are accustomed to doing what they please, regardless of its effect on each other, and then lying about it, especially when they're playing certain roles. But if they can follow these policies for just a few weeks, they begin to see how their dishonesty and thoughtlessness had created the emotional distance they were experiencing. As they try to apply these policies to each of their daily plans and activities, they begin to feel cared for by each other and are encouraged by each other's thoughtfulness. Over time, their emotional bonding becomes increasingly secure, and the policies become easier and easier to follow as they learn how to make thoughtful choices.

Those who follow the Policy of Joint Agreement think about their spouse throughout the day, because as they make decisions they ask themselves how their spouse would feel. Phone calls are made whenever there is any doubt. And by giving radically honest answers to each other's questions, they become increasingly sensitive to each other's feelings.

If spouses consider each other's feelings in every decision they make, asking each other when there is any uncertainty, they eventually create a compatible lifestyle. The Policy of Joint Agreement and the Policy of Radical Honesty help create understanding, emotional bonding, intimacy, and romantic love in marriage. Over time, they experience what every couple hopes to create in marriage: a loving and compatible relationship.

By the time Brian and Kay had invited each other into every room in their houses and had made adjustments that created a mutually comfortable lifestyle, Kay could no longer even imagine leaving Brian. That's because she wasn't standing in the hallways of his house feeling like a stranger. All his rooms were her rooms as well, and she was welcomed into his entire home as his cherished life partner.

Using Successful Negotiation to Overcome Independent Behavior

When you decide to become interdependent, you will not have fewer conflicts—you will have more of them. At least there will seem to be more conflicts because you will address each of them as they arise. In fact, you will welcome them if you can dispatch them as fast as they arise.

Joyce and I have at least one conflict every hour we're together. And yet we have a terrific marriage. That's because it's not conflicts that make a marriage miserable. Marriages fail because couples don't know how to negotiate when a conflict arises. Since Joyce and I know how to handle conflicts the right way, they actually make our marriage stronger, not weaker. Whenever we have a conflict, an area of weakness is identified, and when we resolve the conflict, our marriage is strengthened.

If conflicts are not resolved the right way, independent behavior, or sometimes dependent behavior, is the result. It's essential for you to rid your marriage of every Love Buster, but the one we are presently discussing is so complicated, and so pervasive in marriage, that I will take the next five chapters to address the five types of conflict that get the most attention.

But first, let's review three of my basic concepts that will help you resolve your conflicts the right way so that you will avoid independent behavior.

I've given you two rules to help you identify conflicts: The Policy of Radical Honesty (Basic Concept #6) and the Policy of Joint Agreement (Basic Concept #9). When you've been honest, and you can't seem to be in agreement about something, you've identified a conflict. But how do you get from identifying the conflict to resolving the conflict with a mutually enthusiastic agreement? In chapter 3, I answered that question when I introduced the Four Guidelines to Successful Negotiation (Basic Concept #10).

Let's quickly review that procedure once more.

ACTION STEP

Set ground rules to make your discussion pleasant and safe.

Guideline 1: Set ground rules to make your discussion pleasant and safe.

Before you discuss anything, you should guarantee to each other that it will be **pleasant** and **safe**. It must be pleasant in that you should try to make sure that you and your spouse are enjoying the conversation. Have a smile on your face as you're discussing the issue and some of the alternatives to resolving the conflict. And it must be safe by completely avoiding selfish demands, disrespectful judgments, or angry outbursts. You should both maintain zero tolerance for these three destructive instincts. If one of you fails to keep the discussion pleasant or safe, postpone it to a later time after you've had a chance to regain emotional control.

ACTION STEP

Introduce the conflict and try to understand each other's perspective.

Guideline 2: Introduce the conflict and try to understand each other's perspective.

What is the issue and how do both of you feel about it? What would you like? And if you were to have your way, how would it affect your spouse? Is there a way to have what you want with your spouse's enthusiastic agreement?

During this phase of problem solving, radical honesty is essential in understanding each other's perspective. But be careful to avoid being critical of each other's opinions. And try to understand each other's opinions well enough to repeat them accurately to each other.

One of the biggest mistakes people make in this phase of problem solving is to be disrespectful. Many people think that their honesty must include their criticism of an opposing opinion. But radical honesty does not require disrespectful judgments, even when you feel like being disrespectful. You're not being dishonest when you keep your critical thoughts to yourself—you're being respectful.

Disrespect is a poison pill when it comes to negotiating. The quickest way to end a discussion, and to completely eliminate all efforts to come to an enthusiastic agreement, is to be critical. On the other hand, your effort to understand each other and to try to accommodate another perspective when trying to resolve a conflict encourages further discussion.

Guideline 3: Brainstorm with abandon.

For many conflicts, it isn't easy to find a resolution that accommodates the perspectives of both spouses. So you will need to give

ACTION
STEP

Brainstorm with
abandon.

your brains a chance to do some of the hard lifting by letting the problem incubate.

When a conflict is first discovered, a mutually agreeable resolution may not occur to either of you immediately. You may need time to brainstorm about possible solutions. Carry a pad around with you so that you can write down solutions as they occur to you. It may take days before you have accumulated several possibilities. But remember, whatever you write down should take both you and your spouse's perspectives into account simultaneously.

Guideline 4: Find the solution that provides a mutually enthusiastic agreement.

Check each other's lists daily to see what each of you wrote until you find a solution that clicks. Spend a little time discussing each idea, even if it's rejected. Explain how the idea works and how it doesn't work. Be willing to test ideas that may work.

In some cases you may not be able to find a solution. I know of many happy marriages where some conflicts have never been resolved. That's because the way you go about trying to resolve a conflict is more important to the success of marriage than the resolution itself. You are more likely to hurt each other in an argument over a conflict than to leave the conflict unresolved. And a conflict is never really resolved unless both spouses agree enthusiastically.

The Choice Is Yours

ACTION
STEP

Find the solution
that meets with
your enthusiastic
agreement.

Marriages usually go one of two ways: Nature takes its course and marital compatibility is eventually lost, or a couple can decide to build compatibility by eliminating independent behavior and replacing it with interdependent behavior. My years of marriage counseling have taught me a very important lesson: Unless couples create compatibility throughout their marriage, the compatibility they had at the time of their wedding will be destroyed.

When couples divorce or separate because they're "incompatible," does this mean they were doomed from the start? Is there some basic personality clash they just can't overcome? No, it just means they've failed to *create* compatibility. Very likely they developed interests and activities independently of each other. They weren't thoughtful enough to try to include each other in the most enjoyable moments of their lives.

> Unless couples create compatibility throughout their marriage, the compatibility they had at the time of their wedding will be destroyed.

What a shame! It doesn't have to be that way. A marriage, a family, and personal happiness can be saved if a couple would apply thought and consideration to the decisions they make.

When you learn how to resolve conflicts using the Four Guidelines for Successful Negotiation, you will not only be able to get what you need from each other, but you will also create a lifestyle that makes you compatible. And you won't be arguing with each other—you'll be discussing your conflicts safely and enjoyably.

But you'll need plenty of practice before you become experts at this essential marital skill. So in the next five chapters of this book, I'll introduce you to the five most common conflicts in marriage—friends and relatives, career choices and time management, financial planning, child discipline, and sex. Failure to resolve any of these types of conflict with mutual enthusiasm usually leads to independent behavior, and that can make any marriage very unpleasant. As I introduce one conflict after another, we will review the right approach to their resolution. It will not only give you some ideas as to how you might solve some of the conflicts you are now facing, but will also give you invaluable practice in learning how to resolve any conflict with radical honesty and mutual enthusiastic agreement.

Then, I will introduce two very destructive types of independent behavior—infidelity and substance abuse. They are both absolutely devastating to marriage if they are allowed to run amok. They are so incredibly thoughtless that they set every marriage on a course of almost certain ruin. In these chapters, I will illustrate how the Policy of Joint Agreement can protect a marriage from unbearable independent behavior.

Key Principles

Independent behavior is the activities of one spouse that are conceived and executed as if the other spouse did not exist.

Interdependent behavior is the activities of a spouse that are conceived and executed with both spouses' interests in mind.

The most important reason independent behavior is tolerated in marriage is that it's instinctive.

Whenever you ignore your spouse's interests and feelings, you are eroding the love he or she has for you, and you are destroying your emotional bond.

Two policies help create interdependence: (1) the **Policy of Radical Honesty** (Basic Concept #6—reveal to your spouse as much information about yourself as you know: your thoughts, feelings, habits, likes, dislikes, personal history, daily activities, and plans for the future), and (2) the **Policy of Joint Agreement** (Basic Concept #9—never do anything without an enthusiastic agreement between you and your spouse).

Unless couples create compatibility throughout their marriage, the compatibility they had at the time of their wedding will be destroyed.

The **Four Guidelines for Successful Negotiation** (Basic Concept #10) help couples resolve conflicts the right way—with honesty and thoughtfulness.

Consider This...

1. What is independent behavior? Think of a few instances of independent behavior that have been a problem for you in the past, but that are no longer a problem for either of you. How did you go about ridding yourself of those Love Busters? Think of other examples that are still a problem for one of you. What are you presently doing to try to overcome them?

2. How has your Taker tried to justify your existing independent behavior? Has it tried to convince you that you have the right to make independent decisions, that those decisions will make

you more attractive to your spouse, and that when your spouse challenges your decisions he or she is being disrespectful? Are there other arguments your spouse has used? Regardless of your spouse's arguments that you should engage in independent behavior, what's the bottom line?

3. Describe each of your own imaginary houses. Which rooms are easy for you to both enter and which are more difficult to enter? Which are locked shut to the other spouse? What are the advantages and disadvantages of inviting each other into all of your rooms?

4. An invitation to enter a room is not enough to build compatibility in marriage. What must you do after you invite each other in?

5. What are the Four Guidelines to Successful Negotiation? How do they help eliminate existing independent behavior? How do they help prevent the creation of new independent behavior?

Part 3

Resolving Marital Conflicts with

THOUGHTFUL
NEGOTIATION

9

RESOLVING CONFLICTS OVER FRIENDS AND RELATIVES

Many of us value loyalty to our family and friends with almost religious fervor. Since our parents endured a great deal of sacrifice in raising us, we usually assume that we have a responsibility to care for them in their hour of need. The same kind of thinking applies to our siblings and possibly even to extended family members—if any of them are in trouble, we will be there to give them a helping hand.

Our loyalty often extends to lifelong friends as well. Those you've known since childhood may have helped you at a time of great personal need. And so you may feel obligated to help them as well when they have a problem. After all, that's what friends are for, to help and support each other.

Given our sense of responsibility to our family and friends—along with our enjoyment of their company, a question almost invariably comes up after marriage: *What do we do when our relationships with family and friends conflict with the interests of our spouse?*

If a member of your family or a friend needs your help, should you be there for them even if you don't have your spouse's enthusiastic

175

agreement? If your mother cannot care for herself and wants you to care for her, possibly in your own home, should you provide that care even if your spouse is unenthusiastic about the invasion of your privacy? If one of your friends is about to move and that friend had helped you move, should you help your friend even if your spouse would prefer that you spend the weekend at home with your family? Or, if you simply want to relax and have a good time with your best friends, should your spouse have the right to ruin it all by objecting?

> What do we do when our relationships with family and friends conflict with the interests of our spouse?

Those are tough questions and in many cases, they require answers almost instantaneously. When one of these conflicts arises, you usually don't have the luxury of days or weeks of negotiation with your spouse. So let's take some time now, while you can carefully think it through, to resolve some of the conflicts that you may be having over friends and relatives.

In this book, we've discussed three different marital problem-solving strategies. The first, and most common, was introduced in the first five chapters of this book. It's the use of abuse and control to try to force your spouse to do what you want even when it's not in your spouse's best interest to do so. You tell your spouse that your parents will be coming over for dinner (selfish demands). If your spouse objects, you blame his or her reluctance on an uncaring attitude (disrespectful judgments). And finally, when all else fails, you raise your voice, stomp from room to room, and throw things around until you get your way (angry outbursts).

That's not the right way to resolve marital conflicts, and most couples who fight know it. It not only fails to help them resolve conflicts, but it destroys the love they have for each other. So many spouses try to use a second strategy that I introduced in the last chapter, independent behavior. *If you don't enjoy having dinner with my parents, I'll have dinner with them by myself.* It's not mutual agreement, but rather a unilateral choice that is sprung on a spouse with little or no notice. It introduces a "family-and-friends room" in the imaginary house, and the other spouse is locked out. This strategy leads to marital alienation that will cause the couple to eventually lose their emotional bond. Instead of being lovers, partners, and best friends in life, they become ships passing in the night.

The third strategy for problem solving that I've introduced to you is the only one of the three that actually resolves marital conflict the right way. It helps find solutions that strengthen an emotional bond and build romantic love in marriage. When you use this strategy, you're inviting your spouse into your family-and-friends room by following the Policy of Radical Honesty (explaining your desires and describing tentative plans before they are implemented), and then making your spouse an equal partner in deciding how to resolve any conflicts that may appear by following the Policy of Joint Agreement (making a final decision only after you both agree to it enthusiastically).

This strategy begins with the first guideline to successful negotiation—you guarantee each other a pleasant and safe discussion by being cheerful, and by avoiding demands, disrespectful judgments, and angry outbursts. If either of you cannot make that guarantee, you postpone the discussion until you feel better.

The next step is to follow the second guideline to successful negotiation by introducing what it is you want, and learning how your spouse would feel about fulfilling your request. You tell your spouse that you would like to invite your parents over for dinner (without having discussed it with them first). Then you ask your spouse how he or she would feel about it, letting your spouse reveal any objections without countering with disrespect.

With your request on the table and your spouse's objections (if any) understood, you are ready for the third guideline—brainstorming. For example, what are some of the ways that you could have your parents for dinner without your wife having to cook a meal and clean up after a busy day at work?

Finally, you're ready for the fourth guideline. You make a decision that is in the best interest of both you and your spouse. Your final decision may be to take your parents out to dinner, and then invite them to your home for dessert.

The illustration I've used here to describe the best strategy for marital problem solving is a fairly easy conflict to resolve. We're assuming that your parents are delightful to entertain. But what happens when your wife simply doesn't want to get anywhere near your parents? They may be disrespectful or downright cruel to your wife. If she feels obligated to be with your unpleasant parents, you risk making Love Bank withdrawals every time she even thinks about them.

But if you follow the Policy of Joint Agreement, that won't happen.

The Policy of Joint
Agreement helps recreate
your relationships.

Neither spouse is obligated to spend time with people who make them unhappy because the default condition for the policy is to do nothing until an enthusiastic agreement is reached. You can't force your parents to treat your wife with respect, but you don't have to spend time with them, either. If you resolve this conflict the right way, your parents will come to realize that they won't be seeing much of either of you until they change their ways.

The Policy of Joint Agreement helps recreate your relationships with family and friends to satisfy both of you. Unless they treat both of you thoughtfully and respectfully, and you enjoy their company, you shouldn't make them a part of your lives.

It Pays to Be Prepared

Because many of the decisions you make regarding the care of your parents or friends have to be made instantly, you and your spouse should discuss many of these issues before they actually arise. For example, if your parents or your spouse's parents were to require your care, what kind of care could you provide with an enthusiastic agreement? Neither one of you should feel pressured into making an agreement that is not actually in your own best interest. So now is the time for you to start thinking about what kind of care you can provide and how long that care should continue.

What would you do if a friend needed help moving? Or if a friend invited you both out to dinner? Or if a friend invited one of you out to dinner but didn't invite the other? Or if the friend had been a former lover?

Trust me. Former lovers should be left completely out of your lives. But what about friends of the opposite sex in general? How friendly do you really want these relationships to be? I have warned couples for years that most affairs begin with opposite sex friendships.

If you can anticipate problems you may face with family and friends, and then make some tentative decisions about how you would address them, it will be much easier to come to a quick and enthusiastic agreement when one finally arises.

The wisdom in the Policy of Joint Agreement is that it forces you and your spouse to negotiate fairly with each other. When you reject the option of gaining at the other's expense, it keeps you focused on each other's best interests. It keeps you thoughtful when you're tempted to be selfish. If you follow the Policy of Joint Agreement, your family and friends will never come between you.

Get into the habit of discussing all invitations with your spouse before responding. When somebody invites you, say to them, "Let me get back to you after I've discussed it with my spouse." Your family and friends will get used to the idea that you make your decisions together.

A Crusade for Religious Freedom

Shortly after their wedding, Sherrie told Dwight that to keep peace in her family he must join Trinity Church, where her parents attended. Having been a member of St. Paul Community Church all his life, he preferred continuing to attend there. Besides, he and Sherrie had attended his church together before their wedding, and she loved it. But Sherrie insisted on the switch, so he agreed.

For about a year, Dwight attended Trinity with Sherrie but was never able to make the adjustment. He complained to her all year about how unfair it was that her parents determined what church they should attend.

One day he'd had it. "Sherrie, I just can't do it anymore. I will not attend a church just to make your parents happy."

"Well, then do it to make me happy."

"But I'm not comfortable at that church. Besides, you always enjoyed being at my church before we were married. What's so bad about it now?"

"Dwight, I enjoy the services at your church but I can't disappoint my parents."

"So you *can't* disappoint your parents, but you *can* disappoint me?" Dwight countered.

The following Sunday, without discussing it with Sherrie, Dwight announced that he would be attending St. Paul Community Church by himself. She could attend Trinity with her parents, but he would attend the church of his choice alone.

When the couple saw me for counseling, I pointed out to Sherrie that she'd been making a selfish demand, gaining peace with her parents at the expense of her husband's feelings. She knew Dwight did not enjoy the church services at her parents' church, yet she forced him to attend so she would not have to deal with her parents' objections.

Dwight had made the correct response to her selfish demand: He rejected it. He told her he would not continue to do something that made him uncomfortable. They needed to find a solution that would satisfy them both, and his attending Trinity was not it.

But when Dwight unilaterally chose to attend St. Paul Community Church, he made the mistake of engaging in independent behavior, making a choice that failed to take Sherrie's feelings into account. I explained to them that neither selfish demands nor independent behavior would solve their problem. And both approaches to their problem were eroding their love for each other.

Sherrie had struggled with the issue of whom to please, Dwight or her parents, ever since they'd married. She now saw clearly that she'd chosen to please her parents at Dwight's expense, and when I brought that fact to her attention, she immediately saw her mistake. She felt as if she'd had a heavy burden lifted from her shoulders.

With the help of the Four Guidelines for Successful Negotiation, Sherrie and Dwight went to work finding a solution to their problem. They had already attended several other churches and discussed these alternatives. None of them would have pleased her parents, but with their new perspective they moved beyond that restriction. Now they were simply looking for a church they would both enjoy.

If Sherrie had not enjoyed the services at St. Paul Community Church, they would have visited other churches until they found one they both enjoyed. But after lengthy discussions and brainstorming, they agreed that they enjoyed and benefited most from the services at St. Paul Community and should return to that church. Sherrie was very happy with the outcome.

When told of the couple's decision, Sherrie's parents announced that they would not speak to Sherrie and Dwight until they changed their minds. Sherrie had experienced this reaction in the past, because her family frequently used demands and intimidation. But this time she didn't buckle under the pressure. She and Dwight decided to honor her parents' request for silence. It took two full years, but her parents finally broke the silence and admitted they'd made a mistake.

Dwight and Sherrie's solution to the problem met the conditions of the Policy of Joint Agreement, and they found it by using the Four Guidelines for Successful Negotiation. They rejected other solutions until they had each other's enthusiastic support for one. Their final solution deposited love units into both Love Banks and the way they went about finding that solution protected their Love Bank accounts.

In the end, Sherrie's parents adjusted to their decision. But even if they had continued to be stubborn, it still would have been correct. As their counselor, I witnessed a noticeable improvement in the love Dwight and Sherrie felt for each other, and their entire family benefited from the wisdom of their decision.

Taking Generosity One Step Too Far

Judy's Giver worked overtime. Whenever someone was in need, Judy rushed to the rescue. Bill was attracted to that trait when they were dating, especially when he was on the receiving end of her generosity. But after marriage, it became a source of conflict when Judy's sister, Barbara, and Barbara's husband, Jack, moved in with them while Jack was "looking for work."

Bill didn't have any say in the matter. He came home one day to find his in-laws' possessions filling his house. That alone upset him, but it got worse as the weeks dragged on. Barbara and Jack seemed to be permanent fixtures.

"We cannot continue to support your sister and brother-in-law," Bill finally told Judy. "He'll just have to find a job like everyone else."

"But he's tried," Judy pleaded, "and if we don't help, who will? I can't just put my sister out on the street."

Our Giver can get us into a lot of trouble because it is willing to see us suffer for the sake of others. And when we're married, it's not just our Giver that we have to watch out for. Our spouse's Giver can also give us fits when it's generous at our expense. That's what Bill faced: Judy's Giver wanted him to join her in sacrificing for her sister.

When is it wrong to be generous? It's wrong when your generosity takes advantage of someone who is an unwilling participant—in this case, Judy's husband. Granted, she willingly suffered to help her sister survive. But she forced her husband to suffer along with her.

As time went on, Bill began to think that Judy cared more for her sister than for him. That thought was reinforced by her inability to meet his emotional needs the way she had in the past because of their lack of privacy. He was also resentful that they had to support four people on an income that could barely support two. He was having trouble paying his bills.

Again and again Bill asked Judy to tell them to leave, but she insisted on letting them stay until Jack found a job. "I just can't turn my sister away. You'll have to be patient," she told Bill.

But his patience finally ran out. He had come to the conclusion that Judy didn't care at all about how he felt, and he decided it was time to leave. So he moved out.

Bill's decision brought them to my office for counseling, and Judy admitted that her generosity had been at Bill's expense. During that first appointment with me, she agreed to follow the Policy of Joint Agreement from that day on.

But Judy raised a very important issue. How should the Policy of Joint Agreement be applied to a decision that has already been made unilaterally? The damage was already done, so why not see it through to the bitter end? She suggested that her sister and brother-in-law stay until Jack could find a job, and from then on she and Bill would follow the Policy of Joint Agreement on all other decisions. From Bill's perspective, it would have been more of the same, and he probably would have walked out of my office had he been present when Judy made that suggestion.

I explained to her that when the Policy of Joint Agreement has been violated, and a decision has been made without a joint agreement, a couple must correct the decision as quickly as possible. In this case, it meant going back to the conditions that existed before the decision was made, and then negotiating anew, this time with the Policy of Joint Agreement in mind. So she asked her sister and brother-in-law to find another place to live that very day. As soon as Jack and Barbara moved out, Bill moved back in.

Now they could apply the Policy of Joint Agreement to their care of Judy's sister. They learned to follow the Four Guidelines for Successful Negotiation, and started to brainstorm. How could they help while taking Bill's interests into account? They finally arrived at a solution that was a sensible way to handle the problem. Bill enthusiastically offered to cosign for a loan to give Jack and Barbara enough money to pay their rent for a few months, and he even agreed to let them use some of the furniture from their home. Bill and Judy were in enthusiastic agreement because they were not sacrificing anything they needed to be happy.

From that one experience that almost ruined their marriage, they learned to apply the Policy of Joint Agreement to all their decisions, and as far as I know, Judy's generosity never again got them into such serious marital trouble. She continued to be generous, but it was with the enthusiastic agreement of her husband.

There are many situations where you cannot please your friends and family and please your spouse at the same time. In those situations the Policy of Joint Agreement protects your marriage from the common yet tragic mistake of pleasing your friends and family at your spouse's expense. It demonstrates the fact that you care for each other, and that you are each other's highest priority. But most important, it preserves the love you have for each other.

"I Just Don't Like Her!"

Craig knew there was really nothing wrong with Joan's friend, Bev, but she annoyed him. In fact he felt annoyed whenever Joan talked to Bev on the telephone. He believed Joan should be able to freely choose her friends, and she had known Bev long before she met him. He didn't want to break up that friendship but he just didn't like Bev, and Joan's relationship with her was beginning to affect their marriage.

When they came to me for counseling, I helped them recognize that Joan's friendship with Bev fell into the Love Busters category of *independent behavior*. It was innocent, as many independent behaviors are. Joan did not want her relationship with Bev to hurt her relationship with Craig, but each time Joan saw Bev, love units were withdrawn from Craig's Love Bank.

Craig had no choice in the matter. His emotional reactions to Bev were strongly negative and consistent. He tried to like Bev, but it didn't work. Compromises had been attempted, but to no avail.

Every one of us knows someone whom we dislike. I can't believe that even Will Rogers wasn't annoyed by someone! It's normal to like some people and dislike others. Furthermore, just because you love your spouse there's no guarantee you'll like your spouse's friends.

Most of us who are married notice that the friends we had before marriage are not the same as those after marriage. Look at your wedding pictures. How many of those people do you still regard as close friends? For most of us, only those who were friends of *both* spouses before marriage remain friends after marriage.

Friendships are more difficult to develop than most people think. And they depend on individual taste. In general, there is nothing wrong with people I don't like, and there is nothing wonderful about people I do like. It seems that I'm programmed to like certain people and not others. Most people find this true.

The Policy of Joint Agreement helped guide Joan and Craig toward a resolution of this conflict. They had to find a solution that would make them both happy. After encouraging them to practice the Four Guidelines for Successful Negotiation for a few days on issues that were not emotionally charged, they went to work explaining to each other how they felt about Bev. They did it respectfully and did not try to force their opinions on each other. Craig was open to the idea that he might come to like Bev if she stopped being so annoying, but Joan realized that she really didn't have the right to try to change her, especially when she found those "annoying" characteristics to be part of her charm. What Joan liked about Bev, Craig happened to hate.

They finally arrived at a solution to the problem that made the most sense: They would develop friends that Joan and Craig both liked, and end their relationship with Bev. That may sound like Joan capitulated and gave in to Craig's solution. But her decision was made with enthusiasm, not reluctance. Through thoughtful negotiation, she was able to see that her friendship with Bev had no hope for the future. And she also became aware of how her gain had been at Craig's expense—something that would ultimately destroy the marriage that she wanted far more than her relationship with Bev.

As part of their enthusiastic agreement, they planned to carve out time each week for the purpose of developing new friendships. They invited several couples they knew to join them in weekend activities and eventually found one that clicked. Today Joan is just as happy with her new friend as she was with Bev. And her new friendship is helping her deposit instead of withdraw love units in Craig's Love Bank.

This example of a conflict regarding friends introduces two problems that I want to mention before going on to the next example. First, there is the problem of friends taking up so much time that you don't have enough private time for each other. And second, there is the problem of a spouse being so controlling and jealous that he or she won't agree to any friendships.

The first problem is solved if you follow the advice I give in chapters 16 and 17, building romantic love with care and time. If you want to stay in love with each other throughout life, you must spend a minimum of 15 hours together each week for the exclusive purpose of meeting each other's intimate emotional needs. These intimate emotional needs are affection, conversation, recreational companionship, and sexual fulfillment. When you schedule that amount of time together, and use it to meet those needs, you deposit so many love units that your Love Banks will overflow. But if you spend all of your dating nights out with your friends, these intimate emotional needs will not be met, and you will lose your love for each other. So don't let friendships keep you from having enough private time with each other to keep your romantic love alive.

The second problem, having a spouse who doesn't want you to have any friendships, is almost always in the context of abuse and control. While the Policy of Joint Agreement would suggest that you have no friendships unless your spouse agrees enthusiastically, there are exceptions in an abusive and controlling marriage. For example, you have the right to separate from your spouse if you are in danger, even if he or she does not agree to your decision. You have a right to call the police and file a report of domestic violence if your spouse is physically abusive. You have a right to let others know about your spouse's affair, without having to first obtain his or her enthusiastic agreement. In other words, if your spouse is hurting you, you have the right to protect yourself.

I regard the exclusion of friendships as a form of abuse, and just about every marital therapist will agree with me. If your spouse tries to prevent you from having contact with others, I suggest that you see a professional therapist to help you understand why it's abusive, and what you can do to free yourself from the trap you're in, without having to divorce. In many of these cases, I recommend a separation until the controlling spouse learns to let go.

"You Like Her Too Much!"

Sometimes a problem develops in marriage when you like your spouse's friend *too* much. If you find yourself infatuated with a mutual friend of the opposite sex, you're headed for trouble.

Tom and his wife, Alice, bought a mobile home in a resort community when they retired. They liked the area so much they encouraged their best friends, George and Emma, to buy the home that was for sale next door to them. It turned out to be a great idea—until George died.

After his death, the three of them remained very good friends. Tom was more than willing to help Emma with repairs and he often went over just to keep her company. Within a few months he had fallen in love with her. He didn't tell Alice about it but he did tell Emma. She was also in love with him. Before long he was doing more than keeping her company.

This went on for more than a year before Alice caught them. They were both ashamed and begged her forgiveness, but she could not be consoled. She didn't know what to do. Should she forgive her friend's offenses and continue the friendship? Or should she abandon the relationship forever?

This problem affects married couples of all ages. But it is particularly troublesome among retired couples who have been lifelong friends. I know of more than twenty cases where the offending spouse was over seventy years of age. It's remarkable, yet predictable. Why *wouldn't* you fall in love with a lifelong friend?

Tom made his first mistake by failing to follow the Policy of Radical Honesty. He didn't tell Alice he was falling in love with Emma. If he had avoided the Love Buster of dishonesty, the problem might have been nipped in the bud. Many affairs in the making can be safely sidetracked with honesty.

Tom had a million excuses for why he kept the truth from Alice: He didn't want to hurt her feelings; he knew how important Emma's friendship was to Alice; it was a short-term fling that would end soon with no one the wiser.

Dishonesty always has its reasons. But it always brings the same result—solutions to marital problems become impossible because information critical to a solution is distorted.

Tom's second mistake was independent behavior. He created a secret second life, hidden from Alice, so he could have an affair with Emma—a clear violation of the Policy of Joint Agreement.

When they came to see me for counseling, I first focused their attention on radical honesty. Over the next few days, Tom told Alice the details of the affair, and gave her a complete accounting of his daily activities. His life was an open book that she could investigate freely. Transparency was the key word, and he made every effort to invite Alice into every room in his house.

The first step for recovery after an affair is to never see or talk to the lover again. In that community, it would have been impossible to avoid bumping into Emma, so Tom and Alice agreed to sell their mobile home and move to another retirement community in another state. Years of experience have taught me that people cannot be trusted with former lovers, and the close proximity to Emma would have been extremely tempting to Tom and emotionally stressful to Alice. Besides, even if a rekindling of the affair would not be at all tempting to Tom, any contact would have been a terrible offense to Alice.

They had to move quickly to get away from Emma, and yet the choice of where to move had to be with their mutual enthusiastic agreement. So I suggested that they move to a temporary location while negotiating with each other to find a permanent residence, which they eventually found. The transition and ultimate move was costly, something that stretched their retirement budget, but the affair could have been much worse, and more expensive—it could have ended their marriage.

All of their trouble could have been avoided if Tom had been radically honest with Alice. They could have worked together to ease them out of their relationship with Emma before the affair took place. During the transition, Alice might have continued to help her during her time of greatest need. But she would have been completely off-limits to Tom.

Don't Let Friends and Relatives Destroy Your Love for Each Other

Many conflicts regarding friends and relatives pit the interests of a spouse against those of the friends and relatives. In our first example, Sherrie had to decide who had the highest priority—her parents or her husband. When she chose her parents, she risked the loss of love in her marriage, a poor choice. But when she returned her husband's interest to its rightful place, her top priority, their love was restored, and her parents eventually made the adjustment.

I could have related many other examples of parents' influence in marriage. One particularly difficult situation is where the parents' judgment seems clearly superior to the couple's. But even in those cases, it's wiser in the long run for the couple to make the final decisions for themselves, taking each other's emotional reactions into account. Parental wisdom sometimes fails to take romantic love into account, and unless a couple applies the Policy of Joint Agreement to their conflict, the solution will sacrifice their love for each other.

Judy and Bill's case represented another common type of marital conflict regarding relatives—in this case, relatives with economic need. Under no circumstances should one spouse's generosity toward relatives be imposed on the other. All gifts and acts of kindness should be mutual decisions, and your relatives should give *both* of you credit.

The remaining two cases in this chapter dealt with friendships. In the first case, Craig simply didn't like Joan's friend, Bev. But again, the Policy of Joint Agreement led them to pick friends they both enjoyed. Many can't see the wisdom of Joan ending her friendship with Bev. But once a couple sees that the Policy of Joint Agreement is the most thoughtful way to make marital decisions, it seems like common sense. Joan's friendship with Bev had been a Love Buster.

Likewise, even though Tom and Alice had a long mutual friendship with Emma, when Emma and Tom had an affair, she had to go. You are more likely to have an affair with a mutual friend than anyone else, and if you begin to have romantic feelings toward that friend, tell your spouse about it right away—and never tell the friend. Then, ease out of the relationship entirely.

Your spouse is your most important friend and relative. No other should ever be allowed to come between you. Follow the Policy of Joint Agreement to make sure they don't.

Consider This...

1. What are three strategies to resolving conflicts over friends and relatives? Why should you always avoid two of them and learn to become experts at using the third?

2. Think of a conflict you have over friends and relatives. If you used the first strategy to resolving conflicts that I describe in this chapter, how would you try to resolve it? If you used the second strategy, what would you do? Why would both of these strategies for marital problem solving diminish the love you have for each other?

3. Use the third approach I suggested to help you resolve your conflicts over friends and relatives (the Four Guidelines to Successful Negotiation, introduced in chapter 3, and described again in chapter 8).

4. Try to anticipate some of the conflicts you may have with family and friends. If your parents or your spouse's parents were to require your care, what kind of care could you provide with an enthusiastic agreement? Where will you be spending Christmas? What would you do if a friend needed help moving? Or if a friend invited you both out to dinner? Or if a friend invited one of you out to dinner, but didn't invite the other? Or if the friend had been a former lover? Think of other situations with family and friends that might lead to conflict in the future. How will you handle these situations so that you'll have an enthusiastic agreement?

5. What are exceptions to following the Policy of Joint Agreement? Think of some examples that you might face in your marriage where those exceptions might apply.

6. The Policy of Joint Agreement is a rule that applies uniquely to marital relationships. Why can't you use it when you make decisions with friends and relatives? (Hint: "Never do anything . . ." only makes sense in marriage because you have agreed to be exclusive lifelong partners, sharing everything with each other.)

10

RESOLVING CONFLICTS OVER CAREER CHOICES AND TIME MANAGEMENT

Joyce was nineteen and I was twenty-one when we were married, and my career plans were anything but settled at the time. After graduating from college with a degree in philosophy, I had absolutely no idea what I'd do to earn a living. So I attended graduate school for two years taking courses in philosophy, religion, mathematics, and computer sciences—searching for direction. But the birth of our daughter, Jennifer, ended the searching. We were forced to make a career decision quickly. After Joyce rejected two career possibilities that I suggested, we eventually agreed on psychology, and I completed my education with a PhD degree in that field.

Joyce and I decided my career path together. It was easy for me to reject careers that didn't appeal to Joyce, because I hadn't prepared for them yet. But today many couples don't marry until they're in their late twenties or thirties, long after they've made decisions regarding careers. If I had earned a professional degree and then had ten years of experience, I might have thought twice if Joyce had expressed reservations. Yet it's been proven to me time and time again that unless spouses have enthusiastic agreement about each other's careers, a career choice can destroy a marriage. And that enthusiasm must persist throughout life if a marriage is to be successful.

When couples are dating, they usually don't have much information about the implications of a career decision. They want to encourage each other, so they usually express enthusiasm for each other's career preferences, not knowing exactly how it would affect them if they ever married.

> A career choice can destroy a marriage.

But after marriage, and especially after children arrive, the effect of a career is clearly revealed. It either supports or threatens a marriage. And making a career choice even more complicated, it may support a marriage in one phase of life but threaten it in another.

In this chapter, I combine two types of conflict because they are so interwoven with each other—career choices and time management. As I've tried to help couples resolve just about every conflict imaginable, when it comes to conflicts over how time is to be used, the most common obstacle to a simple solution is their choice of career.

In the chapters you've already read, I've made it clear that if you want to be in love and stay in love, your decisions must be made with mutual and enthusiastic agreement. And that applies to the way you spend every hour of every day. But how can you have a mutual enthusiastic agreement about your daily schedule when you have enlisted in the army and have just been assigned to a year's tour of duty? Or when you're on call at a hospital for emergency care? The demands of a career will usually trump the Policy of Joint Agreement when it comes to how you schedule your time.

Marital conflict over a career often has more to do with the way it dominates a time schedule than it does with the career itself. Some careers are so flexible regarding time schedules that the interests of a marriage can be easily accommodated. But other careers are notoriously damaging to marriages because of the time constraints that are imposed. This is especially true when a career separates a couple or prevents them from having enough time to meet each other's emotional needs.

If your spouse is unhappy with what your career requires you to do, you're making Love Bank withdrawals every time you go to work. You may think that when it comes to earning a living, you don't have any choices. Your spouse simply must learn to adjust to your career. But after complaining about it for a while, the way your spouse is likely to adjust is to disconnect from you emotionally so that the effects of the career don't hurt as much. In other words, your spouse will simply fall out of love with you.

Take it from me, a seasoned veteran when it comes to changing people: It's much easier to change a behavior than it is to change an emotional reaction to a behavior. If you tell your spouse not to feel the way he or she does when you do something, you're making a terrible mistake, because your spouse's reactions are very unlikely to change. On the other hand, if you change your behavior to produce a positive reaction instead of a negative reaction in your spouse, that reaction will also persist as long as you continue your new behavior.

If your work schedule or career requirements make your spouse unhappy, change them. And if necessary, create a new career that gives you enough flexibility to keep your marriage healthy and happy.

> Your career should support your spouse and family— not the other way around.

When I introduce this idea of changing careers to couples, many of them think I'm nuts. And yet when you consider the career paths of most people, careers usually change several times during a person's lifetime. One way or another, your career is likely to change during **your** lifetime. Are you willing to change your career path out of consideration for your spouse or will you let some of the random factors of life make those changes for you?

I'm a firm believer that your career should support your spouse and family and not the other way around. The purpose of a career is to earn a living so that you can have a satisfying lifestyle. But what if the career itself causes you or your spouse to lose your love for each other? Then the career is defeating its very purpose. Instead of creating a comfortable lifestyle, it's creating a miserable lifestyle.

Some people have tried to argue that their career choice is a personal decision. Since it's something that they will be doing most of their waking hours, the first and foremost consideration should be whether or not they like doing it. People who use this argument are usually afraid that their spouse will force them into a career that they really don't want. But the Policy of Joint Agreement handles that problem. It requires both of you to be enthusiastic about your final decision. It guides you to a career that you will enjoy because that's one of the conditions that must be met.

But your spouse must enjoy it too. If you follow the conditions of the Policy of Joint Agreement, when your negotiations are over you will have a career that's just as fulfilling as the one you have now, if not more so. And your spouse will be as enthusiastic about it as you are.

Is He Ambitious or a Workaholic?

Renee didn't know exactly what she wanted in a husband, but she knew one thing: She didn't want to marry some lazy oaf! So when Jim came along, his tireless ability to work impressed her. He had not only put himself through college but had saved enough to pay cash for his car. It made her feel secure to know he was not the type to pile up debts.

While they were dating, he saw her or at least called her every day. Being with her was a part of his schedule. But after they married, his career took off, and his time with Renee gradually tapered off.

"Jim, you're working too hard," she would tell him. "Why don't you relax a little? Let's take a vacation together!"

He would just smile. "I am relaxed! Have you ever seen me on a vacation? I'm a bundle of nerves."

Jim didn't realize—and Renee didn't explain—that the problem with his nerves was insignificant compared with the problem that was developing in their relationship. Jim was not with Renee often enough to sustain her love for him. With his work schedule, he couldn't possibly meet her emotional needs, and it wasn't long before Renee had fallen out of love with him.

Renee came to me to express her dissatisfaction with life. She lived in a beautiful home, had wonderful children, and all the freedom a mother could ever want. But her emotional needs were not being met. In fact she was seriously considering an affair, just to see if it would help.

The Love Buster dishonesty was partly to blame for Renee's dissatisfaction. She didn't want to appear unappreciative of all the material things he provided, so she had not explained to Jim that she was un-happy with their relationship. And she didn't dare tell him she was thinking of having an affair. He might leave her, and then where would she be?

Arranging for an appointment with Jim was a Herculean task. He was scheduled for months ahead. So I adjusted my schedule to fit his. Even then, he canceled his first appointment at the last minute when a "business emergency" arose.

When I finally did see him, I asked if he felt his daily schedule was any of Renee's business.

He was puzzled by my question. "Of course it's her business," he responded.

Then I wanted to know if he had ever asked her how she felt about his schedule. He thought he had, but Renee was right there to tell him he had not.

Finally, I asked him if Renee's feelings would affect his schedule. If she were unhappy with something he planned, would he change his plans to accommodate her feelings?

By the end of the session, Jim understood where I was headed and he got the message. His work schedule had become his highest priority, and even though he said he was working to make Renee happy, it was actually ruining his relationship with her. He had imposed his work schedule on Renee, and his career fulfillment came at her expense.

Fortunately, we caught the problem before Renee had tried having an affair. And it was also before she was in the state of withdrawal, where she would not have wanted him to meet her emotional needs, or even to spend time with him. If Renee had wanted him to remain at work, I would have had a more difficult time restoring their marriage. But, thankfully, she still wanted to be with him.

I gave them both the assignment of creating a daily schedule that would be carefully negotiated. No time would be spent on any activity, including work, unless they first agreed enthusiastically. They used the Four Guidelines for Successful Negotiation to create that schedule, and literally every hour had to be spent doing what they had negotiated.

Jim began by clearing his work schedule for the rest of the day so that he had time to negotiate with Renee. He was hoping it could be done that very afternoon and evening. But after talking with Renee that day, and realizing how far she had drifted from him, he did the right thing and took the rest of the week off to be with her. They used that time to learn how to use the Policy of Joint Agreement and the Four Guidelines to Successful Negotiation to make every scheduling decision.

One of my cardinal rules for couples is to schedule a minimum of fifteen hours each week to meet each other's intimate emotional needs (see chapter 17). So while still in my office, I asked them to schedule those hours together for the next week. During that time they were to be affectionate, talk to each other, enjoy recreational activities together, and make love. So from that moment on, they were not to let a week go by without giving each other the attention they needed to make much-needed Love Bank deposits.

> Your career should serve your marriage; your marriage should not serve your career.

In the final analysis, Jim was still a workaholic in the sense that he enjoyed work more than most people do. But by following the Policy of Joint Agreement, he made Renee his highest priority, a position that she deserved to have as his wife. In making that decision, he saved his marriage and possibly his career as well.

Renee's habit of dishonesty was part of their problem. Jim would have tried to accommodate her feelings much earlier if she had complained more often, or at least they would have sought counseling earlier. She had to express her dissatisfaction before he could make an adjustment.

I've counseled others, however, who were not as accommodating as Jim. They argue that unless they devoted all their energy and effort to their career, their family would become homeless! These people have their priorities backward.

Your career should serve your marriage; your marriage should not serve your career. You and your spouse should work with each other to help develop each other's career, but the success of your careers should never be more important to you than the success of your marriage. To put it another way, the success of your career should never be at the expense of your spouse's interests and feelings. If you're in a career where its demands are so great that your spouse's interests simply cannot be considered, you're in the wrong career.

I've spoken to many people who are close to death, and none of them have ever told me they should have spent more time at work. If people have regret later in life, it's that they didn't spend more time with their spouse and children.

Flying into Clouds of Conflict

Sarah loved her job as a flight attendant. She liked the work itself, earned a good salary, and could travel almost anywhere as an employee benefit. But her husband, Rich, didn't like her job at all. She had applied for it without consulting him, knowing he wouldn't like the idea and thinking she probably wouldn't get it anyway. But when they actually offered it to her, she was delirious with excitement.

When Rich came in the door from work, Sarah flung her arms around his neck. "I got it! I got it!"

He smiled and hugged her back. "Got what?"

"I got a job as a flight attendant. Isn't that great? Oh, I'm so happy!"

Rich's smile faded. But Sarah didn't notice. She ran all around their apartment, screaming, "I got it!"

"Hey, wait a minute, Sarah, you didn't tell me you were applying for a new job. Don't you like the one you already have?"

"It was okay, but I never thought I'd be able to work as a flight attendant. It's all right with you, isn't it?"

Rich didn't seem to have a choice. "Well, I guess we can try it for a while to see how it works, but I'm not too crazy about your being away so much."

Six months later the job was becoming a major issue in their marriage. Rich was not only being left alone for up to three nights at a time, but he was becoming jealous of the pilots and passengers who asked his wife out to dinner. Sarah would come home to find a beast in her apartment, and by the time he'd settle down, she'd be off on another trip.

When they came to me for counseling, Sarah was not sure she was in love with Rich anymore. And she was secretly meeting with a man she had met on a flight. A separation might be a good idea, she suggested, so she could decide how she felt about her marriage.

Rich didn't know about any of this and simply wanted me to tell her to quit her job.

Their marriage was hanging together by a thread. If I had followed Rich's advice, Sarah probably wouldn't have shown up for the next appointment. Besides, it would have been a very bad precedent for future negotiations—demands don't work, as Rich should have discovered by then.

Neither Rich nor Sarah was a good negotiator. They didn't make their discussions safe for each other, and they didn't try to understand each other's perspectives. The Policy of Joint Agreement seemed like a joke when they first heard about it.

Rich's demands, disrespectful judgments, and angry outbursts regarding Sarah's independent behavior had turned him into a most unpleasant husband. And it made his position regarding her work totally uncompelling. Instead of persuading her that her job was ruining their marriage, he was persuading her that **he** was ruining their marriage. His abusive way of handling this conflict had done nothing to resolve it, and had punched a gaping hole into Sarah's Love Bank.

I explained that he would need to learn to control his abusive behavior before Sarah would be willing to negotiate with him regarding her independent behavior. He had to make discussion safe and enjoyable for her. It was in his best interests to stop making demands, start showing respect, and avoid losing his temper. In return for his commitment to avoid these Love Busters, Sarah agreed not to separate while in counseling.

Rich's success in avoiding angry outbursts was probably the most crucial step toward their recovery. Once Sarah felt he could control his temper, she explained her feelings to him and even went so far as to tell him that she had been planning to move out, that she might be in love with someone else, and that she didn't love him.

Even after these revelations, Rich didn't become angry. Instead, he simply expressed his desire for reconciliation.

At that point in the counseling process, I had the opportunity to explain to Sarah that she had engaged in the Love Buster of independent behavior. She had been inconsiderate of Rich's feelings when she took her job. She had gained a career advantage at his expense.

Her face turned red. "Well, I suppose you want me to quit my job. That's what you really want, isn't it?"

I explained that I had no right to demand anything of her, and neither did Rich. But the truth was that her happiness led to his unhappiness.

Sarah could have walked out of my office never to return. But Rich's proven ability to stop trying to control her with demands, disrespect, and anger encouraged her enough to begin a process of negotiation with the Policy of Joint Agreement. After they agreed that neither of them should gain at each other's expense, they began asking each other how they would feel about alternative jobs that would give her the advantages she enjoyed without the disadvantages to Rich. Eventually, Sarah found another job with the same airline company, one Rich enthusiastically supported because it gave her many of the same benefits yet didn't require being away nights.

The happy ending did not take place immediately. There were many times that I thought their efforts might end in failure. But Sarah and Rich both used their intelligence to override their destructive instincts, and their combined wisdom trumped the foolishness of their Takers. His complete elimination of demands, disrespectful judgments, and angry outbursts gave them the opportunity to negotiate thoughtfully. Before they ended their sessions with me, her new job and their new approach to resolving conflicts helped restore her love for him.

Any career that takes you away from your spouse overnight is dangerous to the health of your marriage. The more often you're gone, the more dangerous it is. That's because most of the important emotional needs are usually met in the evening, and when you're apart they can't easily be met. If emotional needs are unmet, Love Bank balances fall, and if a couple eventually falls out of love, they no longer feel like meeting each other's needs, even when they are together.

But you risk more than the loss of love when you are apart overnight. You also risk infidelity. I can thank the airline industry for giving me the opportunity to make a living as a marriage counselor. By being separated from their spouses overnight, pilots and flight attendants helped me become an expert on the subject of infidelity, because many of these folks were having affairs in almost every way possible. They also gave me confidence in my methods, since they provided such a difficult testing ground, and the methods I used proved successful even under those conditions.

Joyce and I have avoided overnight separation ever since we were first married, even though both of our careers require extensive travel. When either of us is called away, the other comes along. That way, we are not only more integrated into each other's careers, but we also continue to meet each other's emotional needs, even when on business trips.

If your job does not allow your spouse to come along when you travel, I strongly recommend that you change that condition of your job or change the job itself to keep your marriage from being at risk. Pilots and flight attendants, over-the-road truckers, traveling salesmen, and train engineers tend to have disappointing marriages because their jobs keep them away from their spouses for days or even weeks.

Other jobs that are hard on marriages are those that require a spouse to be on call twenty-four hours a day, seven days a week. Physicians, for example, who are not in control of their own schedule can develop a lifestyle where the demands of their career control their day-to-day schedules. Scheduled time between the husband and wife is always at risk and can always be interrupted. To overcome this sad state of affairs I've encouraged many doctors to simply avoid being on call when they're with their spouse or family. They learn to leave their cell phones at the office.

No matter how much satisfaction you may find in a particular job, if it keeps you away from your spouse overnight, or interferes with the time you schedule to meet each other's important emotional needs, it's time to make a change.

The Unhappy Wanderer

Moving is never easy but it's excruciatingly painful when you don't *want* to move. Jean was in tears all day as she packed.

"Brian, Duluth may be a wonderful city with wonderful opportunities, but I like it here in Sioux Falls. Please, don't do this to me," she begged.

"I'm sorry," he replied, shaking his head, "but we can't turn back now. I was fortunate to be offered this job and I can't pass it up."

Jean moved to Duluth with Brian. Then she moved to Des Moines, Kansas City, and finally Minneapolis. Their children had not been in one school for any two-year period and they were having trouble adjusting socially. Jean had experienced severe symptoms of anxiety, so she made an appointment with me to help her and her children.

During my first interview with her, she avoided the subject of her marriage and focused on her symptoms. But eventually she mentioned that her anxiety had threatened her marriage. Sometimes it's difficult to know if emotional symptoms cause a bad marriage or vice versa. I tentatively concluded it was probably the marriage that caused the symptoms and asked to see her husband.

Brian loved Jean dearly, tried to put her first in everything, and valued his time with his family. He seemed to be a perfect husband. But in my interview with him, he mentioned that Jean had been cold toward him ever since they moved from Sioux Falls. In further conversations with Jean, she admitted that the move had caused a change in her feelings toward Brian and she wasn't sure if she loved him anymore. During the past year, they had made love very infrequently.

The more we talked about Sioux Falls, the more visibly depressed Jean became, mentioning on several occasions having no hope of ever going back "home."

I explained to Brian that Jean could take medication to relieve the anxiety symptoms that seemed to be caused by all their moving around, or he could move the family back to Sioux Falls. If they moved, I predicted that within two to five years, she'd be back to normal.

But I didn't want Brian to move entirely on my recommendation. I wanted him to learn how to use the Policy of Joint Agreement, and the Four Guidelines to Successful Negotiation to come to an agreement. Otherwise, whenever they had a conflict, they'd have to call me for a decision.

The first of the four guidelines, making their negotiation pleasant and safe, was easy for them to follow. They never had argued with each other over conflicts. Even when they moved, Jean would complain, but she didn't fight with Brian. She felt that as his wife, she had to submit to his final decision. My advice that they come to a mutually enthusiastic agreement before making a decision changed all of that. She was now being encouraged to express her opinions, and that no decision could be made unless those opinions were addressed.

The second guideline, expressing their perspectives with mutual respect, was also easy for them to do. The difference this time was that Jean's perspective had to be considered in the final decision.

Jean loved Sioux Falls and the friends she had come to know there. But until Brian loved living there just as much and was willing to stay there for the rest of his life, there wouldn't be much enthusiasm on his part for a move back.

So as they were brainstorming, guideline number three, they decided that a test of my recommendation would satisfy both of them. If Brian could find a job he liked in Sioux Falls and Jean were "cured" of her symptoms as I had predicted, Brian would be just as enthusiastic about living there as Jean would be.

The fourth guideline, making a mutually enthusiastic decision, was met when Brian was offered a very attractive position in the company he worked for when they had lived in Sioux Falls. And Jean's anxiety symptoms eventually all but disappeared. Most important, however, was that her love for Brian was completely restored. The results of their test confirmed the fact that they had made the right decision, and today they enthusiastically live in Sioux Falls.

You usually know what you need more than anyone else. Jean knew she would suffer if she moved away from Sioux Falls. And she did suffer. But short of a divorce, she thought there was no way to return.

She experienced a conflict that commonly causes severe emotional symptoms: an avoidance-avoidance conflict. If Jean were to continue moving from one strange community to the next, she would suffer; and if she were to choose a divorce, she would suffer. In other words, regardless of what she did, she would experience pain. Conflicts like this tend to make people neurotic. In some cases, these conflicts lead to suicide.

Brian's insistence that the family move from one city to another was a selfish demand. He forced the move on Jean. If, on the other hand, he had formulated his desire to move from Sioux Falls to Duluth as a thoughtful request, Jean might have agreed to the move as a test, to see if they would thrive after the move. Upon finding that it made her miserable, they would by previous agreement move back to Sioux Falls. After all, the move to Duluth would have been only a test, and relatively few love units would have been lost.

Joyce and I have experience with that same situation. I was offered an attractive career opportunity in Chicago, but Joyce was not at all happy about moving from our home in beautiful Santa Barbara. After discussing alternatives, we came to an agreement: She was willing to go to Chicago on the condition that we would move back if she found that she preferred living in Santa Barbara.

After a year in Chicago, I was offered another opportunity in Minneapolis. Again, we discussed the alternatives, and Joyce agreed to the move as long as a return to Santa Barbara was possible if she found Minneapolis to be undesirable.

During that year, our daughter, Jennifer, was placed in four different schools, and Joyce's father died suddenly and unexpectedly. It was a time of unprecedented emotional upheaval. But through it all Joyce knew I'd be willing to return to Santa Barbara as soon as she said the word. It was a test, and as such, she was still enthusiastic about the move.

There were disadvantages to be sure, but there were also advantages to living in Minneapolis. Joyce was able to weigh them in her mind and each year she chose to remain in the Twin Cities. We have lived here for over thirty-five years now, and Joyce could still decide to move back to Santa Barbara if it was what she wanted to do. In fact, we own a home in Santa Barbara. But to this day she has never expressed a bit of resentment toward me regarding the move, because it was a *joint* decision that was in her best interest. And she's still enthusiastic about living here.

What If God's Calling Is the Issue?

When he was nine, Al committed his life to the ministry. At a church service, when the preacher asked for those willing to become full-time ministers, he responded and never forgot that decision. In college he majored in Bible to prepare for the ministry.

Toni was also a Bible major and had thought she would become a missionary. She and Al took many of the same classes and studied together. They dated and before long they were in love.

But before graduation Toni decided against becoming a missionary, changed her major to social work, and eventually completed that major. Al figured social work would be a great background for a minister's wife and encouraged her in her professional training.

They married immediately after college graduation. Al enrolled in seminary, and Toni found a job as a social worker. But after only one year of seminary, they both realized she would not be comfortable in the role of a minister's wife. She had become acquainted with a few of these wives and didn't like what she saw. They all seemed to be complaining about the criticism they received from parishioners, and Toni hated criticism in any form.

"Toni, we're in this thing together. You have an important role to play," Al explained. When that didn't work, and she continued to express reluctance to accept that role, he read her verses from the Bible on the subject of a man's authority over his wife.

Toni became furious. "Don't you lecture me! If I don't want to play Mrs. Reverend, I won't."

Then they broke into the biggest fight they'd ever had. But when it was over, Toni agreed to support Al in his ministry because he had made a commitment to God. She didn't like it at all and it certainly wasn't an "enthusiastic agreement." Al's selfish demands, disrespectful judgments, and angry outburst would eventually come back to haunt him.

After graduating from seminary, Al took a position in a rural church of fifty members. He was happy with his career, but Toni suffered. She could not fit into the role that was expected of her. There was little privacy in the church parsonage—she hated living in a fishbowl. And even in a church of fifty, there were those who were critical of her. She put on a cheerful face when she met parishioners but when she was home alone, she cried.

Al felt her problems were spiritual and that Toni had not given herself to God's work. Her "rebellious spirit" was keeping her from enjoying the ministry as much as he enjoyed it. She believed him and her depression became so serious that she could no longer hide it from others. Eventually Al felt she should see a psychologist.

It didn't take me long to discover the problem. Toni explained that she was not cut out for the role of a pastor's wife. What's worse, she had come to hate her husband, because he'd forced her into it. She could see no escape from a lifetime of misery, and was on the brink of suicide.

Al had imposed his career choice on Toni, even though he knew it was the cause of her suffering. The solution to their problem was easy to understand but difficult to implement—he had to find another career.

Pastors are in the business of making moral judgments from the pulpit. It's what their parishioners expect them to do. But they often make the mistake of carrying their preaching into their home. When that happens, it becomes a disrespectful judgment. Al had to learn to discuss their conflicts without any reference to "shoulds" and "oughts."

He also came to understand the foolishness of selfish demands. Instead of obtaining Toni's cooperation, his demands caused her to resist doing whatever it was he needed. If he had negotiated with thoughtfulness, he might have been able to find a way to be a pastor with her enthusiastic agreement. But by the time I saw them, she had developed such an aversion to the entire scene that Al had no choice but to make a career change—if he wanted to save his marriage.

As they discussed alternatives with each other, they eventually settled on a career in counseling as mutually acceptable. Toni was able to find a full-time job as a social worker, which supported Al's retraining. The work was good for her, and I saw them long enough to see her recover completely from depression.

Today, Al has completed his retraining and has a job as a psychologist. He works closely with churches and supports ministers in their pastoral counseling. And Toni is in love with him again.

It's a matter of priorities. In Al's case, he had to realize that once he was married, Toni had to be his highest priority. His marriage could not serve his career. His career had to serve his marriage.

Al's choice was not between God and Toni—it was between his career and Toni. He had made a commitment to God to become a full-time minister. But he also made a commitment to God to be a caring husband. Al thought that his career was more important to God than his marriage. But the question I put to him was, *Which one of those roles is really more important to God?*

Over the years, I've counseled many pastors and their wives. In many cases, these men made a commitment to become a minister of the gospel at an early age, much like Al's commitment. However, in the course of life, these men discovered that they'd married women who, for whatever reason, had failed to adjust to the role of pastor's wife. At that point each had a decision to make: *Does God want me to follow my commitment to Christian ministry and remain a pastor, or does he want me to reevaluate that commitment in light of the needs of my spouse?*

They struggle with that question. They think God might be disappointed with them if they choose to consider their wife's feelings in making career decisions. But I point out to them how foolish that sounds. How could God be disappointed with thoughtfulness toward their spouse? He's in *favor* of thoughtfulness, not *opposed* to it! He wants us to treat our spouses with the utmost care and consideration, and that includes how we make career choices.

The Policy of Joint Agreement provides the wisest solution to this problem. When a wife realizes her husband is willing to consider a new career that she would enthusiastically agree to, she will usually take her husband's love for the ministry into account. The decision often keeps them in some form of ministry, but also provides her with an emotionally satisfying role.

Don't Let Your Career Destroy Your Love for Each Other

As I explained in the beginning of this chapter, I planned my career with my wife in mind. My first career choice was to become a minister and my second was medicine. Joyce didn't like either of them for various reasons. But by the time we had been married three years, we both agreed on my profession, psychology.

It would have been pointless for me to start my career development without her enthusiastic agreement. After all, my career was to be a joint effort with joint compensation. Without her support, the career would not serve our mutual purposes in life. Her encouragement has made my choice particularly satisfying and undoubtedly accounts for much of its success.

Joyce's career choices were made with the same consideration for my feelings. I support her career as enthusiastically as she supports mine. I consider her work as a gospel singer and radio host/producer to be an effort we make jointly. I never resent the time she spends pursuing her career interests, because she is willing to accommodate my feelings with her schedule and choice of career activities.

> Make your career and schedule a Love Builder, not a Love Buster.

Since we are both ambitious people, our career interests could have wrecked our marriage. Our careers could have driven us in opposite directions. But instead, our careers have strengthened our marriage, because we consider each other more important than our work. Our deep love for each other is the result.

I have counseled hundreds of couples whose marriages were threatened by foolish career choices and thoughtless time management. I gave you a few examples of these cases in this chapter. In every case one or both spouses felt that they should be able to make independent career and time management decisions without adversely impacting their marriage. But their gains were made at the expense of their spouse's love for them.

Don't lock your spouse out of your career room. And when it's time to lay out your schedule for the week, be sure that your spouse is sitting next to you to discuss each activity. The career you choose, and the way you schedule your time, should always be carried out with your spouse in mind. Make your career and schedule a Love Builder, not a Love Buster.

Consider This...

1. How are selfish demands, disrespectful judgments, and angry outbursts used to force career choices? How are they used to force time schedules? What are some common excuses spouses use to justify their selfish demands, disrespectful judgments, and angry outbursts? Have you used any of these forms of abuse to try to force your spouse to agree with your career choices or time schedules?

2. What is the likely outcome when a spouse is expected to adjust to a decision that has not been enthusiastically accepted?

3. When does a career choice or a time schedule become the Love Buster of independent behavior? How is that decision different than trying to obtain agreement through demands, disrespect, or anger? Do either of you feel you have the right to make decisions about your career or schedule independently of the other's interests and feelings? Are you willing to give up that right for the sake of your love for each other?

4. Why should your commitment to your career be less important than your commitment to care for each other?

5. Are you in agreement with each other's career choices, what you do while at work, and the way you schedule your time? Make a list of all aspects of each other's careers that bother one of you. Then, use the Policy of Joint Agreement and the Four Guidelines to Successful Negotiation to try to resolve these conflicts by modifying your schedules and work assignments with enthusiastic agreement.

11

Resolving Conflicts over Financial Planning

A few years ago I read an article announcing that conflicts over finances had been shown to be the number one cause of divorce. That's not really true, but if a couple doesn't know how to resolve their conflicts, they're likely to be arguing about money almost every day.

The reason most people divorce is because they've lost their love for each other. They stop depositing love units because they stop meeting each other's emotional needs. And they start withdrawing love units by not taking each other's feelings into account when they make decisions. Since so many decisions in marriage have to do with finances, it may seem that conflict over money is the number one cause of divorce. But it's actually only a symptom of the real cause.

When a couple first comes to see me for counseling, I often ask them how they make their financial decisions. Do you have a joint checking account? Does the money that both of you earn go into that account? Do you make decisions together on how that money is to be spent?

For most of the couples I counsel, that isn't the way it's done at all. For most couples with bad marriages, each spouse makes unilateral decisions about how money is to be spent. In many cases, the husband's salary goes into his checking account and the wife's salary goes into hers. They may have some sort of agreement on how the bills are to be split up so that he pays some of the bills and she pays others. Or they may decide that one of them takes full responsibility for all the bills. All their earnings go into one account, but only one spouse has the right to make decisions as to how that money is spent.

By now, I'm sure you can see that these and other common approaches to making financial decisions violate the Policy of Joint Agreement. If a couple wants to avoid Love Bank withdrawals, they should be thoughtful toward each other as they spend every dime. The money that both of them earn should be deposited into a joint checking account, but no check should be written unless they are both in enthusiastic agreement. In some cases I've encouraged spouses to print checks with two signature lines so that they can be reminded to practice making all financial decisions with joint agreement.

If conflict over financial planning is causing Love Bank withdrawals in your marriage, I suggest that you take the first step toward recovery by depositing all of your income into a joint checking account. Then, agree not to write a check unless you both enthusiastically agree. Set aside a time each week to pay your bills, and write each other checks for personal discretionary spending.

> If a couple doesn't know how to resolve their conflicts, they're likely to be arguing about money almost every day.

For most monthly bills, there will be no conflict. But if you can't agree on the purchase of a particular item or how much to pay toward a particular bill, you should use the Four Guidelines for Successful Negotiation to resolve the issue.

First, remind each other that your conversation must be pleasant and safe if you are to come to an enthusiastic agreement. And also remind each other that the default position on the Policy of Joint Agreement is to do nothing. If you can't come to an enthusiastic agreement, the money should remain in your checking account.

Second, discover each other's feelings about the issue in a nonjudgmental way to understand what kind of a solution would work for both of you. Granted, there are some who simply don't want to spend any money—they're tightwads. The default condition, not doing anything, is precisely what they want. I'll address that problem in the next section of this chapter. But most couples try to find common ground when they're respectful toward each other.

The third step is to brainstorm—think of solutions that might make both of you happy. If you can't think of anything immediately, let the problem incubate for a day or two, and then come back to it again. It's amazing what your brain can do when you give it a chance to process information for a while.

Finally, take the fourth step by finding a solution that you can both agree to enthusiastically. Again, I want to remind you why I want you to find enthusiastic agreements as opposed to reluctant agreements. Enthusiastic agreements create a lifestyle that deposits love units while reluctant agreements create one that withdraws love units. If you want to be in love, don't settle for reluctant agreements.

> What ruins marriage is not delaying a purchase—it's making a purchase where one spouse gains at the other's expense.

While you negotiate, don't spend anything on the item in question, regardless of how much one spouse senses urgency. Instead, wait until you have enthusiastic agreement regardless of how long it takes.

For many couples this is a very difficult assignment. They feel that if they don't buy a particular item the earth will swallow them up and send them into oblivion. But I try to convince couples that their love for each other is far more important than a particular purchase.

What ruins marriages is not delaying a purchase—it's making a purchase where one spouse gains at the other's expense. You may feel that what you're doing is right, but if in the process of being right your spouse loses his or her love for you, what kind of victory does that turn out to be? Besides, it's been proven to me again and again that a decision made with mutual agreement is usually far wiser than one made unilaterally by either spouse. So joint agreement not only insures your love for each other, it also helps you make wiser choices.

If you and your spouse are not in the habit of using the Policy of Joint Agreement and the Four Guidelines to Successful Negotiation when you make decisions, you'll probably be very frustrated when you use them at first, and feel that they are not for you. But if you give this method of resolving conflicts a chance to become a habit, making sure that you don't use demands, disrespect, or anger as a shortcut to a solution, you'll find that it becomes easier, and you'll find solutions faster.

You will also find that your agreements will set a standard for similar financial decisions in the future. Reluctant agreements must be renegotiated every time a conflict arises, but once an enthusiastic agreement is made, you will know what to do whenever the problem comes up. Enthusiastic agreements may take longer to discover, but they lead to less negotiating overall. And as your negotiating skills improve, when new financial conflicts arise, you will be able to resolve most of them quickly.

Married to a Tightwad

Frank didn't seem to worry about money. He earned enough to get by, and that was always good enough for him. But he never took out a loan, and he had no credit cards.

After high school, he had moved from his home into a mortuary where he worked (while he slept) as night attendant. His meals cost him nothing at his part-time job as a waiter and he took the bus for transportation. He paid for college with grants and money he earned. By the time he graduated, he had not borrowed a dime.

Beth realized Frank couldn't afford much while he was attending college and admired his financial discipline and resourcefulness. While their dates and his gifts to her were inexpensive, they were thoughtful and reflected his deep love for her.

But after they married and were both earning a good income, financial conflicts began to develop. Frank insisted from the beginning that they deposit both of their paychecks into a bank account that he controlled. This selfish demand set the stage for many unresolved conflicts over money.

Beth knew he was a good financial manager and that he wasn't squandering their income. But Frank was not only demanding, he was also engaging in the Love Busters of dishonesty and independent behavior—dishonesty because he didn't tell her how the money was being spent, and independent behavior because he was making financial decisions without her enthusiastic agreement.

One day Beth posed an important question. "Frank, do you think we're ready to raise children?"

"Not yet," he replied. "It'll be a while before we can afford them."

Beth bristled. "We can afford children now! We both earn good incomes and we've been saving most of it—haven't we?" Suddenly she felt uncomfortable. "By the way, how much have we saved?"

There was a long pause. "We just haven't saved enough. Take my word for it," Frank said.

His selfish demands, dishonesty, and independent behavior had caught up with him. The next day, when Beth was home alone, she started poking around Frank's papers. What she found blew her away. Frank had all their investments in *his* name. Savings accounts, money market accounts, and stocks—all in his name. The most remarkable part of it was that he had managed to save over forty thousand dollars in just two years!

That evening Beth confronted him with her discovery.

"Why are all our savings in your name? And how can you say we can't afford children when we've saved forty thousand dollars?"

Frank was furious. "I handle all the finances and I do it the way I see fit. Besides, you wouldn't understand it even if I tried to explain it to you. So stay out of my desk!"

Frank may have been *saving* money but he was *losing* love units. Beth was terribly offended and ended the conversation.

The very next day she opened her own checking account. When she was paid, she deposited her check into it.

That evening, Frank said casually, "You haven't given me your check. Do you have it yet?"

"Yes, I do," she said flatly, "and you're not getting any of it!"

Frank's independent behavior had inspired Beth to carry out her own independent behavior. It seemed fair to her. After all, why should she deposit money into an account that she had no control over? But just as his independent behavior caused losses in her Love Bank, she made Love Bank withdrawals each time she deposited her check into her own account.

By the time Frank and Beth saw me for marriage counseling, their complaint was that they'd "grown apart." She had her life and he had his. Their inability to resolve their financial conflicts had implications in many other parts of their lives, and their separate checking accounts had inspired them to separate everything!

Their problems began with Frank's selfish demands, dishonesty, and independent behavior. He wanted to control the finances and didn't want her to interfere. With incomplete information, Beth gradually suspected that Frank was cheating her.

Frank's motives were pure: He was saving money for both of them and was not trying to cheat her, but his arrogant approach destroyed her trust in him.

Beth contributed to the problem when she set up her own checking account. Even though Frank had been secretive with her about their finances, she should not have made the same mistake. As an interim solution, she would have helped the situation by depositing her check into a joint checking account that required both of their signatures. It would have set an example for Frank as to how all of their financial decisions should be made.

Of course, it was Frank who set the stage for Beth's defensive reaction, and many wouldn't blame her for what she did. When she explained that his method of financial planning had upset her, he refused to address her complaint. He knew his decisions had been at her emotional expense but did nothing to protect her feelings. If he had simply added her name to all their investments and thoughtfully requested that she deposit her check into a joint account, she might have enthusiastically agreed. But his arrogance and thoughtlessness proved to her that he could not be trusted.

The resolution to their financial conflicts began with the Policy of Joint Agreement and the Policy of Radical Honesty. I advised Frank to add Beth's name to all of his investments and to his checking account, which he did. Then he explained his investment strategy to her and asked her a crucial question: "How do you feel about it?"

That question was the first step toward negotiation. Without it, there can be no discussion leading to an enthusiastic agreement. The next step was a willingness to put off a final decision until an enthusiastic agreement is reached. In other words, their paychecks would remain in their joint account until they could decide how the money would be spent.

But that essential rule for marriage created a new problem for Beth. Frank was happy to leave the money in the joint account indefinitely.

The default condition for the Policy of Joint Agreement is to do nothing until an agreement is reached. It's usually such an uncomfortable position, that a couple will put the issue on the front burner so that they can get on with life. But what should you do when your spouse doesn't find the default condition unpleasant? What if your spouse wants to remain in limbo?

That was Beth's problem. Frank didn't like spending any money on anything. They had no loan payments, house payments, or car payments. So Frank was in no hurry to negotiate an agreement on how their income was to be spent, because they had very few bills.

If you find yourself in a similar position, where it seems that making no decision actually works to your spouse's advantage, you may need to see a mediator to break the logjam. That's what Beth and Frank did when they counseled with me.

In helping them negotiate through this conflict, I emphasized the importance of creating a lifestyle that would make both of them happy. The default condition of the Policy of Joint Agreement, spending no money, would not make Beth happy, so that alternative could not be tolerated much longer. Frank agreed.

They followed the first guideline for successful negotiation by keeping their conversation regarding their finances pleasant and safe. No demands, no disrespectful judgments, no angry outbursts. Then they asked each other to express feelings and opinions regarding household spending. I encouraged them to do that by making a tentative budget that they could enthusiastically accept. The budget was to list basic needs, such as food and utilities, but I also encouraged them to include discretionary expenses for items of personal interest. Beth was pleasantly surprised to discover that Frank was willing to buy guns and cartridge reloading equipment. He had never discussed hunting with her in the past and she was happy to see that he was willing to buy something that they didn't need. While they weren't the items she would have chosen, it seemed to be a crack in his façade of wanting only the barest essentials. For the first time in their marriage, they were talking to each other about finances, and were trying to come to an agreement. But they were not making much progress on a final budget that they could both agree to enthusiastically. Beth was faced with the prospect of accepting Frank's budget reluctantly, or Frank would reluctantly accept Beth's budget.

So I introduced an idea that I've mentioned several times in this book—a trial solution. If their brainstorming would result only in reluctant agreements, they could tentatively try one of them to discover if it would eventually lead to an enthusiastic agreement.

Technically, even if they had enthusiastically agreed to a budget in my office, a trial period would still have been wise. That's because the Policy of Joint Agreement does not hold spouses to an agreement if either person reacts negatively once the decision is enacted. For example, if you agree enthusiastically to go to a baseball game together, but after two innings one of you is bored and wants to leave, you should leave and do something else that you both enjoy.

Remember that the purpose of this policy is to keep love units flowing into both of your love banks simultaneously. An enthusiastic agreement means that you predict you will both enjoy the outcome of the decision. But if the actual event causes Love Bank withdrawals instead of deposits, you should cancel the decision and renegotiate. If you want to be in love with each other, you should place far more importance on mutual enjoyment than on trying to follow through on commitments that cause one of you to suffer.

Frank and Beth could not predict accurately how they would feel under a specific budget, so they selected one that Frank had proposed on a trial basis. I explained that the one who made the proposal would have to take initiative in demonstrating its value to the other spouse. If the other spouse was not enthusiastic about the budget after it was implemented, it would be that person's turn to have their budget proposal tested.

This is the *try it, you'll like it* approach to brainstorming. With a few adjustments made during the trial period, Beth became enthusiastic about Frank's budget, and their marital crisis was over.

Their cooperation in financial matters spread to other aspects of their marriage. Instead of walking down independent paths, they joined each other in a single interdependent path in life. Conflicts in financial planning never again threatened their love for each other.

Married to a Spendthrift

For many of us, spending more money than we have seems to be instinctive. We usually know of at least one of our ancestors who was financially undisciplined. We probably inherited the trait from him!

Shirley had inherited the trait in its purest form. From early childhood she couldn't resist buying things she wanted. Her father had tried to help control her spending, but usually gave in to her demands for the money she needed if she became upset.

While Joe dated her, he bought her gifts for special occasions and as an occasional surprise, because he enjoyed seeing her reaction: She seemed to live for her next gift from him. Joe's generosity brought out the best in her and made her appear very attractive to him. Within six months, they were head over heels in love with each other.

Joe was an executive in a growing company and earned a very good living. After paying for his living expenses and gifts to Shirley, he had plenty left over every month. So it never occurred to him that marrying her would cost him far more than he earned.

While they were dating, Shirley never asked Joe for money. She got all she needed from her father. But after marriage, she expected Joe to take her father's place in supporting her spending habits. And at first, Joe was happy to fill his shoes.

In the first few years of their marriage, he justified many of her purchases as necessary for their new home. But soon she wasn't satisfied with her initial purchases and had to buy replacement items. The closets in their home became so filled with her clothes that she gave away many items to make room for new wardrobes.

It wasn't long before Joe became alarmed. "Shirley, I think it's time we discuss something. You're spending more than we can afford."

She became genuinely concerned. "Oh, Joe, are you having financial problems?"

"*We* are having financial problems! My income is better than ever, but you're spending more than we can afford," he complained. "We'll have to start a budget so we can keep our expenses under control."

"That's okay with me," she responded cheerfully. "Just give me an allowance each month, and I'll stick to it!"

Joe worked out a budget for Shirley, but in the first month she *didn't* stick to it. When Joe tried to talk to her about it, she shrugged it off as a bad month and promised to be on target the next month. But the next month was no better.

Joe's concern turned to anger. "Shirley, are you trying to ruin me? You're spending money we don't have."

Shirley's voice remained calm. "Take it easy, Joe. You must be upset about something that happened at work. I think you're overreacting."

He couldn't control his temper any longer. "Overreacting? My problem is that I haven't reacted soon enough. I've got to put an end to this immediately. I'm taking your name off our checking account and canceling all our credit cards. I'm sorry, but it's the only way I can get your irresponsible spending under control!"

Shirley was visibly hurt by Joe's outburst. She felt he had no right to talk to her the way he did. And he was treating her like a child. So his anger had a predictable effect—she ignored his demands. The next time she saw something she wanted to buy, she simply withdrew money from their savings account. Within six months, all their savings were gone.

By the time Joe and Shirley came to my office, Joe was threatening divorce. "How can she say she loves me—and steal me blind? I just can't go on like this."

"I admit I have a problem controlling my spending, but I love Joe and I think he still loves me. He knew I liked to shop before we were married. I'm no different now than I was then," she said in her defense.

Shirley's excuse that she had a "problem controlling her spending" was nothing more than admitting her selfishness, and unwillingness to accommodate Joe's feelings. She knew Joe would be furious when he discovered their savings gone but she cared more about buying that next item than protecting Joe's interests.

It's important to realize that Shirley really loved Joe. That's because he had done a very good job of meeting her emotional needs. And he still loved her, in spite of the fact that she was driving them into bankruptcy. She was meeting his emotional needs, too. But her irresponsible spending was draining her account faster than she could make deposits. It wouldn't be much longer before she'd be the only one in love.

Joe was on the right track when he tried to negotiate with Shirley, but when his initial effort failed to change her spending habits, he should have continued negotiation, perhaps with the help of a marriage counselor. She was not only addicted to shopping, but, like most addicts, she would agree to anything just to get him off her back. Then, when he least expected it, she'd sneak out and shop again.

Psychologists often call Shirley's behavior passive-aggressive. It's passive, because she doesn't want to fight about an issue, and seems to give in when confronted with it. And it's aggressive because she ends up doing what she pleases, regardless of her promises. How do you negotiate with someone like that?

My problem as a counselor was to tap into Shirley's Taker, because that's the part of her personality that was causing Joe fits. Remember the Taker's rule? *Do whatever you can to make yourself happy, and avoid anything that makes yourself unhappy, even if it makes your spouse unhappy.* If she had not been in love with Joe, it would have been more difficult to reason with this selfish side of her. But she didn't want to lose this man who was perfect for her in every way—except letting her spend them into bankruptcy.

I took the direct approach. "Why did you spend all of the money in your savings, knowing that Joe would eventually discover what you did?" I asked.

"I was angry with him," was her reply. "He had no right telling me what to do."

"But before he told you what to do, he tried to come to an agreement with you. Why did you break that agreement?"

She gave me an answer that was quite encouraging: "I wanted to spend less, but I couldn't help myself. I guess I'm addicted to shopping."

There are some forms of addiction that require no compromise. Alcohol and drug addiction, for example, leave no room for a middle ground—the addict must avoid the addictive substance at all costs. But in Shirley's case, compromise was possible. The issue for Joe was not Shirley's shopping per se, but rather the amount of money she spent. So as they discussed possible ways to allow shopping without breaking the bank, one strategy that they agreed to was for her to shop differently—at garage sales and discount stores, instead of the high-priced stores that emptied their bank account.

Technically, she had already considered that approach when Joe first wanted her to control her spending. So we needed something else to make it work—accountability. But whatever we did had to be approved by her Taker, or it wouldn't work. Takers have a way of sabotaging a plan that is not agreed to enthusiastically.

Shirley's Taker, the selfish part of her personality, did not want to lose Joe. So as long as the plan we considered did not require her to be unhappy, she would follow it. And the plan was designed to create new habits where she would shop regularly, but at places where her purchases were within their budget.

At first, Shirley's every move had to be monitored. She had to go to discount stores and garage sales to get into the habit of shopping that way. She even hosted a garage sale of her own. But she did have a few slips along the way. Remember, habits take time to form, and the new behavior must be repeated often before it becomes so natural that it seems almost effortless. Once in a while, the old behavior will pop up out of nowhere, making it seem that all the effort has been wasted. Psychologists call that *spontaneous recovery*. But the effort is not wasted because the old habit has become very weak compared with the new habit. It's much easier to get back on track, and avoid the undesired habit, after practicing the desired habit for a while.

By the time Shirley's shopping habits had changed, she shopped as much as ever, but didn't spend nearly as much money. She stayed well within the budget that had been set aside for shopping, and that change in her behavior plugged the leak in Joe's Love Bank.

What If You're Both Spendthrifts?

Financial problems trigger many divorces because of the way people treat each other when the risk of financial disaster looms before them.

Mel and Cindy were a happy-go-lucky couple who never missed an opportunity for a good time. He had a decent job but didn't earn nearly enough to support their standard of living. She worked when she felt like it, which wasn't very often. Most of the time, they got along very well but whenever they had a conflict over money, sparks would fly.

When money was tight and Mel would try to reign in Cindy's spending, she would remind him that Nate, a former boyfriend, earned more money than he did. After a bitter argument, he would give in and let her buy whatever she wanted—whether or not they could afford it.

And Mel wasn't much better in his spending habits. When he saw something he wanted, he bought it on credit.

A point was finally reached where Mel could no longer borrow enough to pay all the bills. So without telling Cindy, he stopped making their house payment while trying to get a new loan just one more time.

Cindy had a few friends over the morning the sheriff arrived to serve her with a foreclosure notice. She was embarrassed beyond words. When Mel came home that evening, he received the tongue-lashing of the century, and then she kicked him out of the house.

"When you have all this straightened out, you can return home. But until then I don't even want to look at you. You disgust me!"

"Listen to me for just one minute," Mel pleaded. "If it weren't for your reckless spending, we wouldn't be in this mess. I've done the best I can to keep us from bankruptcy, and you just keep spending money as if it's water."

"What about your motorcycle and your hunting and fishing equipment? You spend a lot more than I do!" she fired back. "The reason we are losing our house is that you can't control your spending. Get yourself in gear or say good-bye."

Mel came to my office to see if I could help him save his marriage. I arranged for an appointment with Cindy and discovered that she didn't want a divorce any more than he wanted one. She was terrified at the prospect of supporting herself.

Neither of them took responsibility for their financial woes, yet they were both to blame. In a way, they had conspired with each other to create a house of cards. They both wanted more than they could afford, but they just weren't willing to accept the inevitable consequences.

Foreclosures often lead to divorce because both husband and wife become vicious in their effort to shift blame to the other. Whenever Mel tried to discuss finances with Cindy, she would throw in his face the last toy he bought for himself, and then they'd have a fight. Because they couldn't control their anger, a thoughtful resolution never got off the ground.

So the first step I took was to teach them how to control their angry and defensive reactions. There was no hope for an intelligent solution to their financial conflicts if they continued to blame each other. For the first time in their marriage, they were able to discuss financial problems with consideration for each other's feelings.

Then, I introduced them to the Policy of Joint Agreement. Prior to my intervention, they had never really considered a mutually enthusiastic agreement to be possible in marriage. They assumed that most couples fought until one was exhausted. And since Cindy usually had the upper hand in an argument, she was reluctant to give up her position of control. But it didn't take long for her to see that control hadn't given her what she really wanted in life—a fulfilling marriage. Both of them had to learn to apply the Policy of Joint Agreement to every dime they spent. And they had to do it with a budget in mind.

After consulting with a financial planner, Mel and Cindy eventually lost their house and filed for bankruptcy. Their new budget proved to them that they had lived far beyond their means for much too long, and they needed to make a fresh start in life. But because they had both learned to avoid disrespectful judgments and angry outbursts, their marriage survived the ordeal.

With this new start, Mel learned to be radically honest with Cindy, partly because she stopped throwing a fit in response to disappointing information. They learned to share financial information with each other and to make decisions using the Policy of Joint Agreement. Before long they were in a rented home they could afford, and their standard of living kept pace with their income.

I'm almost certain Mel and Cindy will have financial problems again in the future. Almost all married couples do. But when these problems develop, they won't use the abusive tactics of the past that prevented them from finding solutions. Instead, they'll use thoughtful tactics that lead to enthusiastic agreements and preserve their love for each other.

Deciding between Two Worthy Causes

A husband and wife often have legitimate positions when they disagree. They both have a point, and that's why mutual respect is so important as they try to resolve the conflict. While they don't agree with each other's perspectives, they must understand them if their goal is enthusiastic agreement.

The issue that divided Kevin and Marcia was how to budget their income. Kevin had a good job but he was afraid that if he were laid off, their family would have nothing to fall back on. So he insisted on saving part of each paycheck.

Marcia, on the other hand, was more confident of Kevin's job security and felt that helping their children pay for college was more important than saving money. She agreed that it was a good idea to set aside part of each paycheck for unforeseen emergencies, but that helping their children through college was a better idea. What should they do?

Kevin and Marcia came to my office in the hope that I would decide the issue for them. The solution to their problem, of course, was not mine to provide. They had to decide for themselves.

To begin, I explained that whatever they decided had to take each other's feelings into account. They should both be enthusiastic about their final decision. I asked each to explain why his or her position was important. Kevin told Marcia about his fear of losing his job and having difficulty finding another. Having savings that would carry them for a year would make him feel much more secure, since he felt he could be reemployed within that time.

Then Marcia expressed her point of view. She felt that it was the obligation of parents to see their children through college by providing financial help, and that a college education would be essential for their success.

Marcia felt that Kevin's insecurity was irrational. There was nothing to suggest that he might lose his job. And he felt that her belief that college was so important was irrational. After all, he hadn't graduated from college, and he was doing just fine, except for his fear of being unemployed.

I reminded them that they had to respect each other's perspective while searching for a solution. If they both concluded that the other person was being irrational, how could they ever come to an enthusiastic agreement?

"How would you feel if . . . ?" took the place of "Stop being so stubborn!" Marcia suggested that she work more hours and that her extra income go to their children's education. When she asked how Kevin felt about that idea, he said that if they gave the kids money for college, he wanted it to come from both of them. He was also concerned that by working more, she would have less time to be with him.

Kevin suggested that he wouldn't object to cosigning student loans. If they had the money later on, they could pay off those loans for their children. When she was asked how she felt about that idea, Marcia explained that she didn't want their children to face life with debts, even if there was the possibility that they would be paid later.

Through their discussion of possibilities, they learned not to challenge each other's opinions. Even when they seemed unreasonable, their perspectives were respected. This created a much greater willingness to cooperate. They became more creative in the discussion and finally arrived at a solution they both liked.

When their negotiations ended, they both agreed that the most important outcome of their discussion was the love they felt for each other. In fact, at one point both had reversed their original positions: He was willing to sacrifice his savings for the children's education, and she was willing to use the money for his savings. It was their Givers at work—encouraging them to sacrifice so that the other spouse could be happy. But I don't like the Giver's solution any more than the Taker's solution because in either case, someone gets hurt. I wanted them to negotiate until they reached an enthusiastic agreement—one that would make them both happy.

> When financial decisions consider the feelings of both spouses, it's a wiser plan that also builds the feeling of love.

Their ultimate compromise was a combination of taking some money from savings (but not enough to make Kevin uncomfortable), and cosigning a student loan that Marcia did not feel would be burdensome for their children. The compromise did not sacrifice love units, and that was the most important outcome.

Don't Let Financial Planning Destroy Your Love for Each Other

In each case I introduced to you, a financial decision came between a husband and wife. And whenever that happens, the decision is usually unwise, and the way it's made is always unwise because it causes Love Bank withdrawals.

When one spouse spends money without considering the interests of the other, love units are lost. It's that simple. But when financial decisions consider the feelings of both spouses, it's a wiser plan that also builds the feeling of love.

In *His Needs, Her Needs*, the companion to this book, I explain (in chapter 9—Financial Support) how important it is to negotiate a realistic budget and to stick to it. And in *Five Steps to Romantic Love: A Workbook for Readers of Love Busters and His Needs, Her Needs*, you will find worksheets that are designed to accompany that chapter. They'll help you create what I call the Needs and Wants Budget. If you need help with a budget, I encourage you to complete those worksheets.

Consider This...

1. How are selfish demands, disrespectful judgments, and angry outbursts used to force financial decisions? What are some common excuses spouses use to justify those Love Busters when making decisions about money? Have you used any of these forms of abuse to try to force your spouse to agree with your financial decisions?

2. What is the likely outcome when a spouse is expected to adjust to a financial decision that has not been enthusiastically accepted?

3. When is a financial decision independent behavior? How is that different than trying to obtain agreement through demands, disrespect, or anger? Do either of you feel you have the right to make decisions about your finances independently of the other's interests and feelings? Are you willing to give up that right for the sake of your love for each other?

4. Do you and your spouse have conflicts over financial planning? Are your conflicts at all similar to any of the examples I used? Describe your conflicts as clearly as possible, and respect each other's interests and opinions. Then, use the Policy of Joint Agreement and the Four Guidelines to Successful Negotiation to try to resolve them.

5. Create a budget that you both accept enthusiastically, and that you are both willing to follow. Use the Needs and Wants Budget worksheets in *Five Steps to Romantic Love* to help you create that budget.

6. Do your financial decisions seem to make money a higher priority to you than your love for each other? How does the Policy of Joint Agreement always remind you to make each other your highest priority?

12

RESOLVING CONFLICTS
OVER CHILDREN

It's been known for some time now that children are hard on marriages. Research on the subject has consistently shown that marital dissatisfaction increases with the number of children born to a couple. The year that divorce is most likely is the first year of marriage. But the next most likely year for divorce is the year a couple's first child is born. You might think that a child would help unite a couple, or at least motivate them to take their marriage seriously. But for many couples, it does the opposite.

We also know that the divorce rate for blended families is astronomically high. A family is *blended* when a husband and/or wife bring children from previous relationships into their marriage. I read a recent report that found only about 20 percent of these marriages survive. The report viewed blending families as the single most important risk factor for marriage.

Why does marital satisfaction tend to decrease with the number of children, and why do blended families have such a high divorce rate?

There are two answers to those questions, and I'll take them one at a time.

The first answer is that the care of children often takes the place of spouses' care for each other. With more children to raise, there is less time and energy to meet the most important emotional needs in marriage. And when those needs go unmet, spouses lose their love for each other. Parents can be so committed to the care of their children that they forget about the care of each other.

> With more children to raise, there is less time and energy to meet the most important emotional needs in marriage.

The way to overcome this first reason for the adverse effect of children on marriage is to make your time together for undivided attention your highest priority. Nothing, not even your children, should prevent you from meeting each other's intimate emotional needs, such as affection, conversation, recreational companionship, and sexual fulfillment. Don't neglect this time together, because what your children need most from you is parents who love each other. And you will not be in love if you don't meet each other's intimate emotional needs.

At the end of this book, I have included two "bonus" chapters, "Building Romantic Love with Care" and "Building Romantic Love with Time." If care for your children is preventing you from meeting each other's important emotional needs, be sure to read those two chapters.

The second answer to the question why are children hard on marriages is that conflicts over children are usually among the most difficult to resolve, especially in a blended family. And the way most spouses go about trying to resolve those conflicts destroys their love for each other.

This chapter will address this second reason for children's negative effects. I'll show you why it's not really the children who mess up marriages—it's the way their parents make decisions while raising them. You'll learn to make wise decisions that sustain your love for each other, regardless of how many children you have. And if you're in a blended family, I'll show you how to beat the odds and make your marriage the exception by making decisions about your children with mutual enthusiasm.

> What your children need most from you is parents who love each other.

The biggest childrearing mistake is for parents to make unilateral decisions. For example, when parents don't agree on how to punish a child for disobedience, a unilateral decision is almost certain to be offensive. When one becomes the disciplinarian and the other becomes the protector of the children, the spouse doing the protecting often feels the pain of the discipline more acutely than the children do. The one doing the disciplining feels abandoned and unappreciated. It's a Love Buster to discipline your children when your spouse does not agree with you with enthusiasm. You're sure to withdraw love units whenever that happens. And if your spouse does not support your form of discipline, your children will not learn much from it.

Love Bank withdrawals are also made when favors are given to children without mutual agreement. If one spouse gives something to a child that's not approved by the other spouse, the disapproving spouse can sometimes look like the evil parent who doesn't care enough about his children to give them what they really need. Unilateral giving of favors by a parent can sometimes cause as much resentment in marriage as unilateral discipline.

> The biggest childrearing mistake is for parents to make unilateral decisions.

In blended families, these mistakes usually have a greater effect on Love Bank balances than they do in nuclear families (where children are offspring of both parents) because spouses have a natural instinct to protect their own at all costs. The resulting bias creates a strong negative reaction.

So if you want plenty of children, but you don't want them interfering with your love for each other, or if you're part of a blended family and you don't want to end up the way most blended families do, you should make all of your childrearing decisions with mutual and enthusiastic agreement. All disciplinary action and rewards should be decided before you implement them. That way your discipline will be taken seriously, and you'll both be heroes—neither of you become the evil parent.

This approach to parenting will make you better parents. The perspectives that each of you bring to childrearing are both valuable. When you come to an enthusiastic agreement about the way you raise your children, your children will benefit through your joint wisdom. On the other hand, if one of you makes a unilateral decision your children will be frustrated and confused. When one spouse disciplines a child without the other spouse's support, the child rarely learns a lesson from the experience. Instead the child feels that one parent seems to love him more than the other.

> You should make all of your childrearing decisions with mutual and enthusiastic agreement.

And when a child is rewarded by only one spouse he or she receives a mixed message. What he did was valuable from one parent's perspective, but not valuable from the other parent's perspective. Was it or wasn't it valuable? The child doesn't know for sure.

When you come to your children with a united front, with consistency, and with agreement, you deliver to your children a powerful message, lessons that are sure to impress them and point them in the right direction.

Your Daughter's a Thief and a Liar!

Greg was a single parent of two teenagers, thirteen-year-old Allan and fifteen-year-old Vivian. The three had a comfortable lifestyle, and Greg tended to spoil his children. Since the death of his wife eight years earlier, he had dated only two women, Bobbi and Janet. He liked them both very much, but Janet enjoyed being with his children, and Bobbi didn't. That single factor caused him to break up with Bobbi and eventually marry Janet.

Immediately following the marriage, however, conflict developed between Janet and Vivian. Once Janet had moved into their home, Vivian started "borrowing" her clothes without asking. Janet didn't say anything at first, but after her favorite sweater disappeared, she'd had it!

"Vi, have you seen my pink sweater?" she asked.

Vivian didn't miss a beat. "Nope."

"Are you sure?" Janet pressed. "You may have taken it to school and left it there."

"I've never taken any of your sweaters to school! Why would you think I took it?"

"Well, you've taken some of my other clothes, and I thought maybe you'd taken the sweater, too."

"I can't believe this! Look, I haven't taken your sweater. *Okay?*"

There was no way to prove Vivian had worn the sweater, but Janet knew her clothes hadn't sprouted legs. When Greg came home that night, she explained her problem to him. Greg asked Vivian about the sweater. She denied ever wearing it and became angry that they were ganging up on her.

After that incident, more of Janet's clothes disappeared. One day while Vivian was in school, Janet searched Vivian's room and found almost all her missing clothes. When Greg came home, she told him what she'd found. He confronted Vivian with the evidence. His daughter burst into tears and denied having had any of those clothes in her room. It was her word against Janet's, and she accused Janet of putting them there just to get her into trouble. In an effort to calm everyone down, Greg said they'd discuss the matter some other time.

Janet was furious.

Vivian put a lock on her door.

As the months passed, the relationship between Janet and Vivian worsened. When her father was gone, Vivian made rude remarks to Janet and openly challenged her right to live there. Greg tried to stay out of the growing conflict. But one day Janet could take no more.

"Greg, it's either me or Vivian. The two of us can't live in this house together."

Greg was stunned. "What do you want me to do? I can't kick out my own daughter. Besides, she'll only be with us for another three or four years. Can't you hold out that much longer?"

"Yes, Greg, I could. But I won't. It's perfectly clear to me that she comes first in this house—and I'm not living in a home run by a spoiled brat!"

Greg lost control with that remark. "I think we have *two* spoiled brats living in this house. But Vivian's only fifteen! What's your excuse?"

Janet moved out.

In my office, Greg and Janet reviewed their disastrous first year of marriage. Each of them thought it had been a mistake to get married.

But I reminded them that prior to marriage they were highly compatible and loved each other as much as they had loved anyone. Their loss of love was a direct result of the way they had handled Vivian. She had come between them. They needed to discover a way to complete the job of raising her without further destroying their love for each other.

Greg laid his cards on the table. He told Janet he had never punished Vivian for anything. When he knew she had taken Janet's clothes, he didn't know how to respond. So he tried to avoid the issue. He recognized now how much Janet needed him to help her resolve the problem and he apologized for his failure.

I encouraged Greg and Janet to decide how they would handle the situation when Vivian verbally abused Janet or took her clothes. Simply telling Vivian to stop wouldn't work.

Throughout their discussions, they made no demands and tried not to be disrespectful. The discussion itself was difficult for Janet because she felt that Greg was being disrespectful when he kept coming up with ideas that favored Vivian. She was hurt by each suggestion and was very tempted to be disrespectful toward both Vivian and Greg. But she held back her comments. She knew that Greg's care for his daughter was not an expression of disrespect for her. He was simply letting her know that he felt very protective of his daughter, and an enthusiastic agreement had to accommodate that reality.

While they negotiated with each other, I suggested that Janet remain separated from Greg. They could reunite as soon as an enthusiastic agreement was decided and then implemented. I warned them that it might take several weeks of incubation before a solution would occur to them. But in the meantime, they should go out on dates together and meet each other's intimate emotional needs a minimum of fifteen hours a week. In other words, negotiation should not put their romantic relationship on hold.

By reestablishing their romantic relationship, they were able to view their conflict with more empathy toward each other. Janet admitted that the loss of her clothes was not as painful as the feeling of being abandoned by Greg. When her clothes were stolen, he did nothing to protect her. But she could understand why he would have trouble siding with her—he cared about both his wife and his daughter.

Greg admitted that he defended his daughter at Janet's expense. And he knew how much that hurt her. He came to realize that he could not let anyone come between them, not even his own daughter.

This was a significant turning point in their crisis. When Greg understood that protecting Janet's feelings had to be his highest priority, the crisis was essentially ended. That was all she wanted from him. She knew teenage girls can be hard to handle but she wanted reassurance that she would come first in his life.

As they discussed the sweater-stealing incident, Greg agreed that he should have searched the entire house, including Vivian's room, for the sweater as soon as it was missing. And when his daughter accused Janet of planting her clothes in her room, he knew that his daughter was lying. So he should have reprimanded her. By the time their negotiation had ended, they had come to an enthusiastic agreement about what they should have done, and what they would do in the future if such incidents were repeated.

With Janet gone for several weeks, Vivian started feeling guilty. On her own initiative, she invited Janet back to the home, apologizing for being rude and insulting, but never did admit to stealing the sweater.

But it was only a week before she offended Janet again. She called her a lousy cook because she didn't happen to like what Janet had served for dinner. This time, Greg and Janet discussed the problem with Vivian as if it had affected them both. He explained to her that whenever she hurt Janet's feelings, she was hurting him too. She had to learn that her dad was now a part of Janet; if she loved him, she needed to care for his new wife.

From that day on, each time she offended Janet, Vivian could expect to engage in a discussion with Janet and her dad. And he would accept Janet's version of the incident if there was a conflict. Within a year, Vivian's rude remarks had all but disappeared.

By teaching his children to be considerate of Janet's feelings, Greg established an important childrearing objective, thoughtfulness, which helped both children become more successful later in life. But something else was also achieved: He learned that once they were married, every decision had to be made together, with enthusiasm.

From Perfect Lover to Perfect Mother

Wayne had dated many women and was even engaged once, but no one seemed to meet his high standards well enough to make him want to tie the knot—that is, until he met Kris. She was everything he'd always hoped for, and she loved him too. She was absolutely perfect as far as he was concerned.

230

Those who knew Kris well were not surprised by the good job she did as Wayne's new wife. She had a history of doing things well. Ever since early childhood, she was able to focus her attention on personal objectives and achieve them with excellence, one by one. When she fell in love with Wayne, she wanted nothing more than to be everything he needed in a wife, and she was able to achieve it.

Kris was the perfect lover, meeting all Wayne's known emotional needs and some he never knew he had. She was his friend, recreational companion, greatest admirer, and kept herself extraordinarily attractive.

But when their first child, Rachel, was born, Kris's focus of attention changed. Now she had a new objective: to be the perfect *mother*. At first, Wayne was delighted with the care and attention she gave their daughter. After all, he wanted the very best for Rachel and knew that Kris could provide it. After a while, however, it became apparent that Rachel's gain was his loss. Kris couldn't leave Rachel for a moment, and when they were together as a family, Rachel had her mom's undivided attention. Wayne knew that somehow he had to separate his wife and daughter for a few hours so he could get the attention he needed from Kris.

Walking in the front door one evening, he said, "Hey, hon, let's go to the hockey game tomorrow night. A guy at work has tickets he'll give me."

"No, thanks, not this time," she said pleasantly. "But you go ahead, if you'd like, dear."

"What's gotten into you?" he teased. "You used to *love* hockey!"

Kris was not smiling. "We can't go out and have fun and forget about Rachel. She needs our attention. She's in a crucial stage of development, and what we do for her now will affect the rest of her life."

"Now wait a minute! I'm talking about one evening out. Surely her whole life won't be ruined if she spends an evening with your parents."

"I *said* I won't go. That's it!" Kris turned and walked out of the room.

Wayne wondered what had happened to his perfect lover. She apparently left one day, and her twin sister, the perfect mother, showed up in her place. He did go to the hockey game with his friend at the office, and that started a pattern of working late or going out with friends most evenings.

Even though their marriage was suffering, Kris wanted more children. So over the next seven years, they had three more, and she dedicated herself to their care. She took full responsibility for their training in a cheerful and fun-loving way.

Kris wished Wayne would join her in raising their children, but when she tried to discuss it with him, he explained that with four children he had to keep his nose to the grindstone to keep up with the bills.

In my last example of conflicts over children, Greg had let his daughter from another marriage come between him and Janet. But even when the children are your own, they can easily come between you and your spouse. Kris's effort to give their children the best opportunities in life came at Wayne's expense.

People usually enter marriage wanting to be loving and caring partners in life. But when children arrive, a new ideal, to be loving and caring parents, can sometimes sweep the old ideal of partnership out the door. When that happens, the Policy of Joint Agreement becomes essential to the marriage's survival.

Wayne showed up in my office one day to try to gain perspective on his life. He was falling in love with a woman at work but didn't want to start an affair. And yet, he felt that marrying had been the biggest mistake of his life. He couldn't go on living this way but didn't know how to change things without breaking up his family.

"All she really wanted was children. I don't think she ever really wanted me," he said. "I'm not even sure she loved me. How could I have been so stupid?"

I tried to assure him that Kris had loved him and probably still did. She had simply made a choice between two ideals—being a good lover and being a good mother—choosing one at the expense of the other. She had not grasped the consequences of her shift in emphasis. At the end of our conversation, he asked me to speak with her about their marriage.

Kris was upset about the marriage, too. She felt Wayne had abandoned her as soon as their children arrived. By leaving her alone so much of the time, he caused her to focus her attention on the children even more.

I explained to her that it was in the children's best interest for their parents to have a romantic relationship and to be in love. To achieve that objective, they had to schedule time to meet each other's intimate emotional needs. Kris had created a schedule that met her children's needs at her husband's expense. Wayne's schedule didn't take her needs into account, either.

I recommended a plan designed to flush out all the cobwebs: a vacation for just the two of them.

It worked like a miracle. During their vacation together the old Kris returned. Wayne couldn't believe it. He became the center of her attention again, and it brought the best out in him.

When they returned home, I saw them immediately. Habits are usually conditioned by environment, and I knew Kris was likely to revert to old habits on her arrival home. Sure enough, as soon as she was with her children, her twin sister, the perfect mother, arrived.

But they were prepared for the transformation. They had agreed in advance on a schedule that would allow them to be together fifteen hours each week without the children. As part of the overall agreement, Wayne scheduled an additional fifteen hours to be with Kris and the children for what I called Quality Family Time.

At first Wayne didn't think he could find thirty hours to spend alone with Kris and with Kris and their children. But as they discussed his schedule together, he realized that the hours he worked, and some of his recreational activities, did not have Kris's enthusiastic support. Since they'd agreed to apply the Policy of Joint Agreement to all their behavior, including his schedule, he agreed to cut back on some of his work, and abandon some of his interests. In the end everything fell into place.

They had made two mistakes that almost ruined their marriage. The first was Kris's mistake of believing that caring for her husband and caring for her children was an either-or proposition. She didn't realize that caring for her children required caring for her husband. The single most important factor for her children's future success and happiness was their parents' love for each other. And that meant spending time away from the children to meet each other's intimate emotional needs.

The second mistake was Wayne's decision to create an independent lifestyle. He felt that he had no other choice at the time, because Kris had made up her mind and there was no turning back. Unless he wanted to be miserable the rest of his life, he felt that he had to escape into his job and his independent recreational interests. But if he had realized that the choice he made would ultimately lead to divorce, he would have brainstormed a little longer to find an alternative.

Kris knew that her marriage was in trouble, but she couldn't escape the influence of her ideals. The reason I use this illustration is to demonstrate again how the Policy of Joint Agreement can identify thoughtless decisions, even when they're based on important values. When you and your spouse can't agree enthusiastically, you'll be tempted to persuade each other with value judgments. If that happens, be very careful, because many values depend on the context of their application. Reluctant agreement often reflects a flaw in reasoning that requires further brainstorming. Misguided values can help create Love Busters and the Policy of Joint Agreement can protect you from them.

Three in Bed Is One Too Many

Andre and Patti had a great marriage, and when the kids came along it was still great. But there was one fly in the ointment: Susan, their three-year-old, insisted on sleeping with them at night. At first Andre thought it was cute. But after a while, when Susan became a nightly resident in their bed, he didn't think it was so cute anymore.

"Patti, we've got to do something about Susan sleeping with us," Andre suggested one morning over coffee. "Don't you think we need more privacy?"

"Oh, she'll outgrow it. It's just a phase she's going through," Patti responded.

"Well, it's starting to bother me, and it sure has affected our love life!"

Patti shook her head. "If we tell her she can't sleep with us, she may think we don't love her. We can't do that. Be patient."

Andre would raise the issue occasionally, but Patti's response was always the same: She felt it was wrong to create anxiety in Susan by forcing her to sleep in her own room. Besides, whenever they encouraged her to try it, Susan would throw a fit.

The problem persisted for a solid year, and Andre became increasingly upset. The more upset he became, the more love units were withdrawn from Patti's account in his Love Bank.

It never occurred to either of them that Andre's feeling of passion toward Patti would be affected by the situation. All he knew was that his sexual interest had taken a nosedive. When they came to see me for counseling, he blamed the problem on his work or unpleasant experiences with women early in his childhood. In spite of his frustration with Susan's invasion of their bed, he couldn't admit to me, or to himself, that their lack of privacy was the problem.

But I identified the problem immediately because it was so obvious to an outside observer. In most cases I encourage a husband and wife to come to a joint agreement without my interference. But in this case, Patti asked for my professional opinion regarding Susan's emotional welfare if she were to sleep in her own bed. I told her that it was actually much healthier for Susan to sleep alone, with a nightlight on and her door left open. I also warned her that Susan might actually grow up emotionally handicapped by an unhealthy dependence if she were to continue sleeping with her parents.

I helped Patti and Andre with a plan to wean Susan from the bedroom. Patti read bedtime stories to her in her own bedroom, and offered her rewards for staying in her room throughout the night. When Susan would try to come to their bedroom, Patti would take her back, and tuck her in bed again. I warned them that they may go though a week of sleepless nights getting the point across to Susan.

Then I helped them create a bedroom environment that would encourage lovemaking. A lock on their door was the first step toward insuring privacy. And they were not only to keep Susan from invading their privacy—they were to keep pets out as well. I also suggested that they remove their television from the bedroom, so that when they were in bed at night, they would give each other their full attention instead of watching the evening news. They were to go to bed together every night, and cuddle for at least ten minutes before going to sleep. When they awakened in the morning, they were to cuddle again for another ten minutes. Each of them was to wear night clothes that the other person found attractive. Beyond that advice, they needed no further help. Their passion was restored.

The problem that Patti and Andre faced was that they let Susan's interests trump the interests of their marriage. As it turned out, Susan did not actually need the security of sleeping with them at night. But even if she did, their marriage was more important. And their passion for each other was more important. It was in Susan's best interest for her parents to be in love with each other, and to sustain a romantic relationship.

In the last illustration, I made the same point, and you may feel that I'm being redundant. But I don't think I can overemphasize the value of romance in marriage. And romance requires privacy. Children thrive when their parents express passion for each other, and they become very insecure when that passion is lost.

The Policy of Joint Agreement would have prevented Patti and Andre from losing their love for each other. Knowing that Andre objected to Susan joining them for the night should have triggered negotiation, not a unilateral decision on Patti's part.

When Discipline Becomes a Love Buster

Alex had a short fuse. His friends and family all knew it. But when he fell in love with Christine, he cared so much for her that he managed to keep his temper under control whenever he was with her. Christine became his bride because of his victory over this ugly Love Buster.

Their marriage went well because he kept his vow never to subject her to his angry outbursts. He never punished her either verbally or physically.

However, he had been brought up in a tradition where heavy-handed discipline was considered the father's duty. As a child, his father had beaten him on many occasions. If he disobeyed, he could expect disastrous consequences. Alex had learned firsthand all about those disastrous consequences.

When Alex and Christine had their first child, Alex expected the same unwavering obedience that his parents had expected of him. Whenever little David misbehaved, Alex disciplined him the way *he* had been disciplined as a child.

The first time this happened, Christine became very upset and begged Alex to stop. When his violent methods continued, she went to her pastor for help. He recommended that she leave the discipline up to her husband, and gave her examples of children who grew up to be criminals because women raised them without a father's punishment.

The pastor's advice made matters much worse. Alex had been holding back somewhat because he knew that the way he punished David bothered Christine. But now that he had his pastor's permission to do whatever he felt was right regarding discipline, he released all his pent up fury on young David. Whenever he felt irritated about something, he punished his son even more severely than before.

All the while, Alex was careful never to treat Christine abusively. In fact he went out of his way to be sure she understood that his punishment of David was a father's responsibility, something that their pastor had encouraged him to do.

But still she suffered every time he punished the child, crying as if he were punishing her. Even though Alex had shown her exceptional care in other ways, his form of discipline caused a huge withdrawal from her Love Bank.

What should Alex do? How would you try to solve this problem?

The answer should be obvious to you by now. If Alex and Christine had followed the Policy of Joint Agreement, her enthusiastic agreement would have been required before he punished David. And a radical change in his approach to discipline would have been required to obtain that agreement.

In my experience counseling families, I have found that every couple's **joint** methods of discipline are superior to their **independent** methods. In other words, couples are wiser in the way they train their children when they agree on a training method. By discussing options and agreeing to a particular approach, they eliminate many of the foolish and impulsive acts of discipline that either one of them might be tempted to try individually. Furthermore, children take parents more seriously when they both agree.

Christine wanted Alex to focus more attention on David's good behavior than on his bad behavior. She wanted him to reward his son far more often than he was punished. And she wanted the punishment to be nonviolent—taking away privileges rather than physical beatings or verbal assaults.

Deep down Alex knew that she was right. He knew how unfairly he was treated as a child, yet he wanted to respect his father's judgment. To get his father off the hook, he had talked himself into believing that it was somehow a father's responsibility to be abusive toward his children. However, the truth was beginning to puncture his illusion.

Protecting Christine had always been his highest priority, and when he realized that punishing David hurt her even more than it hurt their son, he enthusiastically agreed to her plan. And the more he thought about it, the more he knew that this was the way he should have been raised.

It took some effort on his part to overcome his abusive habits. He had to follow the plan that I described in chapter 5. But in the end he broke the chain of violence that had burdened his family for generations. Under the Policy of Joint Agreement, not only was David spared the traumatic childhood that Alex had suffered, but Christine's love for Alex was restored.

Don't Let Your Children Destroy Your Love for Each Other

Children clearly gain when both parents can agree on how they're to be raised. It eliminates confusion from mixed messages and stupid, emotional, and impulsive decisions made by one spouse in the heat of anger.

Joint decisions of childrearing are not only wise and effective, but they also prevent massive Love Bank withdrawals. Each time you reward or punish your children without your spouse's enthusiastic agreement, you risk losing your spouse's love for you.

Children can easily come between a husband and wife, destroying their love for each other. In most cases, it isn't the children's fault. It's the fault of one or both parents, who assign a higher priority to the care of their children than they do to the care of each other. For further information on this very important subject, I suggest that you read my book *Mom's Needs, Dad's Needs* and chapter 11 ("Family Commitment") in the companion to this book, *His Needs, Her Needs.*

Consider This . . .

1. How are selfish demands, disrespectful judgments, and angry outbursts used to force childrearing decisions? What are some common excuses spouses use to justify their selfish demands, disrespectful judgments, and angry outbursts when making decisions about children? Have you used any of these forms of abuse to try to force your spouse to agree with your childrearing decisions?

2. What is the likely outcome when a spouse is expected to adjust to a childrearing decision that has been forced upon him or her? What outcome can be expected when the decision has been enthusiastically accepted?

3. When is a childrearing decision independent behavior? How is that approach to childrearing decision-making different than trying to obtain agreement through demands, disrespect, or anger? Do either of you feel you have the right to make decisions about your children independently of each other?

4. Describe the conflicts you face over child discipline. Do any of them resemble the examples found in this chapter? After describing a conflict with respect for each other's perspectives, use the Policy of Joint Agreement and the Four Guidelines to Successful Negotiation to try to find an approach to childrearing that you both accept enthusiastically, and that you are both willing to follow. Remember to use the "try it, you'll like it" test of a proposed remedy. And if the test doesn't create an enthusiastic agreement, go back to brainstorming.

5. Explain why some couples consider the care of their children to be more important than their care for each other. It's easier to understand when their love for each other is already lost, but how do couples make that mistake when they still love each other? I'll give you a hint: They don't understand how romantic love is created and destroyed. They think they'll love each other regardless of their priorities in life. Do your actions make care for your children seem like a higher priority than your care for each other?

13

RESOLVING CONFLICTS
OVER SEX

About five thousand years ago, as part of Sumerian culture, a man and woman who planned to marry would write on a clay tablet what they expected of each other during the marriage. If either person was unwilling to sign the list of expectations drawn up by the other, the marriage was off.

I wish that custom could be resurrected today. Today our marriage agreements say almost nothing about what a husband and wife are to expect of each other. And as a result, disappointment is almost a certainty after marriage.

In an attempt to remedy this problem, I've identified four promises for couples to make when they exchange rings. These promises embody what a husband and wife should expect of each other—very much like the marriage contracts that the ancient Sumerians created.

The first is the **promise of care:** *I promise to be your primary source of happiness—to meet your most important emotional needs.* Spouses promise to identify their five most important emotional needs prior to marriage, and then promise to meet them for each other after they are married.

The second is the **promise of protection:** *I promise to avoid being the source of your unhappiness—to avoid Love Busters.* They promise to avoid all six of the Love Busters that I've been dis-

These promises embody what a husband and wife should expect of each other.

cussing in this book—selfish demands, disrespectful judgments, angry outbursts, dishonesty, annoying habits, and independent behavior. And by following the Policy of Joint Agreement, they promise to avoid making decisions that benefit one at the expense of the other.

The third is the **promise of honesty:** *I promise to be radically honest with you.* They promise to be honest about their emotional reactions, personal history, current activities and experiences, and plans for the future.

The fourth is the **promise of time:** *I promise to give you my undivided attention at least fifteen hours each week.* They understand that time should be set aside to meet each other's important emotional needs of affection, sexual fulfillment, conversation, and recreational companionship. So they promise to commit a minimum of fifteen hours each week for undivided attention, regardless of how busy their lives become.

By agreeing to these expectations up front, it is much easier for a couple to get into the habits that will build a loving and fulfilling relationship with each other. They would deposit love units by meeting each other's most important emotional needs, and they would avoid love unit withdrawal by being considerate of each other's feelings.

I share this with you because these four important promises help create a fabulous sexual relationship in marriage. Failure to follow them is at the root of most sexual problems.

Let's start with the promises of care and time: if your spouse has an important emotional need—sex, for example—you're obligated to schedule time to meet it.

This basic principle comes to grips with the fact that goals are rarely accomplished unless time is set aside to achieve them. If you are committed to meet each other's important emotional needs, it had better be on your schedule. But the intimate emotional needs—affection,

If your spouse has an important emotional need—sex, for example—you're obligated to schedule time to meet it.

conversation, recreational companionship, and sexual fulfillment—usually get the short shrift in marriage. They're met when there's extra time. So your most important objectives in marriage become your lowest priority. The promises of care and time encourage you to prevent that from happening.

Let me clear up a misconception that people often make when hearing the promise of care for the first time. It doesn't obligate couples to meet all emotional needs—that's obviously impossible. Instead, it encourages couples to focus their attention on the five most important emotional needs. And those should be identified by each spouse. You don't have to do it all to deposit enough love units to break through the romantic love threshold—you only have to do enough. And I've discovered that couples who meet each other's top two emotional needs with great skill, and meet the next three adequately, find their Love Banks to be overflowing.

Unfortunately, in most marriages spouses don't understand how crucial it is to meet each other's most important emotional needs. When these needs are unmet, the result is disappointment and frustration, to say nothing about the loss of romantic love.

The promise of honesty that I suggested for newlyweds is also crucial in creating mutually satisfying sex in marriage. If you want the best sexual experiences, you and your spouse should honestly express your sexual desires and your sexual reactions to each other. You should teach each other how to make sex so enjoyable that neither of you would ever refuse the other's offer to make love. But remember not to confuse honesty with demands, disrespect, or anger. Honesty is simply reporting what you like and what you don't like about what the other person does sexually. You communicate to each other the conditions that help you desire a sexual relationship and then, while you're making love, the conditions that make the experience most enjoyable for you.

Honest communication about negative reactions to each other's lovemaking habits is not criticism. It's simply the expression of the need for change. And from that honest expression, you should make adjustments to each other that will make your lovemaking great for both of you.

But promising to meet the need for sexual fulfillment, scheduling time to meet it, and being honest in communicating sexual understanding are not enough to guarantee a fulfilling sexual relationship. Couples usually find themselves incapable of meeting that need because of a violation of the promise of protection: to avoid being the source of your spouse's unhappiness.

Love Busters Poison Sex

Violations of the promise of protection make fulfilling a sexual need in marriage difficult, if not impossible. If the Love Busters we discussed earlier—demands, disrespect, or anger—are ever used to force lovemaking, it usually makes the experience so unpleasant that sex is avoided rather than encouraged.

I know of many spouses who have selfishly demanded sex instead of thoughtfully requesting it. They give their spouse no choice about whether or not to make love or in what way they should do it. Instead of applying the Policy of Joint Agreement to their lovemaking, where they would both enjoy the experience simultaneously, they force their spouse into unpleasant or even painful sexual experiences to obtain gratification. If a conscientious spouse tries to meet the need for sex under those conditions, a sexual aversion is likely to form that turns their commitment into a nightmare. Their aversion becomes so intense that they simply can't do it anymore.

Spouses are also known to use disrespectful judgments in their effort to provide motivation. Instead of encouraging a reluctant spouse, they belittle, they criticize, and they make him or her feel totally inadequate. The result is less sex, or no sex at all.

And then there's the Love Buster of angry outbursts, which often ruins what could have been a fulfilling sexual relationship. When a spouse doesn't find the sexual experience to his or her liking, that dissatisfied spouse flies into a rage rather than negotiating for improvement.

Let me remind you that demands, disrespect, and anger make it virtually impossible for your spouse to fulfill your emotional need for sex even if he or she is very committed to doing so. Unless you avoid these Love Busters, your need will not be met.

The Love Buster of independent behavior can also make sexual adjustment in marriage seem almost impossible. When applied to sex, independent behavior refers to having sexual experiences met outside of your marital relationship. Masturbation, pornography, sex chat rooms on the Internet, and infidelity are all forms of sexual gratification that are usually very offensive in marriage—they're major causes of Love Bank withdrawals. But if you do not have an exclusive sexual relationship with your spouse, where he or she is your only source of sexual gratification, you will do more than offend your spouse—you will also find that your own sexual experiences in marriage will tend to be very shallow and unfulfilling.

> Ask yourself if Love Busters may be at the root of your problem.

When a couple has a conflict over sex, the underlying problem can sometimes be due to a failure to understand the importance of meeting that need. In other words, the promise to care has not been kept. But in most cases, the problem can be traced to one or more Love Busters. So I suggest that before you tackle some of the conflicts you may have over sex, ask yourself if Love Busters may be at the root of your problem. If so, by overcoming those Love Busters, you will not only be able to resolve conflicts over sex, but you will be able to resolve most of your other conflicts as well.

Don't Wait Until It's Almost Too Late

Throughout their long marriage, Grace and Ben had been known for the affection and consideration they showed each other. But no one, including Grace, imagined the seriousness of their marital problem.

From their first wedding anniversary on, Ben had expressed his deepest love for his beautiful and charming wife. But on their fiftieth anniversary, an occasion for special appreciation for a long and happy marriage, he gave her a card that read, "Thanks for ruining my life!"

Grace thought she was having a nightmare. It was totally unexpected, and she cried for days. Ben felt ashamed as soon as she read the card and begged her forgiveness. But the cat was out of the bag.

When she finally gained enough composure to discuss the matter with him, Grace wanted him to explain himself. "Ben, I expect an answer. What did I do that ruined your life?"

"Please believe me," he pleaded. "I don't know what got into me. You haven't done anything. It's all my fault."

"What's all your fault?"

"Oh, it's nothing. Please forgive me for wrecking our anniversary."
He insisted, "I'm just an old fool."

"*What is this all about?* I will not let you sleep until you tell me, so
you may as well tell me now and get it over with."

"Okay," he agreed, "but remember, it's not your fault! I know you've
never experienced a climax when we make love, and sometimes I
feel I've missed out on something that's very important to both of us.
That's all."

"Ben, I don't know how."

"Don't worry about it." He shrugged. "We're too old to do anything
about it now anyway."

Throughout their marriage, Grace had not put much effort into
sex. She didn't think it was that important for herself. But because
Ben enjoyed it, she went through the motions just to make him happy.
She thought that someday she'd learn what it was all about, but never
got around to it.

It didn't occur to her that Ben couldn't be sexually fulfilled unless
she experienced arousal and climax with him. *Her* pleasure was an
essential part of his pleasure.

But she took a very important step that day, one she should have
taken years earlier. She decided to get help and made her first appointment with me that week.

I gave her a copy of the book *Woman's Orgasm: A Guide to Sexual
Satisfaction* by Georgia Kline-Graber, RN, and Benjamin Graber, MD
(New York: Warner Books, 1975). The book not only showed her how
to climax but also how to climax during intercourse, a difficult achieve-
ment for most women. I suggested she bring her husband with her for
the next appointment, and encouraged them to read the book together,
and follow the assignments. They worked daily on the prescribed exercises and had never had so much fun with each other.

Within weeks, Grace had learned how to climax while making love,
and was happy that Ben had brought the problem to her attention.
Her regret was that he had waited so long to tell her how much it
bothered him. If he had talked to her about the problem early in their
marriage, she would have done something about it. The solution would
not only have helped Ben, it would have revealed to her how enjoyable sex can be.

The Love Buster that prevented their sexual fulfillment was dishonesty. Ben failed to communicate his frustration until it was almost too late. Although he used an angry outburst to communicate his problem, the revealed truth was more constructive than the anger was destructive. It was not only out of character for him to become angry, but he had apologized to her profusely after it happened.

When Grace discovered the problem, she eagerly set out to solve it. To a large extent, her love for Ben made it rather simple for her to learn to climax. She trusted him completely and felt safe and relaxed in his company. The quality of their relationship made the solution easy.

We're all wired correctly; it's just a matter of learning where the controls are. If you're a woman who isn't sure you've ever experienced a climax, or if you climax very seldom, get a copy of the book I mentioned above or some other book explaining how women can experience a climax during intercourse. If you go through the recommended exercises and still can't quite get it, consider obtaining the help of an experienced sex therapist.

An effective sex therapist won't mind if your husband is part of each counseling session, and all exercises should be done in the privacy of your own home, either alone or only with your husband. A therapist should never touch you or have you experience any form of sexual arousal in the office. Therapy for most sex-related marital problems is completed within three months and is sometimes covered by health insurance.

If you're at all uncomfortable with one therapist, go to another. Your gynecologist should be able to recommend several, and you may wish to consult with two or three before you settle on one.

All He Needed Was Practice

Jeffrey was one of the only men Kathleen had dated who seemed more interested in conversation than sex. In fact they spent their first date discussing how to help the handicapped, one of her greatest concerns. Since they both majored in social work, they shared many of the same values. They would discuss the problems of society and their deep compassion for the underprivileged for hours on end.

Jeffrey also had a profound respect for women, and that respect translated into avoiding any sexual advances toward Kathleen. She appreciated his respect for her, and told him that her past boyfriends seemed to be interested in only one thing—sex. She had made love to some of them, and although she usually enjoyed the experiences, she felt guilty and somewhat used whenever it happened.

When she explained these feelings to Jeffrey, he suggested they wait until marriage to make love. She interpreted his patience as respect for her and a willingness to place her feelings above his selfish desires. He earned hundreds of love units for that "selfless" attitude. But it really wasn't so selfless. It was fear that prompted his willingness to wait. He knew that she was sexually experienced, while he had never made love before.

After graduating from college, they were married, and on their wedding night Kathleen looked forward to making love to Jeffrey, having waited for two years. But he told her that he was too tired, and that it would have to wait. Kathleen was crushed and cried most of the night.

The next morning, however, Jeffrey got up the courage to do something he had dreaded, and they did made love for the first time. But, as Jeffrey feared, Kathleen was visibly disappointed. He ejaculated after less than a minute of intercourse.

Kathleen wanted to try again that afternoon, but again Jeffrey gave the excuse that he was too tired. And that evening he was still too tired. From the beginning to the end of their two-week honeymoon, they made love only five times, and each time it either lasted only a few minutes, or he found himself unable to maintain an erection. Most of the time when Kathleen wanted to make love, instead of explaining his anxiety to her, he would use some excuse to put it off. It was a frustrating way to start her marriage, and eventually she lost her temper. In fact she threatened to get an annulment if he couldn't get his act together.

But Jeffrey did everything else right. He was affectionate and considerate, made her the center of his life, and was a great conversationalist. She couldn't have asked for anything more—except sex!

"What's the matter with you?" she blurted out shortly after they arrived home.

"What do you mean?" he asked.

"Do you realize that when a woman is sexually rejected by her husband it makes her feel unattractive? Maybe I'm not your type!"

"Oh, no, Kathleen, you're the most beautiful woman I've ever seen."

"What does that mean, Jeffrey? Your actions speak louder than words. You really don't find me attractive, do you? All the time I thought you were treating me with respect, you were simply uninterested! Why did you marry me, if you didn't find me sexually attractive?"

"You are sexually attractive, believe me. I simply have a problem expressing it. I want to make love to you, but my body doesn't cooperate!"

"You're not telling me the truth," she pressed. "You must think I'm a fool! If I were attractive to you, your body would work just fine."

After their unpleasant exchange, things went from bad to worse. Instead of solving the problem, it made sex almost impossible for Jeffrey and they both decided that it was time to seek professional help for this crisis.

During their first session with me, Jeffrey admitted to me that he was afraid to make love to Kathleen. He needed sexual fulfillment more than she did, but he simply could not get his body to cooperate. The combination of his fear and his failure to perform was eroding both of their Love Bank accounts.

He sat bewildered, telling me how preposterous his situation was. She was, indeed, very attractive, and most men would have considered her to be the sexual fantasy of all time. But here he was, unable to respond the way she wanted, and finding himself increasingly unwilling to try.

In almost all marriages, one spouse is more ignorant of sex than the other. Usually it's the wife, but in Jeffrey and Kathleen's marriage it was Jeffrey. He had postponed sex until marriage, a commendable decision. But that decision left him sexually inexperienced. And since his sexually experienced wife knew considerably more about it than he did, he felt intimidated by her.

When they made love for the first time, all his worst fears were realized! He completely lost confidence in himself. After their first month of marriage, he had been raked over the coals so many times that he had started to develop a strong aversion to having sex with Kathleen. From there, it was a short trip to impotence.

Kathleen was deeply offended by Jeffrey's poor sexual performance because she thought it meant that he didn't find her attractive. She even wondered if he might have homosexual tendencies and had lied about his sexual attraction to her. It made her feel very angry, and she didn't hold back in expressing that anger to him.

After my interview with Jeffrey, I was convinced that he did find Kathleen to be sexually attractive, and his primary problem was inexperience. I explained to her that angry outbursts and disrespectful judgments don't lead to solutions—they drive them away. So she agreed to be patient, and provide him with the experience he needed to become a good lover. And the best way to communicate that experience was by using the Four Guidelines for Successful Negotiation.

They followed the first guideline by guaranteeing each other safety and pleasure while discussing this sensitive issue. To help them understand each other better, the goal of the second guideline, they used the worksheets from the accompanying workbook *Five Steps to Romantic Love* to guide their discussion. That understanding gave the third guideline—brainstorming—legs. They were able to improve their lovemaking skills by practicing some of the techniques that they had learned from each other.

One example of how their understanding of each other led to improved skill followed a common approach to impotence. They decided that Jeffrey was to take sexual initiative on a prearranged schedule. Whenever they made love, he was to explain to Kathleen what she did to make sex enjoyable for him, and what made it unpleasant. She used that information to make a few changes in her approach to lovemaking. Through practice, while Kathleen avoided disrespect and anger, eventually he was able to achieve an erection whenever he wanted.

Jeffrey also learned how to hold an erection without ejaculating while having intercourse. They used a technique that is described in most self-help books that help men overcome premature ejaculation. It involves thrusting fast enough to keep his erection, but not so fast as to have an orgasm. Whenever he felt an orgasm coming on, he would stop his thrusting movement entirely. At first, Kathleen would lay motionless, so he could completely control all movement. During this phase of the training, she felt very little sexual pleasure, because her motion was crucial to her sexual responsiveness. But eventually, as he developed the ability to hold his erection longer and longer, with increasing stimulation, she was able to become an active participant.

When a woman has the problem with sexual responsiveness, the solution is essentially the same with reversed roles: She learns how to become sexually aroused by taking initiative, and training her husband to do what it takes to create her arousal. Then she learns how to come to a climax during intercourse by voluntarily tightening her vagina and thrusting rapidly. Her husband follows her instructions, and he learns from her how to make love to her in a way that gives her the greatest sexual pleasure.

If Kathleen had used her experience to help train Jeffrey to become a good lover, and had never been disrespectful or angry toward him, he would have been a quick learner. He was eager to make love to her. But Love Busters almost prevented her from having great sex with her very best friend. It taught her an important lesson about marital conflicts in general, and from their rough start, they would apply that lesson to all the other conflicts they would have throughout life.

Jeffrey made a crucial mistake as well. Instead of asking Kathleen for help in making their lovemaking successful, he gave excuses for putting her off. The Love Buster of dishonesty almost ended their marriage. Whenever one spouse declines the other's invitation to make love, there should be a "debriefing" to understand what's behind the refusal. Is it an aversive reaction? Is it fear? Or is it really a headache that has nothing to do with sex, and will be gone by morning?

A person's willingness to make love is usually related to the ease with which he or she can enjoy a sexually arousing experience. The easier it is to enjoy sex, the greater the willingness to accept every opportunity.

Does Sin Make Sex Painful?

Nicole was born out of wedlock, and her mother never married. In fact her mother had sex only once in her lifetime—when Nicole was conceived. That single sexual encounter had been extremely painful, and she felt certain it was God's punishment for her indiscretion.

She told her daughter that God often punishes women by making sex painful and that if she ever married, she should expect pain while having intercourse.

Nicole married Doug, a quiet, hardworking farmer. They didn't make love prior to marriage, but on their honeymoon her first sexual experience was as painful as she had ever imagined. In fact it brought her to tears. Doug didn't know what to make of it and figured that whatever it was, it would go away. He tried making love to her several times on their honeymoon, and each time she cried in pain.

Remembering her mother's prediction, Nicole simply expected to experience pain every time she made love. Over the next few weeks when they tried to make love, the pain not only remained intense, but the opening to the vagina eventually closed each time they attempted intercourse. It became impossible for Doug to penetrate. Nicole thought it was God's punishment for her mother's sin, carried over to her. Doug thought it was her way of keeping him from having sex with her.

A month later they attempted intercourse again, but to no avail. It was just as painful as before. Shortly thereafter, Doug informed Nicole that he was considering an annulment. That brought them to me for counseling.

They were both incredibly naive about sex. Since Nicole had been warned by her mother that God punishes sexual impropriety, she had never engaged in any sexual experimentation. Doug had learned to masturbate but had no other sexual experiences prior to marriage. He felt that reading books on sex was a form of perversion. Coming to a counselor was clearly an act of desperation for both of them.

I assured them that if they followed my instructions completely, their problems would be over within three months. It actually took less than six weeks.

Nicole had a condition called vaginismus, in which a muscle spasm closes the opening to the vagina. It's usually caused by tears in muscle tissue somewhere in the reproductive tract or a vaginal infection. It has nothing to do with sin.

I explained to her that her mother may have had the same condition when she made love her first and only time. Not knowing what it was, and feeling guilty for what she did, she thought it was punishment.

I asked Nicole see a gynecologist first to be certain she was free of infection and had a normal-sized vagina. Sometimes an abnormally small vagina can cause the same symptoms and can be corrected with surgery. The report came back showing that everything was normal.

I asked them to complete a series of exercises designed to desensitize the vaginal opening so that the muscle spasm would be eliminated. The exercises were carried out daily (a very important part of the assignment), and within three weeks they were gingerly having intercourse.

She was completely cured of vaginismus within six weeks and experienced a climax for the first time in her life.

Intercourse without pain opened up a whole new world to Nicole and she wanted Doug to make love at every opportunity—at least twice a day! By their last appointment, they had made an outstanding sexual adjustment to each other.

This case is a good example of how failing to follow the Policy of Joint Agreement can cause physical problems as well as the loss of love units. When Doug tried to make love to Nicole, knowing she was experiencing pain, he made her physical problem worse. He tried to force his penis into her vagina, and then once inside he used quick strokes that were not only extremely painful but also strengthened her painful reflex.

The solution to the problem of vaginismus was a procedure that simply required a very slow and painless penetration of the vagina, enough for stimulation to be felt but not enough to cause pain. Over time the speed of penetration was increased, but slowly enough to be painless. The reflex eventually disappears entirely when that method is used.

If Doug had simply made love to Nicole using plenty of lubricating jelly and going very slowly to avoid any pain, he would have followed the procedure to overcome vaginismus on his own. Thoughtfulness is the solution to most marital problems.

If you ever do something sexually that causes your spouse to experience physical or emotional pain, you may lose more than love units. You may contribute to physical and emotional sexual problems that your spouse may find very difficult to overcome.

The Policy of Joint Agreement should be your guide in solving all of your conflicts over sex. Combined with the Four Guidelines for Successful Negotiation, you will find solutions that are mutually agreeable and enjoyable.

Sex Should Always Be Shared

Whenever a client tells me that her husband is impotent, I'm a little suspicious. While I've treated many men who were truly impotent, more often than not the problem turns out to be excessive masturbation.

I once counseled a man who brought himself to ten climaxes each day. By the time his wife wanted to make love, he was sexually exhausted!

When he stopped masturbating, he had absolutely no problem at all making love to her.

But that wasn't Jerry's problem. He could do both. If Jane, his wife, ever wanted to make love, he was ready and able. He initiated love-making on a regular basis himself. But every once in a while she would discover evidence that he'd been masturbating. It offended her deeply—so much so that she made an appointment for marriage counseling.

When Jerry discussed the problem with me, he couldn't understand why she was upset. "Why should she care if I masturbate? We make love whenever she wants, don't we? And I'm an excellent lover besides. What's her problem?"

Jane had explained to him that she wanted all of his sexual feelings to be shared with her. She felt that his masturbation was like a mistress, and she didn't want to share his sexual feelings with anyone else—even a fantasy.

I explained to Jerry that whenever he masturbated, he was doing something that he enjoyed but that Jane hated. Her alternative suggestion wasn't unreasonable either: She was willing to make love to him anytime he wanted.

Then came the real dilemma. Jerry confessed that he enjoyed masturbation more than he enjoyed sex with his wife. He wasn't sure if he could stop doing it.

Masturbation had become such a pleasurable experience for him that sex with his wife was sometimes boring in comparison. He made love to her out of duty and did a good job of it, but he looked forward to masturbating more than anything else. He felt that since no other woman was involved it was okay for him to develop a sexual habit that brought him so much pleasure.

But he actually *had* another lover: his fantasy. Jane had good reason to feel jealous. Some of the effects of an affair were developing in his marriage: He was robbing his wife of some of the very best feelings he could have toward her, sexual feelings. All those love units that could have been deposited in her account were squandered.

Besides, many married men I've counseled with sexual perversions—such as making obscene telephone calls and exposing oneself in public—were addicted to masturbation. Their embarrassing and illegal perversions could have been avoided if they had limited their sexual experiences to those they could enjoy with their wife. In fact, some of the most remarkable cures I've witnessed for deviant sexual conduct have been with men who made their wife a permanent fixture in the sex room of their imaginary house. I recommended to Jerry that if at all possible, sexual feelings be reserved for marital lovemaking. He should avoid sexual fantasies if they didn't involve his wife, he should avoid sexual arousal if his wife was not present, and he should never experience a climax unless it was while making love to his wife.

In this case my recommendations were followed, and Jerry was able to overcome his habit of masturbating. He knew this Love Buster (independent behavior) offended Jane but he had done it anyway because he enjoyed it so much. In other words, he gained pleasure at her expense. When he decided to protect her feelings, he stopped masturbating. It also may have prevented him from developing an embarrassing sexual perversion. But most important, it helped build romantic love for both of them.

Don't Let Sex Destroy Your Love for Each Other

We've seen in this chapter how sex can come between a husband and wife. Anything, including sex, can drive spouses apart when it has a higher priority than the marriage itself.

Years ago, as I was trying to improve my marriage counseling technique, I shifted my primary emphasis from "communication" to teaching couples the importance of meeting each other's emotional needs. The one emotional need that was identified as important by almost every couple was the need for sexual fulfillment. So I focused most of my attention on helping couples learn to have mutually enjoyable sex. My new method was an instant success. The couples I counseled not only restored their love for each other, but they referred many other couples who were also having problems with sexual adjustment.

Today, I balance my emphasis across many other emotional needs, but I haven't forgotten that without a mutually fulfilling sexual relationship, a marriage is usually in serious trouble. If a marriage counselor succeeds in helping a couple create a fulfilling lovemaking experience, the couple feels that what they spent for counseling was well worth it.

The trick to solving sexual problems is to be certain that sexual desires and behavior do not come between a husband and wife. It's easy to see how in-laws, children, money, or a career can come between spouses, but sex can also be a very important agent of marital destruction, particularly when it is self-serving and not in the interest of both spouses.

One of the most important marital skills is the ability to make love with sexual arousal and climax. All married couples should develop that skill so they can provide sexual fulfillment for each other. I've written more on this subject

> Without a mutually fulfilling sexual relationship, a marriage is usually in serious trouble.

in chapter 4 ("Sexual Fulfillment") of the companion book *His Needs, Her Needs*. And the accompanying workbook, *Five Steps to Romantic Love*, contains worksheets that guide a couple through just about any conflict they have over sex. Consider using these tools to solve your sexual problems once and for all. Don't wait until your fiftieth wedding anniversary to solve a problem that you can solve today.

Sex can bring a man and a woman together in marriage but can also drive them apart if it becomes more important than the marriage itself or is overlooked and ignored.

What's Next?

At this point, I've come to the end of describing common marital conflicts that are relatively easy to resolve once Love Busters are overcome. In the next two chapters, I will describe two examples of the Love Buster of independent behavior, which represent marital conflict itself. The first is drug and alcohol addiction and the second is infidelity. These two incredibly thoughtless violations of the Policy of Joint Agreement create conflicts that are extremely difficult to resolve because the behavior itself is so difficult to eliminate. And even when the behavior of substance addiction and infidelity finally are eliminated, they've often done so much damage that marriages seem doomed.

It's important to include these two chapters in a book of Love Busters because substance addiction and infidelity are so pervasive in our society and lead to unending and intolerable pain. Their elimination ranks in importance among the cures of our worst and most painful diseases.

But in these two chapters, I will not emphasize how these Love Busters are overcome. A description of successful treatment methods requires much more space than is available in this book. Instead, I'll show you how to restore your love for each other once these Love Busters have been eliminated. In most cases, they've had such a destructive effect that couples give up hope of ever being in love with each other again. But my experience demonstrates that, even in these cases, when the Love Busters are gone, romantic love can be restored.

Questions to Consider Together

1. How are selfish demands, disrespectful judgments, and angry outbursts used to force sex in marriage? What are some common excuses spouses use to justify their selfish demands, disrespectful judgments, and angry outbursts when trying to make love? Have you used any of these forms of abuse to try to force your spouse to make love to you? What is the likely outcome when a spouse is expected to adjust to lovemaking when it has not been enthusiastically agreed to?

2. When is sex independent behavior? How is that different than trying to obtain agreement through demands, disrespect, or anger? Do either of you feel you have the right to have sex independently of each other? Are you willing to give up that right for the sake of your love for each other?

3. Explain why you would choose sex over your love for each other as a higher priority in marriage. Is this done intentionally after love is already lost? Do your actions make sex seem like a higher priority to you when in fact it is not?

4. Do you and your spouse have a conflict over sex? Is your situation similar to any of the examples I used? Describe your conflict as clearly as possible, with respect for each other's interests and opinions. Then, use the Policy of Joint Agreement and the Four Guidelines to Successful Negotiation to try to resolve these conflicts by creating a solution that you both accept enthusiastically and are both willing to follow. You may find the worksheets in the accompanying workbook, *Five Steps to Romantic Love*, helpful in guiding you through the creation and implementation of your solution. The worksheets also support chapter 4 ("Sexual Fulfillment") in *His Needs, Her Needs*.

14

Restoring Love after Drug or Alcohol Addiction

In marriage, as in our society as a whole, drug and alcohol addiction has played an incredibly destructive role. Besides being physically and emotionally harmful to those using addicting substances, drugs and alcohol also harm those whose lives addicts touch. Addiction makes people insensitive to the feelings of those who care for them, since they will stop at nothing to feed it—their highest priority in life is using the addicting substance. Even though they know that their use of drugs or alcohol causes their spouse intolerable pain, they continue to use—at the emotional and physical expense of their spouse.

Addiction to drugs or alcohol is a clear example of a Love Buster. Remember, a Love Buster is any habit of one spouse that causes the other to be unhappy—and there are many ways that alcoholics and drug addicts make their spouses miserable.

First, when a spouse is under the influence of drugs or alcohol, it's not a pretty sight. Intoxication undermines confidence and respect,

Intoxication undermines confidence and respect.

two very important ingredients in a fulfilling marriage.

Second, addiction helps create other painful habits that make the addict a miserable marriage partner. The following are but a few of the tragic examples of behavior that characterizes addicts:

Infidelity—Infidelity is common among alcoholics and drug addicts. The fact that a man is drunk at the time is no consolation to the grief-stricken wife who finds him in bed with another woman.

Abuse—Spouses often suffer cruel physical and emotional abuse from their addicted partners. Most instances of domestic homicide and physically disabling abuse are committed while under the influence.

Emotional Turmoil—Children of alcoholics, particularly girls, suffer greatly from the emotional turmoil of their childhood. Mental health clinics throughout America have noticed that a very high percentage of adult clients have alcoholic parents.

Molestation—An Iowa survey once found that about 70 percent of the daughters of alcoholic fathers had been sexually molested while their fathers were intoxicated. Wives of alcoholics usually know about their husbands' sexually abusive behavior toward their children, and offer themselves as "bait" to prevent the abuse. The pain suffered by these women during these frightening sexual encounters is commonly reported in the safety of a therapist's office.

As tragic as they are, these examples of an addict's typical behavior are only the tip of the iceberg. If you were raised by a parent or parents who were addicts, I'm sure you can testify to the nightmare that drugs or alcohol brought to your family.

The only one who can overcome an addiction is the addict.

Much has been written on codependency, where an addict's spouse tries to "save" him or her but ends up making matters worse by enabling the addiction. Codependent spouses find themselves feeding a black hole, where their care is sucked in and not returned. Eventually they become exhausted and disillusioned, finding that their care does nothing but increase the strength of their spouse's addiction.

In most cases, the spouse of an addict must separate entirely, providing no care at all until the addiction is overcome. Separation not only protects the spouse of an addict from destructive behavior, but it also provides the addict with the best hope for recovery. The only one who can overcome an addiction is the addict—the spouse cannot do it for him or her.

One of the first things I do when couples come to me for marriage counseling is to evaluate them for drug and alcohol addiction. If either is addicted at the time, I usually refer the addicted spouse to a treatment program. That's because the Love Buster of drug or alcohol addiction prevents them from overcoming any of the other Love Busters that it creates. As long as they have any contact at all with the addictive substance, hope of marital recovery is very slim.

Marriage counselors usually make a big mistake when they try to treat addiction while conducting marital therapy. Even though I've been trained to treat those with drug and alcohol addiction and have operated ten different treatment centers, I do not begin marriage counseling when a spouse is still using an addictive substance. That's because the addict simply will not follow the plan that leads to marital recovery. Besides, the treatment of drug and alcohol addiction usually requires specialized facilities and resources that most marriage counselors do not have readily available.

> While addiction makes it impossible to resolve marital conflicts, sobriety itself doesn't resolve them.

My job as a marriage counselor begins when an addict has been treated successfully and is sober—when he or she is no longer using the addictive substance. If the former addict slips and returns to drugs or alcohol, therapy is suspended and he or she returns to treatment.

The spouses of addicts are usually so relieved when treatment is successful that they often think their marital troubles are over. But while addiction makes it impossible to resolve marital conflicts, sobriety itself doesn't resolve them—it simply makes them *resolvable*. Once addiction is overcome, a couple is faced with the legions of other Love Busters that were ignored in the shadow of addiction or that were created by addiction. In marital therapy, these Love Busters must be overcome one by one.

In this chapter I will describe a few of the cases I've witnessed where couples came to love each other after the addiction was overcome. They did it by meeting the emotional needs and overcoming the Love Busters that the addiction had made impossible to achieve.

Windshield Washer Fluid to the Rescue

Herb and Char were raised in a religious setting, where the use of alcohol was strictly forbidden. The idea that Herb could become an alcoholic seemed preposterous.

It all started in high school. At a party one evening, Herb had his first taste of alcohol. He drank too much but was able to get home and into bed without his parents knowing he'd been intoxicated. The same thing happened at a few other parties, and while his closest school friends knew what was going on, none of them went to his church.

When he married Char, she never knew about his drinking in high school. And since she was opposed to the use of all alcoholic beverages, he didn't dare drink in her presence.

As an attorney with his own practice, it wasn't too difficult for Herb to figure out ways to slip gin, his favorite drink, into his office. There he would drink enough to satisfy his addiction but not enough to cause him embarrassment in the performance of his duties.

He and Char attended church regularly. He even served as a trustee. But none of his friends at church suspected his addiction.

Over a period of years, their marriage suffered. Herb spent little time at home, and when he was there, he had a low tolerance for conflict. Char walked on eggshells and wasn't able to understand what bothered him. She knew he was under constant pressure at work and thought his emotional distance was caused by a preoccupation with his cases.

Since she had never tasted alcohol herself or known anyone who drank, she never knew when he'd been drinking. He'd always been quiet at home, and his silence was a great way to avoid being discovered when he had too much to drink.

After a few years, Herb discovered a way to drink at home. He took a bottle of windshield washer fluid, emptied it, and put in a gallon of gin with blue food coloring. He kept the bottle in the closet near his garage.

It worked like a charm. Each time he felt like a drink, he stepped into the closet and took a swig.

Both at work and at home he was falling further and further into the pit of addiction. Char found him increasingly distant and unempathetic. He seemed to have lost his personality somewhere along the line. She spent many days in tears, reflecting on the nightmare her marriage had become. Yet she couldn't understand why it was turning out so badly.

One day it all became clear.

Herb's brother, Rob, came over to the house during the morning to borrow a baseball and bat. While he was there, he put what he thought was windshield washer fluid into his car. When he returned the ball and bat that afternoon, he also returned with some real windshield washer fluid to replace what he had taken. Herb came home that night and took a swig of the windshield washer fluid, swallowing it before he realized it wasn't gin.

Herb went into a blind panic. He thought he was about to die! Char came running, to find him more talkative than he'd been in years. "I drank this windshield cleaner! Quick, get me to the hospital!" he shouted.

She was bewildered. "Why'd you do that? Were you trying to kill yourself?"

"No, I thought it was gin! Quick, get me to the hospital!"

"You thought it was gin? I don't understand . . ."

"*Never mind!* Just get me to the hospital, quick!"

At the hospital his stomach was pumped, and he was sent home. But Herb believed God had put him through the ordeal to teach him a lesson. He knew he was an alcoholic, so he admitted himself to a treatment program the next day. Char was overwhelmed.

While he was in treatment, Char asked me to help her sort it all out.

I explained to her how this sort of thing can happen if you create a secret second life, and I also explained how Herb's alcohol addiction affected their marriage. His unwillingness to face conflict, his emotional distance, his lack of empathy, and his apparent disinterest in her and the family were all symptoms of alcoholism. Some people have those characteristics when they're sober, but for Herb they were out of character.

Alcohol withdrawal was very difficult for Herb, and following treatment he was often tempted to sneak gin again. So he joined Alcoholics Anonymous and met three times a week for support. At the same time, he joined Char for marriage counseling.

She explained to him that she had missed intimacy and a sense of closeness in their marriage. He had been distant and difficult to reach because of his addiction. But the addiction itself had created Love Busters that prevented them from meeting each other's marital needs. The most serious of these was dishonesty. So they spent several weeks catching up on a lifetime of misinformation.

Herb went back to his high school days and explained how he'd fooled everyone, including Char. He went on to tell her about his deepest feelings—how important she and their family really were to him now that alcohol was not coming between them. He also admitted how lonely he had felt and that his dishonesty had kept him from being emotionally close to her.

When Herb learned to overcome dishonesty, everything else fell into place. He spent considerably more time with Char and was able to express his feelings openly. He had nothing to hide. It created the emotional bonding that they had both been lacking for years. Within a few months, their love for each other had been restored.

The case of Herb and Char was particularly easy to treat. The Love Busters to overcome were dishonesty and independent behavior. And the worst of the independent behavior was already overcome when Herb's addiction was treated. But in most cases the list of Love Busters that remain in the marriage seems overwhelming.

The remaining cases in this chapter are more characteristic of these difficult cases. But it should be encouraging to know that even when marital conflicts seem impossible to resolve, the power of the Policy of Joint Agreement can come through to help restore romantic love.

Addiction Made Them Feel Compatible

Norm and Ruth had grown up together in the same neighborhood and fell in love while still in their early teens. He introduced her to alcohol and cigarettes, and she introduced him to marijuana while they were still in grammar school. In junior high, whenever one came across a new drug, he or she would share it with the other.

They were raised by alcoholic parents and were taught at an early age that drugs and alcohol were what life's all about. Their home lives were wretched, but they didn't realize that their parents' addiction was primarily responsible for all the sadness.

In the eleventh grade, they dropped out of school and found low-paying jobs. They made enough money to support their drug habits. Selling drugs on the side and living with his divorced mother also helped.

After a year of relative irresponsibility, Norm was kicked out of his mother's home and told to support himself. He invited Ruth to move into an apartment with him, to help cover expenses, and for a while life was rosy. That is, until Ruth became pregnant.

They married, and Ruth gave birth to Linda. Those two events wrecked everything. Drugs had always been their highest priority, and they had learned to respect each other's idol. But marriage and Linda interfered with all that.

It started with arguments over who would take care of Linda. Neither had learned much about responsibility, and parenthood came much too fast. Norm's first solution to the problem was to stay away from home. But Ruth chased him all over creation until she found him, so that strategy didn't work.

Then they tried fighting with each other. Ruth was the first to start swinging, but she was also the first to be thrown across the room. She explained to the doctor that she had fallen on the ice. Norm was sorry he'd lost his temper but warned her not to mess with him again.

She didn't take his advice, and this time she landed in the hospital. There was no way to conceal the abuse she'd suffered, so she did the right thing: She filed a criminal complaint for assault.

Norm was arrested, and the judge convicted him but gave him a suspended sentence on the condition that he receive therapy. During the evaluation, his addiction was identified, and the counselor convinced him he needed treatment.

While in treatment, he became sober for the first time since grade school. He woke up to the world around him, saw his life for what it really was, and made an astonishing recovery. Once out of treatment, he never used drugs again, as far as I know.

Ruth, however, was still addicted. While at first she felt encouraged by his recovery, before long he wanted her to go into treatment, too. That wasn't what she had in mind. Norm was becoming a real nuisance.

While he was learning how to be more responsible, she looked less responsible in contrast. Her favorite drinking buddy was sober. Now she had to get drunk alone, and that wasn't nearly as much fun.

One night she left him with Linda, went to a bar, and met someone. By the end of the evening, she had had sex with four different men. It was the first time she'd ever cheated on Norm, and the next morning she was on the verge of suicide.

Her escapade at the bar was enough of a crisis to convince Ruth that she, too, needed treatment. The program was as successful for her as it had been for Norm, and they were ready to begin their lives together—sober!

I saw them for marriage therapy for the first time three years after her sobriety began. Their marriage was in shambles. Apart from drugs and alcohol, they had little in common. Now that they had achieved sobriety, the only thing keeping them together was their love for Linda.

The first point I made to Norm and Ruth was that marital compatibility is *created*. Because of their addiction, drugs had retarded their ability and motivation to create it in their marriage. During their years of courting and early years of marriage, conflicts were never resolved—they were simply medicated with drugs and alcohol. They hadn't rooted out Love Busters and never bothered to learn to meet each other's marital needs. Drugs seemed to be all they needed.

I explained to them that when they woke up out of their drug-induced stupor, they discovered something that should have been no surprise: they had absolutely no marital skills. Without these skills, the love units that had been artificially created by drugs quickly disappeared. Norm and Ruth didn't know how to replace them.

Second, I told them they had come to the right place. I was trained in teaching couples how to *create* compatibility in their marriages. Since they didn't love each other, they would have to commit themselves to my program for three months. After that time had passed, they could decide if they wanted to continue marriage counseling for another three months. I wasn't certain how long it would take them to build a strong marriage, and I explained that it might take up to two years.

We began with a commitment to time (see chapter 17). I explained that they needed to set aside fifteen hours each week to work on their assignments with undivided attention and without interruption.

The next step was to apply the Policy of Joint Agreement to the way they resolved conflicts. Unless they *both* felt good about a solution to a problem, they were to negotiate until they were in enthusiastic agreement.

They had problems with every Love Buster: selfish demands, disrespectful judgments, angry outbursts, dishonesty, annoying habits, and independent behavior. Systematically, each time a Love Buster would appear, it would become the target of elimination. My job was to keep them both on course and encourage them to continue until the enemy was defeated.

Eventually they could identify and overcome Love Busters without my help. No arguing or defensiveness remained. If one of them felt bad about the other's behavior, it was a Love Buster—it had to be eliminated!

Those with a history of addiction usually have a difficult time learning to be thoughtful. The self-centeredness they perfect as addicts stays with them even when they've overcome the addiction. What looks like thoughtfulness often turns out to be manipulation—they appear to be thoughtful to get their way.

True thoughtfulness accommodates the feelings of others *for their sake*. It is a willingness to *give up* behavior that is offensive to others and create new and appealing behavior. You create romantic love when you do something that is deeply appreciated. It's preserved when you avoid behavior that is deeply resented.

Over time, Norm and Ruth learned to be thoughtful. They not only eliminated the Love Busters in their marriage, they also identified and learned to meet each other's most important emotional needs. By the time marital therapy ended, about nine months later, they were in love with each other again. But this time the love units were not deposited by drugs and alcohol—they were deposited by their care for each other.

Daughters of Alcoholism

How would you like to fall in love with a person who leaves you for other women, is chronically unemployed, beats you, and molests your children? If your father had those characteristics, you would undoubtedly hate that behavior—but you would probably fail to see it in the men you date.

Laura was the daughter of an alcoholic. She'd been divorced five times before she made her first appointment with me, and she was only thirty-seven. The longest any marriage lasted was three years—the shortest was three months, the time it took to get the divorce. Fortunately, she had no children.

Laura was in love again, and this time she wanted her marriage to work. She had met her fiancé, Matt, two months earlier. He'd also been divorced several times. He had five children from an assortment of wives and lovers but didn't have custody.

He was living with Laura because he was "temporarily" out of work and had also borrowed about $1,000 from her. At forty-six, he was broke and a recovering alcoholic.

When I asked them why they thought this marriage would work when the others had failed, Laura explained that this time she hoped a counselor would help them correct their past mistakes.

I told Laura I could help them correct past mistakes if they'd commit themselves to a supervised courtship of at least one year. They could not live together during that time, and Matt had to repay the money he borrowed.

Matt was furious.

We all make a living somehow. Some work for their pay, and others don't. Matt was one of those who didn't work. He made his money living with vulnerable women. But this woman was different from some of the others: He was in love with Laura, at least at the moment.

I told them to make another appointment when they were living in separate apartments. I didn't really expect to see them again, but three months later, there they were. Matt had found a job and moved into a rooming house. He had even paid back part of the money he owed Laura.

Apparently my blunt observations about Matt had made sense to Laura, and she'd kicked him out. But they had enough love for each other to try my courtship plan.

Matt's marriages had failed because he was self-centered and inconsiderate. He had learned many of his inconsiderate habits while he was addicted to alcohol but had never learned to overcome them after he became sober.

Laura had seen those characteristics in her father, but because she loved him, she overlooked them in the men she dated. While most women are warned by self-centered behavior, she was blind to those signs. When men said the right words, that's all she heard.

The men Laura married were more concerned with what they'd *get* than with what they had to *give*. Their marital *needs* motivated them to marry, but their inability and unwillingness to *meet* marital needs guaranteed divorce.

The first step I took in helping to create compatibility was to overcome dishonesty. I asked Matt to reveal to Laura any part of his past that could be a threat to her. I explained that good marriages are based on trust, and if he was hiding something that could later hurt her, he should come clean now.

At the risk of losing Laura, Matt admitted he had served time in prison for assaulting one of his former wives and that he had initially been interested in Laura so she'd support him financially. He also mentioned that one of his children would not see him because he had beaten him two years earlier.

He was willing to answer any and all questions she had for him and allowed her to speak to any of his former wives, old girlfriends, children, relatives, or friends. I encouraged her to take him up on his offer and gather as much information as she could from the people who knew him at various times in his life.

I explained to them that his irresponsible behavior, much of it done while he was using drugs, reflected a basic self-centeredness he had not yet overcome. The fact that he'd been sober for two years was only the first step toward preparing for marriage. The destructive behavior of his past was a present threat to Laura.

Matt was encouraged to do a background check on Laura, too. Each man he spoke to told him she was great to be with until they were married, then she turned mean. Even her brother and sisters told him she was incredibly hard to get along with.

I kept reminding them that the best prediction of the future is found in the past. Unless tremendous effort is made, we all tend to make the same mistakes over and over again.

After they had both made progress in overcoming dishonesty, it became apparent that they needed to overcome all the other Love Busters as well.

With the Policy of Joint Agreement as their guide, they completed assignments that helped them gain awareness of destructive independent behaviors, and then eliminated them.

Then they were ready to negotiate a fair exchange of care toward each other (see chapter 16). First, they explained what they needed from each other in marriage and then looked at what they each had to offer. It became clear that they needed quite a bit but had little to offer.

I explained that care was not just a willingness but an ability to make someone happy. The only way they could actually care for each other was to learn the skills that met each other's needs.

The most obvious skill Matt needed was learning to provide consistent financial support. He also needed to learn to share all financial decisions with Laura. He'd been accustomed to putting money he earned into his own pocket. Now he put his paycheck into a joint checking account that required *both* their signatures.

Laura needed to learn to be less critical and to provide Matt with admiration. The men who had been in her life had so many serious problems that she didn't believe men *could* be admired. Even though she loved Matt, it took her quite a while to learn to compliment him. They worked on other skills as well and within a year had done a good job in preparing for their marriage.

Agreements made *before* marriage are much easier to keep than those made *after* it. Since his employment was a *condition* to their marriage, Matt kept it. Laura learned to meet his needs as well, by pre-agreement. None of her former husbands would have believed the changes she made. Demands were out—admiration was in!

So far, the marriage has worked for Matt and Laura. She married a man who was very much like her father, but Matt was able to overcome her father's most destructive habits.

Don't Let Drug or Alcohol Addiction Destroy Your Love for Each Other

Clearly, drug or alcohol addiction comes between a husband and wife. The addiction itself is a higher priority than marriage, and as a result, the Policy of Joint Agreement cannot be followed and Love

Busters prevail. But even after sobriety is achieved, Love Busters acquired during addiction persist.

In marriages where at least one spouse has been addicted, learning to overcome Love Busters is essential for marital success. But in most cases, even after sobriety, they are not overcome, and these marriages usually end in divorce.

In this chapter, I selected cases where marriages were saved because the couples learned to overcome Love Busters. In the course of counseling, they learned to overcome self-centered and inconsiderate habits. They also learned to develop skills that each of them expected of the other in marriage. The application of the Policy of Joint Agreement helped them beat the odds and build successful marriages.

Whenever I counsel a formerly addicted couple and witness their complete marital recovery, it seems like a miracle. When they first see me, their future together seems utterly hopeless. But their recovery is not a miracle at all—it is the result of steady progress toward a goal of depositing as many love units as possible and avoiding withdrawals. Anyone can do it, but it takes perseverance, and I give those who succeed a great deal of credit for ending in their generation the suffering that drug and alcohol addiction creates.

> Recovery is the result of steady progress toward a goal of depositing as many love units as possible and avoiding withdrawals.

Consider This...

1. How does addiction to drugs or alcohol help create Love Busters? How does it prevent their removal?
2. Why is it almost impossible to be addicted to drugs or alcohol if the Policy of Joint Agreement is followed in marriage?
3. Are you or have you ever been addicted to drugs or alcohol? Has the addiction contributed to the creation of Love Busters? If so, are you willing to eliminate these habits so that love can be restored to your marriage?
4. Have you ever been arrested for driving while intoxicated? Has your spouse ever suggested that your use of drugs or alcohol has

interfered with your relationship? If you completely eliminated all future use of drugs or alcohol today, would you feel resentful or depressed? If the answer to any of those questions is yes, for the sake of yourself and your spouse, see a qualified chemical dependency specialist for an evaluation. If the results indicate addiction, it means drugs or alcohol is your highest priority and marital conflicts will be impossible for you to resolve until the addiction has been overcome. Follow the advice of the specialist and complete a treatment program that will help you eliminate the barriers to a fulfilling marriage.

15

RESTORING LOVE
AFTER INFIDELITY

Infidelity tops the list as the most destructive, cruel, and perverse example of independent behavior. As a marriage counselor, I cannot think of a more effective way to hurt your spouse than to have an affair. Yet infidelity is rampant in our society.

The vast majority of those I've counseled who have experienced both rape by a stranger and an affair by a husband have told me that the affair was much more painful. How can so many people inflict that kind of pain on the one they promised to cherish?

There's no good excuse for infidelity. If a man's wife is not meeting his sexual need, finding another sex partner is the cruelest solution of all. If a woman's husband is uncommunicative or lacks the skills of affection, what right does she have to develop a romantic relationship with another man?

It's no surprise that almost all wedding vows promise to "forsake all others." Most couples tying the knot may not know much about how to have a great marriage, but they know enough to demand assurance that they will not have to go through the worst experience of their lives—their spouse's unfaithfulness.

| There's no good excuse for infidelity. | Infidelity is an addiction to a lover. The highest priority of an unfaithful spouse is being with the lover. He or she thinks about the lover almost constantly and |

needs reassurance that the lover is still available. The need to be with the lover overrides the interests of their betrayed spouse, and an affair usually persists with full knowledge of the suffering it causes.

As a marriage counselor, my first reaction to infidelity was to consider reconciliation hopeless. I wanted to encourage betrayed spouses to file for divorce. But in case after case, that's not what they wanted to do—and neither did the unfaithful spouse. In spite of the affair, they wanted to reconcile. So I developed a plan that would restore love and trust to a marriage, in spite of the devastating experience of infidelity.

My plan for marital recovery after an affair cannot begin until there is no further contact with the source of addiction—the lover. As long as a lover is seen or spoken to by the unfaithful spouse, hope for marital recovery is almost zero. When a betrayed spouse asks what to do while the affair is still active, I give the same advice as I give to spouses of alcoholics—express willingness to create a fulfilling marriage after the addiction has ended, then separate with as little contact as possible.

The unfaithful spouse will either end the affair the right way by making a decision never to see or talk to the lover again, or the affair will end the wrong way—by dying a natural death. Affairs almost always die, because they are nurtured by dishonesty and thoughtlessness, characteristics that eventually destroy any relationship. The passion that keeps an affair alive cannot be sustained without honesty and thoughtfulness. And once the passion has ended, the foolishness of the affair becomes apparent to the unfaithful spouse. In most cases, he or she wants to be given another chance to restore what was lost in the marriage. I prepare the betrayed spouse for that moment, and if both spouses agree, their plan for recovery can begin.

The first part of my plan is to guarantee no contact with the lover. Extraordinary precautions are agreed to and followed by the unfaithful spouse to guarantee that outcome. If contact is made with these precautions in place, the bar must be raised with even more precautions. Many of my clients have had to find new jobs and move to other states to avoid the temptation of seeing or talking to a former lover.

Next, both spouses agree to radical honesty. An affair is almost impossible without a secret second life, so all secrets are exposed. Privacy is not permitted.

If you're having an affair or if you've ever had one, don't think you're protecting your spouse by keeping it from him or her. Reveal it, even if you think the problems that helped create the affair have been resolved. It represents the first step toward protection: giving your spouse information regarding your destructive habits. You may lose some love units at first, but without honesty you'll be unable to explain your feelings completely in the future. How can your spouse ever understand your feelings if there's a part of your life you can never expose?

The final step to my plan for recovery is to teach the couple to make Love Bank deposits and avoid their withdrawal—something every couple should do.

My complete guide to recovery after an affair is described in the book I wrote with my daughter, Dr. Jennifer Chalmers. The book is titled *Surviving an Affair*. In it, we explain each phase of the recovery process and how love and trust can eventually be completely restored.

As in the case of drug and alcohol addiction, separation from the source of addiction—the lover—is only the first step toward marital reconciliation. When an affair ends, there's a lot of rebuilding to do. Love Busters must be overcome, and marital needs must be fulfilled. In the cases that I present in this chapter, I will give you a glimpse of how this has worked for a few of the couples I've counseled.

> Thousands of couples have restored love and trust to their marriage, in spite of infidelity.

But don't get the impression that a fulfilling marriage after an affair is a rare outcome. In spite of my initial misgivings, I've been a witness to literally thousands of couples who have restored love and trust to their marriage, in spite of the most destructive Love Buster—infidelity.

All He Wanted Was a Friend

Dean's first marriage was great until children arrived. Then he had an affair with his secretary, whom he later married.

When his second wife had a child, he had an affair with another secretary, divorced his second wife, and came to see me for counseling. He couldn't understand what made his marriages so fragile and his secretaries so appealing!

Upon examination, the answer was clear.

His first wife, Sandy, had been a constant companion and devoted friend while they were dating. They'd grown up together and fully expected to be married for life. But he expected her to give him undivided attention, which she willingly did right up to the time she had their first child. Then her attention was turned from him to the child. Two more children made matters worse.

Dean wasn't happy with her shift of interest, but he loved his children and wanted them to have their mother's attention. So he devoted his time and energy to becoming a successful businessman.

Dean's private secretary, Kim, was paid to give him attention. So she became his closest friend—and eventually his lover.

Sandy never did discover his affair with Kim. During the divorce, he told her that they'd "grown apart," and he no longer loved her. She could do nothing to stop him. But after their divorce and his eventual marriage to Kim, she suspected he might have had an affair with her.

Kim didn't continue as Dean's secretary after their marriage. Instead, she wanted to raise children, which he encouraged. But after her child arrived, Dean struck up a deep friendship with his new private secretary, Joan. Needless to say, after Kim's second child arrived, Dean was in love with Joan and divorced Kim—who was totally surprised. She didn't suspect Joan, because Dean had always told her she wasn't his type. But after their divorce, she knew he'd lied.

Before he married a third time, Dean thought it would be helpful to consult a marriage counselor. He'd already seen the pattern, and he wanted Joan to be his third and *final* wife. What could he do to avoid a third divorce?

In most cases, I do not help an unfaithful spouse and their lover create a lasting relationship. Instead, I try to help restore the broken marriage after the affair dies a natural death. But in Dean's case, both of his former wives wanted nothing to do with him, and without their cooperation, reconciliation was impossible. So I helped Dean make his next marriage his last.

As with most cases of infidelity, Dean's marital needs had not been met. His wives had shifted their attention from caring for him to caring for their children. When the change took place, Dean willingly took a backseat to children, whom he also loved. Since he wanted them to have the best care, instead of complaining, he simply had his needs met by someone else.

But to make his plan work, he had to engage in the Love Buster of dishonesty. He lied so effectively that neither of his first two wives ever suspected him of infidelity until it was too late.

He thought, *what they don't know won't hurt them.* I explained to him that what they didn't know *did* hurt them. His dishonesty was thoughtless, because it enabled him to please himself at their expense. If he had been honest about his feelings *and* his activities, the affairs would have been almost impossible to engineer.

I asked him to let Joan join the counseling sessions. I wanted Dean to describe his past marriages and subsequent affairs to her while I listened, to be sure he didn't leave anything out.

He told her that he'd lied to both of his former wives and had already lied to her about a few things. It would be difficult for him to be truthful with her, since he had established the habit of lying to all the women in his life, including his mother.

Over the next few counseling sessions, Dean explained to Joan how he felt toward his wives while having affairs with his secretaries. He cared about them and never thought the affairs would lead to divorce. He even thought they were good for his marriage, since they helped him overcome resentment from his wives' failure to meet his needs.

Romantic love was something Dean never quite understood until then. He didn't realize his feeling of love could be sustained only if his wife were meeting his emotional needs. To allow someone else to meet those needs assured the loss of his love for his wife and the creation of love toward the new woman. He began to understand that love is created and destroyed, and that he had quite a bit of control over what direction it took.

His practice of dishonesty made it impossible for his former wives to adjust to his needs. He would tell them he was satisfied with their behavior, when he was not. No wonder they were shocked when he left them for someone else. They couldn't see it coming.

Another mistake was to let someone else meet his most important emotional needs. By making another woman his best friend, he was setting up a Love Bank account that was sure to eventually trigger his feeling of love. In his marriage to Joan, he had to "forsake all others," which meant he could not even have friends of the opposite sex. Joan had to be his best, and only, female friend.

I taught him to express his feelings about the way Joan treated him and encourage changes in her habits when he felt the relationship was suffering. I also recommended that they continue to spend the same amount of time together after marriage as they did while they were having an affair.

They've been married for about ten years now, and the last I heard, it has been very successful. Joan had no children, and she still plays an active role in his business as his secretary and lover . . . and best friend.

Every Woman's Dream

Cheryl wasn't getting any younger and was starting to worry if she'd ever find a man who could meet her standards. Then she discovered Nate. He was the most incredibly helpful and thoughtful person she'd ever known. He fixed her car and washing machine; he mowed her lawn, and he painted one of her rooms. He did anything she'd ask him to do. What a man!

Within a year, they were married, and two years later they had their first child. Cheryl had no idea what a mess children could make, and she was thrilled to have a husband who'd help her make dinner and clean up the house after he came home from work. Every evening she'd make a list of things for him to do that would keep him busy until bedtime. Weekends were also filled with projects. She was delighted to see so many things accomplished, but she rarely told him how much she appreciated his work. If he ever complained about all the work, she'd become angry. What had started out as thoughtful requests had become selfish demands.

Over a period of time, however, Cheryl found Nate helping the neighbors more with their household projects and helping her less. In fact, he became a legend in their neighborhood because he was such a skilled repairman and was always willing to help. The neighbors praised Nate for his helpfulness and Cheryl for her willingness to put off her own projects so that he could help others. Cheryl wasn't exactly thrilled with his being gone from home so much, but since she got some of the credit, she tolerated it.

One day, Norma, a neighbor whose husband had died three years earlier, called Cheryl to ask a favor. "I hate to bother you, but something's wrong with my water heater. I haven't been able to find a repairman to fix it this weekend, and I was wondering if Nate would be willing to look at it for me."

Now that was the right approach! "Oh, certainly," said Cheryl. "I'll send him right over."

Within an hour, Nate had fixed Norma's water heater. He also fixed the garbage disposal unit and her garage door opener. By the time he was ready to leave, she was in tears.

"I can't tell you how much this has meant to me. Since Roger died, I've had one problem after another, with no one to help me. And I've been so lonely. You've made me happier than I've been in years." She gave him a big bear hug.

Nate was speechless, but hugged her back. As he left, he told her to call him if she ever needed help.

The next Saturday, Norma didn't call Cheryl for permission to use Nate. She called him instead, and he was right over. He helped her clean up a pile of leaves that had been rotting in a corner of the front yard for two years.

When he was ready to go, she invited him inside for coffee, and they spent three hours talking to each other. She shared many of the struggles a widow faces, among them, her loneliness and sexual frustration. He shared some of his problems, which included Cheryl's constant demands and lack of appreciation. By the end of the conversation, they were making love.

Slowly but surely, Cheryl's love units had been withdrawn from Nate's Love Bank. Every time she demanded work from him, he felt offended. Once in a while he would tell her how he felt. When he did, she'd remind him that if he didn't mind helping all the neighbors, why wouldn't he help his own wife? A compliment would have meant so much to him. But she took his help for granted.

Norma, on the other hand, showered him with praise, cooked for him when he came over, and made love to him besides.

While Nate's excuse for visiting Norma was that he helped her with projects, he eventually spent very little of his time working. Instead they talked and made love. When he did fix something, she was with him, saying how much she appreciated his effort.

Cheryl didn't suspect a thing at first. When Nate came home, he got right to work on her projects and didn't go to bed until he completed them. Their sexual relationship didn't suffer, either.

Over the next six months, however, Nate began to neglect his own home. Cheryl's lists of projects began to gather dust, and Nate visited with Norma several times a week. She praised every effort he made on her behalf, and he just loved all the attention he was getting from her. They made love two or three times a week but were very careful so that they wouldn't be discovered. Love units poured into both of their Love Bank accounts.

Cheryl eventually became suspicious, particularly when their own sexual relationship started to fall apart. Nate claimed to have lost interest in sex. She finally confronted him, but he lied about his relationship with Norma.

Over the next two years, Cheryl tried very hard to determine if Nate was having an affair. She never caught them making love, but she appeared at Norma's house unannounced on several occasions. Nate finally became alarmed with her increasingly suspicious behavior. He told her if it would make her happy, he simply wouldn't see Norma any longer. She replied that it would certainly help, and that apparent concession made her much more relaxed—at least until Norma's neighbor called several weeks later.

Nate and Norma were seen driving into Norma's garage, her neighbor reported. She thought Cheryl should know about it.

Cheryl walked right over and found them together. Now she *knew* Nate was having an affair and insisted that they see a counselor. He agreed to go with her but continued to deny the affair.

My first conversation with Nate was typical for those having an affair. He simply couldn't be pinned down. He told me that his wife was perfect; he was happily married, and he merely had compassion for a widow in the neighborhood. But the evidence was so overwhelming that I knew he was lying to me.

I told Cheryl I wanted to counsel Nate alone for a few weeks before I could begin marriage counseling, and they agreed to that plan. The next time I saw Nate, he told me about his relationship with Norma but made me promise I wouldn't tell Cheryl about it. We discussed the pros and cons of marital reconciliation, and within three weeks Nate decided to save his marriage.

His primary motive for reconciliation was his children—by then they had three. He realized he had a lot to lose in a divorce. Besides, Cheryl was more attractive to him than Norma, and they had more interests in common. He knew he wouldn't marry Norma, even if he divorced.

The first assignment I gave Nate was to overcome the Love Buster of dishonesty. So he admitted to Cheryl that she'd been right about his affair but that he'd decided to end his relationship with Norma and rebuild his marriage. Even though she had suspected it all along, she did what most spouses do when they first discover an affair—she became very angry and depressed. At first, she wasn't even sure she wanted to save their marriage, or that she could ever trust Nate again. But eventually she agreed to give their marriage a chance to succeed.

Since affairs are incredibly difficult to end, Nate had to create extraordinary precautions to avoid ever seeing or talking to Norma again. Since she lived in their neighborhood, I recommended they move away.

Nate and Cheryl had invested thousands of dollars and hours into their home, and it was hard for either of them to even think of selling it. But I felt that the home represented a way of life that had enslaved him, and a new home would give them a fresh start. I also mentioned that I didn't feel he could be trusted living so close to Norma, and Cheryl would be constantly suspicious.

They eventually sold their home and moved about thirty-five miles away, far enough so that he could avoid seeing Norma but close enough to his job so he wouldn't need to find another.

We began marriage counseling with an emphasis on honesty. Nate had never shared his deepest feelings with Cheryl, and he used work to help him remain superficial. I taught him how to talk to her about what he thought and felt and recommended that, for the next few weeks, he spend all his leisure time at home talking rather than working.

In his conversations with Cheryl, he told her how unhappy he'd been with her lack of appreciation. She explained that she had the greatest admiration for him but had simply neglected to tell him how she felt.

Cheryl's list of projects for him to complete had become a selfish demand. She had to learn to ask how he felt about doing them, and Nate needed to tell the truth about his emotional reactions. To her surprise, she discovered that when he came home from work, he wanted her to have his dinner ready and the house cleaned. He preferred watching television to doing one of her projects.

When he did agree to do something for her, she saw it as an act of care on his part, and she learned to compliment him for it.

Instead of spending all his time on projects around the house, Nate used some of it to be alone with Cheryl, where they could meet each other's most important marital needs. They already had countless interests in common and had little difficulty enjoying recreational activities together. Their sexual relationship had never been a problem until Norma came along. By limiting home projects to those he really felt like doing and receiving appreciation from Cheryl whenever he did them, Nate's love for her was quickly restored.

Two years later Cheryl told me that her marriage was better than it had ever been and that her mistrust of Nate had disappeared. She didn't get quite as many projects done, but she was much happier than she had been when every task had been completed—and so was Nate.

Don't Let Infidelity Destroy Your Love

Dishonesty is the primary agent of infidelity. Without it, it's extremely difficult to get an affair off the ground. But infidelity itself is another Love Buster. As in the case of drug and alcohol addiction, it's a destructive independent behavior.

Infidelity is the result of allowing important marital needs to be met outside marriage. It's often motivated by the fact that those needs are not being met inside marriage. But whatever the reason, it creates untold pain and sorrow for an entire family.

In this chapter, I do not explain how couples learn to end infidelity (I do that in my book *Surviving an Affair*). Instead, I selected three cases to illustrate the process of restoring romantic love once infidelity has ended. As long as infidelity is still in process, I don't begin marriage counseling. Infidelity is such a powerful barrier to the resolution of marital conflicts that there is no way to resolve them while it persists.

But once an affair is over, marriage can be restored to a level of satisfaction never before achieved.

Consider This...

1. Which Love Buster provides the opportunity for infidelity? Which Love Buster is infidelity? What other Love Busters can it create?
2. How does the Policy of Joint Agreement prevent infidelity?
3. Have you ever engaged in infidelity? Have you ever discussed it with anyone? Have they encouraged you to keep it a secret or to confess it to your spouse? If you've kept it a secret until now, are you willing to eliminate the Love Buster of dishonesty in your marriage?
4. Have you ever had fantasies about having an affair? Have you ever fallen in love with someone else? Have you ever been infatuated with someone else? Have you ever been tempted to have an affair? If you fail to tell your spouse about these "close calls," you're engaging in dishonesty. Are you willing to restore honesty to your marriage?

Part 4

Bonus
CHAPTERS

16

BUILDING ROMANTIC LOVE WITH CARE

When Jo and Pete married, the most clearly understood part of their wedding vows was that they would care for each other throughout their lifetime. They understood that care means more than a feeling; it's a commitment to make every reasonable effort to meet each other's needs.

While they were still dating, Pete told Jo that if she married him he'd make her the happiest woman in history. She would be the center of his life, and his world would revolve around her. Jo knew that if the marriage was to work she had to treat him the same way. She had to make him happy as well and make every effort to meet his needs.

While they each had the right intentions and the correct understanding of care as a marital commitment, they did not understand how difficult it would be to *learn* to care for each other. They both thought care was something you could decide to do, and that once the decision was made, acts of care would be spontaneous.

But because their care for each other was not carefully planned, it fell far short of their expectations. Both Jo and Pete felt neglected.

Care is the *willingness* to change your own personal habits to meet the emotional needs of the person you have chosen to marry and then *making sure* that those habits are effective. Jo and Pete had the willingness part of care right—but they failed to *deliver* the care they had promised.

Care

The willingness to change your personal habits to meet the emotional needs of your spouse and to make sure those habits are effective.

There are some people who object to the quality of care I recommend in marriage. They think that by changing personal habits rather than doing what comes naturally, they sacrifice their true identity—they become robots. But care does not cause anyone to lose their identity or become a robot. Our habits are very often developed through chance and are not necessarily a reflection of our character or our values in life. When we change them to accommodate our spouse's needs, we are actually controlling our behavior to fit our character.

But the process of discarding old habits and developing new ones can be difficult and stressful. This is one reason well-intentioned couples often fail in their efforts to learn more accommodating habits. It's not only difficult for us to change for our spouse, but it is also difficult to put our spouse through the stress of making changes to accommodate us.

Jo and Pete were very compatible when they were married. They got along with each other extremely well and felt that they were made for each other. It did not occur to them that after marriage their prior acts of care would fade away if they were not deliberately nurtured. Their marriage gave them the illusion that their care was somehow on autopilot and that the marriage itself would guarantee that care.

But life can get very complicated after marriage, especially when children arrive. It's easy to understand why spouses become distracted and focus their attention away from each other. And yet, failure to meet each other's emotional needs with consistency and effectiveness will ruin any marriage.

> The process of discarding old habits and developing new ones can be difficult and stressful.

But care is much more than just learning to meet another's needs at one point in time and then sustaining those particular habits for a lifetime; it also requires the willingness

286

and ability to meet changing needs—adjusting to a moving target. Jo's emotional needs changed after their first child arrived—she needed a husband who would be committed to the development and education of little Jessica. She had always assumed that when the time was right, Pete would be a good father. But it turned out to be something that he had to learn to do—it wasn't as natural as she thought it would be.

One of the more popular reasons cited for divorce today is that a husband and wife have "grown apart from each other." One of them may have completed an education, while the other did not. One may have developed a new career interest, and the other did not join in that interest. Children can also impact a couple's interests and send them in different directions.

At the time of our marriage, my wife, Joyce, dropped out of college after completing her second year while I went on to earn a PhD degree. Did that make us incompatible? Not a bit, because we were able to make adjustments in our care for each other. But most couples do not make those adjustments. Instead of learning how to meet each other's needs under new circumstances, couples assume that their instincts will carry them. Then when instinct seems to fail, they conclude that they must be incompatible.

> Growing apart simply means that a couple has not grown together.

Growing apart simply means that a couple has not grown together. They have let nature take its course, and the new circumstances and new needs that are inevitable in marriage are left unmet, because no effort has been made to create new habits to meet them.

Extramarital affairs and multiple marriages represent one strategy in adjusting to the failure to meet important emotional needs. Over a period of time, as needs change and a relationship falls apart, a new relationship is developed with another individual who happens to be prepared to meet those new needs.

If we were unable to adjust to each other's changes in life, then I suppose multiple marriages would be about the only solution to satisfying relationships. But we have an enormous capacity for adjustment. Learning to meet each other's marital needs is far less destructive and complicated than going through the agonizing ritual of divorce and remarriage.

In this book, I have shown you how to avoid making Love Bank withdrawals. But there is another side to the coin—Love Bank deposits.

Without deposits, you have no hope of ever being in love with each other.

In the companion book, *His Needs, Her Needs: Building an Affair-proof Marriage*, I focus attention on making those Love Bank deposits. In this bonus chapter and the next, I will summarize some of the main points I make in *His Needs, Her Needs*.

How do you learn to care for your spouse so effectively that he or she will be in love and stay in love with you? There are two essential steps you must take.

Discover Your Spouse's Most Important Needs

The first step in learning to care for your spouse is discovering his or her emotional needs and identifying the most important ones.

Men and women usually have the same basic emotional needs, but their priorities are often very different. What is most important to men is usually much less important to women and vice-versa. That makes this first step more complex and difficult than you might first think.

When men and women don't understand each other's most important emotional needs, they tend to meet those that are most important to them—husbands try to meet needs most important to men, and wives try to meet needs most important to women. In most cases, that strategy completely misses the mark.

When the best efforts of a husband and wife go unappreciated and needs are not met besides, they often give up trying. If they had only directed their efforts in the right places, they would have been effective *and* appreciated.

My experience as a marriage counselor has helped me identify ten of the most important emotional needs that can be met in marriage. While all ten are important, five are of critical importance to most men, and the other five are of critical importance to most women. All these categories may not apply to your marriage, but they can help you begin a discussion with your spouse to identify each other's most important emotional needs—the ones that when met will deposit so many love units that they will cause you to be in love with each other.

His Needs

A man's five most important needs in marriage tend to be:

1. *Sexual fulfillment.* His wife meets this need by becoming a terrific sexual partner. She studies her own sexual response to recognize and understand what brings out the best in her; then she shares this information with him, and together they learn to have a sexual relationship that both find enjoyable.
2. *Recreational companionship.* She develops an interest in the recreational activities he enjoys most and tries to become proficient at them. If she finds she cannot enjoy them, she encourages him to consider other activities that they can enjoy together. She becomes his favorite recreational companion, and he associates her with his most enjoyable moments of relaxation.
3. *Physical attractiveness.* She keeps herself physically fit with diet and exercise, and she wears her hair, makeup, and clothes in a way that he finds attractive and tasteful. He is attracted to her in private and proud of her in public.
4. *Domestic support.* She creates a home that offers him a refuge from the stresses of life. She manages household responsibilities in a way that encourages him to spend time at home enjoying his family.
5. *Admiration.* She understands and appreciates him more than anyone else. She reminds him of his value and achievements, and helps him maintain self-confidence. She avoids criticizing him. She is proud of him, not out of duty, but from a profound respect for the man she chose to marry.

When a man is married to a woman who has learned to meet his most important needs, he'll find her irresistible. Love units are deposited into his Love Bank in such great numbers that he finds himself helplessly in love. That's because the fulfillment of these needs is essential to his happiness.

Her Needs

A woman's five most important needs in marriage tend to be:

1. *Affection.* Her husband tells her that he loves her with words, cards, flowers, gifts, and common courtesies. His hugs and kisses are symbols of his willingness to be there for her when she needs him and his deep concern about her welfare. His acts of affection are repeated daily, creating an environment that clearly and repeatedly expresses his love for her.
2. *Conversation.* He sets aside time every day to talk to her. They may talk about events in their lives, their children, their feelings, or their plans. But whatever the topic, she enjoys the conversation because it is never judgmental and is always informative and constructive. She talks to him as much as she would like, and he responds with interest.
3. *Honesty and openness.* He tells her everything about himself, leaving nothing out that might later surprise her. He describes his positive and negative feelings, events of his past, his daily schedule, and his plans for the future. He never leaves her with a false impression and is truthful about his thoughts, feelings, intentions, and behavior.
4. *Financial support.* He assumes the responsibility to house, feed, and clothe his family. If his income is insufficient to provide essential support, he resolves the problem by upgrading his skills to increase his salary. He does not work long hours, keeping himself from his wife and family, but is able to provide necessary support by working a forty- to forty-five-hour week. While he encourages his wife to pursue a career, he does not depend on her salary for family living expenses.
5. *Family commitment.* He commits sufficient time and energy to the moral and educational development of their children. He reads to them, engages in sports with them, and takes them on frequent outings. He reads books and attends lectures with his wife on the subject of child development so that they will do a good job training their children. He and his wife discuss training methods and objectives until they agree. He does not proceed with any plan of

290

training or discipline without her approval. He recognizes that his care of the children is critically important to her.

When a woman is married to a man who has learned to meet her most important emotional needs, she'll find him irresistible. Love units are deposited in her Love Bank in such great numbers that she finds herself helplessly in love. That's because the fulfillment of these needs is essential to her happiness.

Identify Your Needs

Of course, *these categories do not apply to everyone.* Some men look at my "man's needs" list and throw out two of them to make room for two from my "woman's needs" list. Some women do the same. Believing that these categories are right for everyone is a big mistake!

I simply suggest these needs to help you start the process of identifying what you need most in marriage. It is simply a way of helping you think through what makes you the happiest and most fulfilled. I also want you to realize that what a man needs in marriage is usually quite different from what a woman needs. That makes the whole process of discovering your needs very personal; it's something you must do for yourself. Then you should reveal your discovery to your spouse.

Prioritizing Needs

To make this process more accurate and reliable, I suggest that you first select the need you think is the most important for you. Pretend that, in your marriage, it's the only need you'll have met. The other nine needs will *not* be met. What need would you select if you knew you would never get the rest? That's probably your most important emotional need. When it's met, the most love units are deposited.

Then do the same for need number two. If you will *not* get the other eight needs met, what two would you pick? Continue this process until you've picked five. Those are the needs you want your spouse to be particularly proficient in meeting.

Take a hard look at the needs you left behind. For example, if you did not include financial support, you should not expect your spouse to earn a dime! Are the needs you chose more important to you than that one? How about physical attractiveness? If your spouse neglects her appearance, gains weight, or dresses carelessly, what would your emotional reaction be?

Some of my clients tell me that all ten are of critical importance. They could not survive a marriage that neglected any of them. But my experience has shown me that if you can learn to do an outstanding job meeting only the *five* most important needs, you build more romantic love than if you do a mediocre job on all ten.

Most of us cannot be outstanding at everything; we must pick what is most important and concentrate on that. If you want to build romantic love with your spouse, be proficient at meeting only the *most important* emotional needs.

Once you and your spouse have communicated your five most important emotional needs to each other, you're ready for the second step in learning to care for each other.

Learn to Meet Your Spouse's Most Important Needs

Learning to meet your spouse's five most important marital needs usually requires hundreds, maybe thousands, of new habits. But the habits all eventually come together to form a whole. It's like learning a part in a play: You begin by learning each line, each motion, each cue, but eventually it comes together. It's naturally whole; it doesn't seem like hundreds of little pieces.

To build the myriad of habits necessary to meet your spouse's needs, you must have a carefully planned strategy. *His Needs, Her Needs* provides a few strategies for you to consider for each of the ten needs. And you may benefit from professional help as well. The need for financial support, for example, may require you to consult a vocational counselor. The need for sexual fulfillment may require help from a sex therapist.

However you develop it, a strategy—a plan—should be created that has a good chance of improving your ability to meet the needs your spouse identified as most important.

Once you implement your plan, you may need someone to report to for accountability. Your spouse is not a good choice, because your mentor may need to criticize your effort, and your spouse should not be forced into that role. A pastor or professional counselor may be better suited.

If you are successful, you will see it in his or her eyes, and in the way your spouse talks to you and responds to you. The "look of love" is unmistakable.

> Compatibility is created.

I view marriage as a profession. The skills I learn are designed to meet my spouse's most important emotional needs, and if I'm successful, she'll be in love with me. If she's not in love with me, I'm probably at fault and need to develop new skills. Of course, if I'm not in love with her and I've been honest about my feelings, it's her problem to solve.

As I've said earlier, *compatibility is created.* As a couple increases the number of habits that meet each other's marital needs, they improve their compatibility and their romantic love for each other.

We have such an opportunity in marriage to give each other exactly what we need. Many couples squander that. Don't let it happen to you!

17

BUILDING ROMANTIC LOVE
WITH TIME

Before Jo and Pete were married, they spent the majority of their free time together. Her girlfriends knew that spending time with him was one of her highest priorities. Whenever they invited her somewhere, she would first check to see if she'd be missing an opportunity to be with Pete. Her girlfriends thought it was silly. On some occasions, she even broke dates with her girlfriends if he had time to be with her.

Pete did the same. Soon he found that many of the things he enjoyed doing were abandoned because he was spending so much time with Jo.

They tried to see each other on a daily basis. On days when they couldn't get together, they called each other and sometimes talked for hours. When they were together, they gave each other lots of attention.

The total amount of time spent with each other in an average week was fifteen to twenty-five hours. This included time on the telephone. But they weren't counting. They just took advantage of every opportunity.

After they were married, Jo and Pete were with each other more often, but a change took place in the quality of their time together— they spent much less time giving each other attention. Pete came home and watched television all evening. Sometimes he barely said a word to Jo.

Before they were married, they scheduled time to be with each other. But after marriage, they felt that "dates" were not as important, so their time together was incidental to other priorities.

Courtship is a custom that gives people a chance to prove they can meet each other's marital needs. If enough love units are deposited, love is the result and marriage usually follows. Without time together, the test would fail because it takes time to deposit enough love units to create the feeling of love.

Policy of Undivided Attention

Give undivided attention to your spouse a minimum of fifteen hours each week, meeting his or her most important emotional needs.

As a reminder to couples who tend to neglect spending time together, I've suggested the Policy of Undivided Attention: *Give undivided attention to your spouse a minimum of fifteen hours each week, meeting his or her most important emotional needs.*

One difficult aspect of marriage counseling is scheduling time for it. The counselor must work evenings and weekends because most couples will not give up work to make their appointments. Then the counselor must schedule around a host of evening and weekend activities that take the husband and wife in opposite directions.

Another difficult aspect of marriage counseling is arranging time for the couple to be together to carry out their first assignment. Many couples think that a counselor will solve their problems with a weekly conversation in his or her office. It doesn't occur to them that it's what they do after they leave the office that saves their marriage. To accomplish anything, they must reserve time to be together. This may be painful, but eventually they get the point, and little by little they rearrange their lives to include each other.

It's incredible how many couples have tried to talk me out of the Policy of Undivided Attention. They begin by trying to convince me that it's impossible. Then they go on to the argument that it's impractical. Then they try to show me that it's impractical for *them*. But in the end, they usually agree that without scheduling at least fifteen hours for undivided attention, they cannot possibly achieve romantic love.

To help explain how the Policy of Undivided Attention is to be applied in marriage, I've broken it down into three parts: privacy, objectives, and amount.

Privacy

The time you plan to be together should not include children (who are awake), relatives, or friends. Establish privacy so that you are able to give each other undivided attention.

It is essential for you as a couple to spend time alone. When you have time alone, you have a much greater opportunity to meet each other's emotional needs and make Love Bank deposits. Without privacy, undivided attention is almost impossible, and without undivided attention, you are unable to meet the emotional needs of affection, conversation, and sexual fulfillment.

ACTION STEP

Establish privacy so you can give each other undivided attention.

First, I recommend that you learn to be together without your children present. I'm amazed at how difficult this is for couples, especially when the children are very young. Many couples don't think that children interfere with their privacy. To them, an evening with their children is privacy. And, technically, when they are with their children they are meeting at least one emotional need—the need for family commitment. The problem is that if they are never together without their children, they are not able to meet other needs that usually have a higher priority.

Of course, they know they can't make love with children around. But I believe that the presence of children prevents much more than lovemaking. When children are present, they interfere with affection and intimate conversation, which are crucial needs in marriage. Besides, affection and intimate conversation usually lead to lovemaking, and without them, you will find that your lovemaking suffers. And if your recreational companionship always includes your children, you will be so restricted in what you find mutually enjoyable that you will be tempted to make one of the biggest mistakes in marriage—spending your most enjoyable leisure time apart from each other.

Second, I recommend that friends and relatives not be with you in your time together. This may mean that, after everything has been scheduled, there is little time left for friends and relatives. If that's the case, you're too busy, but at least you will not be sacrificing your love for each other to have time with friends and relatives.

Third, I recommend that you understand what giving undivided attention means. It's what you did when you were dating. You probably would not have married if you had ignored each other on dates. You may have parked your car somewhere just to be completely alone and to rid yourselves of all distractions. That's the quality of undivided attention I'm referring to here.

When you see a movie together, the time you spend watching it would not usually count toward your time for undivided attention—unless you behave like the couple who sat in front of my wife and me last week. It's the same with television and sporting events. You should engage in these recreational activities together, but the time I want you to commit yourselves to is very clearly defined—it's the time you pay close attention to each other.

Now that you're alone with each other, what should you do with this time? The second part of the Policy of Undivided Attention deals with objectives.

Objectives

During this time, create activities that will meet your most important emotional needs: affection, sexual fulfillment, conversation, and recreational companionship.

Romance for most men is sex and recreation; for most women it's affection and conversation. When all four come together, men and women alike call it romance, and they deposit the most love units possible. That makes these categories somewhat inseparable whenever you spend time together. My advice is to try to combine them all.

After marriage, women often try to get their husband to meet their emotional needs for conversation and affection without meeting their husband's needs

ACTION
STEP

Create activities that will meet your most important emotional needs.

297

for sex and recreational companionship. Men, on the other hand, want their wife to meet their needs for sexual fulfillment and recreational companionship without meeting her needs for affection and conversation. Neither strategy works very well. Women often resent having sex without affection and conversation first, and men resent being conversant and affectionate with no hope for sex or recreation. By combining the fulfillment of all four needs into a single event, however, both spouses have their needs met and enjoy the entire time together.

A man should never assume that, just because he is in bed with his wife, sex is there for the taking. In many marriages, that mistake creates resentment and confusion. Most men eventually learn that if they spend the evening giving their wife their undivided attention, with conversation and affection, sex becomes a very natural and mutually enjoyable way to end the evening.

> Your time for undivided attention should be the best time of the week for both of you.

But there are some women who don't see the connection either. They want their husbands to give them the most attention when there is no possibility for sex. In fact, knowing that affection and intimate conversation often lead to a man wanting sex, they try their hardest to be affectionate when they are out in a crowd. That tactic can lead to just as much resentment in a man as nightly sexual "ambushes" create in a woman. Take my word for it, the fulfillment of the four needs of affection, conversation, recreational companionship, and sexual fulfillment is best when they are met together.

Your time for undivided attention should be the best time of the week for both of you. But if you have not been "dating" lately, it may not begin that way. If you do not yet know how to meet each other's emotional needs, you may find your time together boring or even unpleasant. This is particularly true if your conversation includes demands, disrespect, and angry outbursts. If you want to meet the need for conversation, you must learn to avoid hurting each other with what you say.

But if you do not schedule this time to be together now, you will never have the opportunity to learn how to make it enjoyable for both of you and how to avoid making it unpleasant. The time that you schedule for each other will eventually become the best time of the week, when you have finally learned to meet each other's needs and avoid hurting each other.

Don't waste precious weeks, months, and years hoping that somehow your relationship will improve. Take the first step toward insuring your success by actually putting each other in your schedules. And once you are there, do whatever it takes to make it the best fifteen hours of your week.

But why do I suggest fifteen hours each week for undivided attention? Won't five hours work just as well? The next part of the Policy of Undivided Attention helps explain why I am so adamant in encouraging couples to spend that amount of time alone with each other.

Amount

Choose a number of hours that reflects the quality of your marriage. If your marriage is satisfying to you and your spouse, plan fifteen hours. But if you suffer marital dissatisfaction, plan thirty hours each week or more, until marital satisfaction is achieved. Keep a permanent record of your time together.

How much time do you need to sustain the feeling of love for each other? Believe it or not, there really is an answer to this question, and it depends on the health of a marriage. If a couple is deeply in love with each other and find that their marital needs are being met, I have found that about fifteen hours each week of undivided attention is usually enough to sustain their love, as long as they use the time to meet each other's emotional needs. When a marriage is this healthy, either it's a new marriage or the couple has already been spending that amount of time with each other throughout their marriage. Without fifteen hours of undivided attention each week, a couple simply can't do what it takes to sustain their feeling of love for each other.

ACTION STEP

Choose a number of hours that reflects the quality of your marriage.

When I apply the fifteen-hour principle to marriages, I usually recommend that the time be evenly distributed throughout the week, two to three hours each day. When the time is bunched up—all hours only on the weekend—good results are not as predictable. Spouses need to be emotionally reconnected almost on a daily basis to meet each other's most important emotional needs.

How can a workaholic businessman find time to have an affair? The man who couldn't be home for dinner because of his busy schedule is suddenly able to fit in a midafternoon rendezvous three times a week! How does he get his work done?

The answer, of course, is that he had the time all along. It's simply a matter of priorities. He could just as easily have spent the time with his wife. Then they would have been in love with each other. Instead, he's in love with someone else, all because of a shortsighted schedule.

The reason I have so much difficulty getting couples to spend time with each other is that when I first see them for counseling, they have forgotten how to have a good time. Their relationship does not do anything for them, and the time spent with each other seems like a total waste at first. But if I can motivate them to schedule the time together every week, they use that time to learn to re-create the romantic experiences that first nurtured their love relationship. Without scheduling that time, they have little hope of restoring the love they once had for each other.

> Fifteen hours a week is often not enough time for couples that are not yet in love.

But fifteen hours a week is often not enough time for couples that are not yet in love. To help them jump-start their relationship, I usually suggest increasing the number of hours spent alone with each other so that they can learn more quickly the skills that will meet each other's emotional needs. I sometimes suggest abandoning most other responsibilities so that they can spend twenty-five or thirty hours a week on undivided attention until they can meet each other's emotional needs almost effortlessly. By the time that happens, they are both in love with each other again. In some cases I have even recommended a two- or three-week vacation together so they can give each other undivided attention around the clock.

Your time together is too important to the security of your marriage to neglect. It's more important than time spent doing anything else during the week, including time with your children and your job. Remember that the fifteen hours you should set aside is only equivalent to a part-time job. It isn't time you don't have; it's time you would use for something much less important, if you don't use it for each other.

If you have not been in the habit of spending fifteen hours a week on undivided attention, it will mean that something else that takes fifteen hours will have to go. But you have about 110 total waking hours each week that are spent doing something, and if you schedule your time productively, you will find that the fifteen hours you lose will have been spent on your least important goals. And you will put in its place fifteen hours for your most important goal. Think of it—your highest priority will take the place of your lowest priority. It will radically change your life for the better, because in exchange for something that really isn't that important to you, you will be investing in the single most important factor in your life—your relationship with your spouse.

It should be obvious to you that it will take time to meet most of each other's emotional needs, and unless you schedule that time, you simply won't get the job done. Time has a way of slipping away if you don't set it aside for important objectives. And what objective is more important than you and your spouse being in love with each other?

To help you plan your week with each other's emotional needs in mind, I encourage you to meet with your spouse at 3:30 on Sunday afternoon to look over each other's schedule for the coming week. That's the time for you to be sure that you have provided for each other. And while you're at it, try to plan a little extra time just in case an emergency arises that prevents you from being together the full fifteen hours you originally plan.

You and your spouse fell in love with each other because you met some of each other's most important emotional needs, and the only way to stay in love is to keep meeting those needs. Even when the feeling of love begins to fade, or when it's gone entirely, it's not necessarily gone for good. It can be recovered whenever you both go back to being experts at making Love Bank deposits.

> Learn to become experts at making Love Bank deposits, and then keep your balances secure by avoiding Love Busters.

As you've seen in this book, though, meeting important emotional needs is only half of the story. While that's how couples make the most Love Bank deposits, they must be sure that they're not depositing into a sieve. They must also avoid making Love Bank withdrawals.

In this book, I have introduced to you some of the most common ways that spouses hurt each other. Unless you protect each other from your destructive habits and instincts, you will hurt each other so much that eventually your Love Bank accounts will be in the red. Instead of loving each other, you will hate each other. Don't let that happen to you. Instead, learn to become experts at making Love Bank deposits, and then keep your balances secure by avoiding Love Busters.

APPENDIX

SUMMARY OF MY BASIC CONCEPTS TO HELP YOU FALL IN LOVE AND STAY IN LOVE

Basic Concept 1: The Love Bank

In my struggle to learn how to save marriages, I eventually discovered that the best way to do it was to teach couples how to fall in love—and stay in love—with each other. So I created the concept of the Love Bank to help couples understand how people fall in and out of love. This concept, perhaps more than any other that I have created, has helped couples realize that almost everything they do affects their love for each other either positively or negatively. That awareness has set most of them on a course of action that has preserved their love and saved their marriages.

Within each of us is a Love Bank that keeps track of the way people treat us. Everyone we know has an account and the things they do either deposit or withdraw love units from their accounts. It's the way your emotions encourage you to be with those who make you happy. When you associate someone with good feelings, deposits are made into that person's account in your Love Bank. And when the Love Bank reaches a certain level of deposits (the romantic-love threshold), the feeling of love is triggered. As long as your Love Bank balance remains above that threshold, you will experience the feeling of love. But when it falls below that threshold, you will lose that feeling. You will like anyone with a balance above zero, but you will only be in love with someone whose balance is above the love threshold.

Not only do your emotions encourage you to be with those who make you happy, they also discourage you from being with those who make you unhappy. Whenever you associate someone with bad feelings, withdrawals are made from your Love Bank. And if that person makes more withdrawals than deposits, his or her balance in your Love Bank can fall below zero. When that happens the Love Bank turns into the Hate Bank. You will dislike those with moderate negative balances, but if a balance falls below the hate threshold, you will hate the person.

Try living with a spouse you hate! Your emotions are doing everything they can to get you out of there—and divorce is one of the most logical ways to escape.

Couples usually ask for my advice when they are just about ready to give up on their marriage. Their Love Banks have been losing love units so long that they are now deeply in the red. And their negative Love Bank accounts make them feel uncomfortable just being in the same room with each other. They cannot imagine surviving marriage for another year, let alone ever being in love again.

But that's my job—to help them fall in love with each other again. I encourage them to stop making Love Bank withdrawals and start making Love Bank deposits. I created all of the remaining basic concepts to help couples achieve those objectives.

Basic Concept 2: Instincts and Habits

Instincts are behavioral patterns that we are born with, and habits are patterns that we learn. Both instincts and habits tend to be repeated again and again almost effortlessly. They are important in our discussion of what it takes to be in love because it's our behavior that makes deposits in and withdrawals from Love Banks, and our instincts and habits make up most of our behavior.

Instincts and habits can make Love Bank deposits, so it is imperative to learn those habits because once they are learned, deposits in your spouse's Love Bank are made repeatedly and almost effortlessly.

Unfortunately, many of our instincts and habits, such as angry outbursts, contribute to Love Bank withdrawals. Since they are repeated so often, they play a very important role in the annihilation of Love Bank accounts. If we are to stop Love Bank withdrawals, we must somehow stop destructive instincts and habits in their tracks. Instincts are harder to stop than habits, but they can both be avoided.

As we discuss the remaining concepts, keep in mind the value of a good habit and the harm of a bad habit, because their effect on Love Bank balances is multiplied by repetition.

Basic Concept 3: The Most Important Emotional Needs

What's the fastest way to deposit love units into each other's Love Bank? I interviewed literally hundreds of couples trying to find the answer to this question when I was first learning how to save marriages. Eventually the answer became clear to me—you must meet each other's most important emotional needs.

You and your spouse fell in love with each other because you made each other very happy, and you made each other happy because you met some of each other's important emotional needs. The only way you and your spouse will stay in love is to keep meeting those needs. Even when the feeling of love begins to fade, or when it's gone entirely, it's not necessarily gone for good. It can be recovered whenever you both go back to making large Love Bank deposits.

Your spouse depends on you to meet his or her most important emotional needs, and it's the most effective and efficient way for you to make large deposits in your spouse's Love Bank.

Basic Concept 4: The Policy of Undivided Attention

Unless you and your spouse schedule time each week for undivided attention, it will be impossible to meet each other's most important emotional needs. To help you and your spouse clear space in your schedule for each other, I have written the **Policy of Undivided Attention: Give your spouse your undivided attention a minimum of fifteen hours each week, using the time to meet the emotional needs of affection, sexual fulfillment, conversation, and recreational companionship.** This policy will help you avoid one of the most common mistakes in marriage—neglecting each other.

This basic concept not only helps guarantee that you will meet each other's emotional needs but also unlocks the door to the use of all the other basic concepts. Without time for undivided attention, you will not be able to avoid Love Busters and you will not be able to negotiate effectively. Time for undivided attention is the necessary ingredient for everything that's important in marriage.

And yet, as soon as most couples marry, and especially when children arrive, couples usually replace their time together with activities of lesser importance. You probably did the same thing. You tried to meet each other's needs with "leftover" time, but sadly, there wasn't much time left over. Your lack of private time together may have become a great cause of unhappiness, and yet you felt incapable of preventing it. You may have also found yourself bottling up your honest expression of feelings because there was just no appropriate time to talk.

Make your time to be alone with each other your highest priority—that way it will never be replaced by activities of lesser value. Your career, your time with your children, maintenance of your home, and a host of other demands will all compete for your time together. But if you follow the Policy of Undivided Attention, you will not let anything steal from you those precious and crucial hours together.

It is essential to (a) spend time away from children and friends whenever you give each other your undivided attention; (b) use the time to meet each other's emotional needs of affection, conversation, recreational companionship, and sexual fulfillment; and (c) schedule at least fifteen hours together each week. When you were dating, you gave each other this kind of attention and you fell in love. When people have affairs, they also give each other this kind of attention to keep their love for each other alive. Why should courtship and affairs be the only times love is created? Why can't it happen throughout marriage as well? It can, if you set aside time every week to give each other undivided attention.

Basic Concept 5: Love Busters

When you meet each other's most important emotional needs, you become each other's source of greatest happiness. But if you are not careful, you can also become each other's source of greatest unhappiness.

It's pointless to deposit love units if you withdraw them right away. So, in addition to meeting important emotional needs, you must also be sure to protect your spouse. Guard your account in your spouse's Love Bank from withdrawals by paying attention to how your everyday behavior can make each other unhappy.

You and your spouse were born to be demanding, disrespectful, angry, annoying, independent, and dishonest. These are normal human traits that I call Love Busters because they destroy the feeling of love spouses have for each other. But if you promise to avoid being the cause of your spouse's unhappiness, you will do whatever it takes to overcome these destructive tendencies for your spouse's protection. By eliminating Love Busters, you will not only be protecting your spouse, but you will also be preserving your spouse's love for you.

Basic Concept 6: The Policy of Radical Honesty

If you and your spouse are to be in love with each other, you must give honesty special attention. That's because it plays such an important role in the creation of love. It is one of the ten most important emotional needs, so when it's met, it can trigger the feeling of love. On the other hand, its counterpart, dishonesty, is a Love Buster—it destroys love.

But there is another reason that honesty is crucial in creating love. Honesty is the only way that you and your spouse will ever come to understand each other. Without honesty, the adjustments that are crucial to making each other happy and avoiding unhappiness cannot be made.

It isn't easy to be honest. Honesty is an unpopular value these days, and most couples have not made this commitment to each other. Many marriage counselors and clergymen argue that honesty is not always the best policy. They believe that it's cruel to disclose past indiscretions and it's selfish to make such disclosures. While it makes you feel better to get a mistake off your chest, it causes your partner to suffer. So, they argue, the truly caring thing to do is to lie about your mistakes or at least keep them tucked away.

And if it's compassionate to lie about sins of the past, why isn't it also compassionate to lie about sins of the present—or future? To my way of thinking, it's like letting the proverbial camel's nose under the tent. Eventually you will be dining with the camel. Either honesty is always right, or you'll always have an excuse for being dishonest.

To help remind couples how important honesty is in marriage, I have written the **Policy of Radical Honesty: Reveal to your spouse as much information about yourself as you know—your thoughts, feelings, habits, likes, dislikes, personal history, daily activities, and plans for the future.**

Self-imposed honesty with your spouse is essential to your marriage's safety and success. Not only will honesty bring you closer to each other emotionally, it will also prevent the creation of destructive habits that are kept secret from your spouse.

Basic Concept 7: The Giver and Taker

Have you ever thought that your spouse is possessed? One moment he or she is loving and thoughtful, and the next you are faced with selfishness and thoughtlessness. Trust me, it's not a demon you're up against, it's the two sides of our personalities. I call them the Giver and the Taker.

All of us want to make a difference in the lives of others. We want others to be happy and we want to contribute to their happiness. When we feel that way, our Giver is influencing us. The Giver's rule is **do whatever you can to make others happy and avoid anything that makes others unhappy, even if it makes you unhappy.** It encourages us to use that rule in our relationships with other people.

But we also want the best for ourselves. We want to be happy, too. When we feel that way, our Taker is influencing us. The Taker's rule is **do whatever you can to make you happy, and avoid anything that makes you unhappy, even if it makes others unhappy.** If that rule makes sense to you, it's because your Taker is in control.

These two primitive aspects of our personality are usually balanced in our dealings with others, but in marriage they tend to take turns being in charge. And that leads to most of the problems that couples encounter. If we take the advice of our Giver, we are willing to suffer to make our spouse happy, and if we take the advice of our Taker, we are willing to let our spouse suffer to make us happy. In either case the advice we are given is shortsighted because someone always gets hurt.

Basic Concept 8: The Three States of Mind in Marriage

The Giver and Taker create moods that I call states of mind. These states of mind have a tremendous influence on the way a husband and wife try to resolve conflicts. Each of the three states of mind discourages negotiation. That's what makes negotiation, in general, so tough in marriage.

When we are happy and in love, we are usually in the **state of intimacy**. That state of mind is controlled by the Giver, which encourages us to follow the Giver's rule: *Do whatever you can to make your spouse happy and avoid anything that makes your spouse unhappy, even if it makes you unhappy.* That rule can lead to habits that may be good for your spouse but can be disastrous for you because you are not negotiating with your own interests in mind.

Sadly, flawed agreements made in the state of intimacy can lead to our own unhappiness, and that in turn wakes the slumbering Taker. As long as we are happy, our Taker has nothing to do, but when we start feeling unhappy, our Taker rises to our rescue and triggers the **state of conflict**. With the Taker now in charge, we are encouraged to follow the rule: *Do whatever you can to make you happy, and avoid anything that makes you unhappy, even if it makes others unhappy.* The Taker also encourages you to be demanding, disrespectful, and angry in an effort to force your spouse to make you happy. Fighting is the Taker's favorite "negotiating" strategy.

When fighting doesn't work, and we are still unhappy, the Taker encourages us to take a new course of action that triggers the **state of withdrawal**. Instead of trying to force our spouse to make us happy, our Taker wants us to give up on our spouse entirely. We don't want our spouse to do anything for us and we certainly don't want to do anything for our spouse. In this state of mind we are emotionally divorced.

How can couples work their way back to the state of intimacy once they find themselves trapped in the state of withdrawal? And once they are back, how can they stay there? The answers to those questions are found in basic concept 9.

Basic Concept 9: The Policy of Joint Agreement

Marital instincts do not lead to fair negotiation. They lead to either giving away the store (state of intimacy) or robbing the bank (state of conflict). And in the state of withdrawal, no one even feels like negotiating. Yet in order to meet each other's most important needs and avoid Love Busters consistently and effectively, fair negotiation is crucial in marriage.

You need a rule to help you override the shortsighted advice of your Giver and Taker. Their advice is shortsighted because regardless of the rule, someone gets hurt. We get hurt when we follow the Giver's advice, and our spouse gets hurt when we follow the Taker's advice. So I've created a rule to guarantee that no one gets hurt, and that's the ultimate goal in fair negotiation. I call this rule the Policy of Joint Agreement: **Never do anything without the enthusiastic agreement of your spouse.**

Almost everything you and your spouse do affects each other. So it's very important to know what that effect will be before you actually do it. The Policy of Joint Agreement will help you remember to consult with each other to be sure you avoid being the cause of each other's unhappiness. It also makes negotiation necessary, regardless of your state of mind. If you agree to this policy, you will not be able to do anything without the enthusiastic agreement of the other, so it forces you to discuss your plans and negotiate with each other's feelings in mind. Without safe and pleasant negotiation, you will simply not be able to reach an enthusiastic agreement.

The Policy of Joint Agreement, combined with the Policy of Radical Honesty, helps you create an open and integrated life-style, one that will guarantee your love for each other. These policies also prevent the creation of a secret second life where infidelity, the greatest threat to your marriage, can grow like mold in a damp, dark cellar.

Basic Concept 10: Four Guidelines for Successful Negotiation

If you and your spouse are in conflict about anything, I recommend that you do nothing until you can both agree enthusiastically about a resolution. But how should you go about reaching that resolution? I suggest you follow four essential guidelines:

Guideline 1: Set ground rules to make negotiation pleasant and safe.

Ground rule 1: Try to be pleasant and cheerful throughout negotiations.

Ground rule 2: Put safety first. Do not make demands, show disrespect, or become angry when you negotiate, even if your spouse makes demands, shows disrespect, or becomes angry with you.

Ground rule 3: If you reach an impasse and you do not seem to be getting anywhere, or if one of you is starting to make demands, show disrespect, or become angry, stop negotiating and come back to the issue later.

Guideline 2: Identify the problem from both perspectives with mutual respect for those perspectives.

Guideline 3: Brainstorm with abandon—give your creativity a chance to discover solutions that would make you both happy. Carry a pad and pencil with you to jot down ideas as you think of them throughout the day.

Guideline 4: Choose the solution that best meets the conditions of the Policy of Joint Agreement—mutual and enthusiastic agreement. Whenever a conflict arises, keep in mind the importance of finding a solution that deposits as many love units as possible, while avoiding withdrawals. And be sure that the way you find that solution also deposits love units and avoids withdrawals.

INDEX

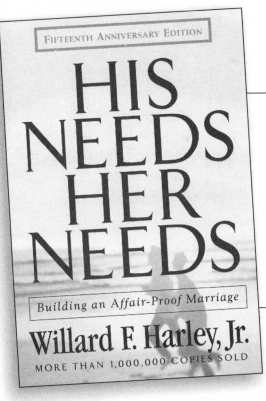
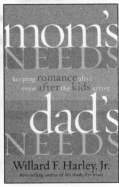

MORE GREAT RESOURCES

MAINTAIN A HEALTHY,

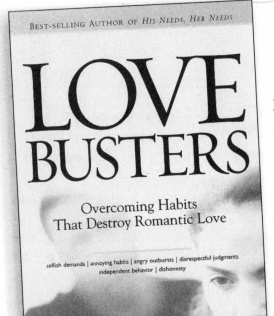

Learn how to identify and overcome the six most common destructive habits that threaten your marriage.

Five Steps to Romantic Love

A helpful workbook containing all the questionnaires and worksheets recommended in *Love Busters* and *His Needs, Her Needs.* A valuable companion to Dr. Harley's bestselling books!

I Cherish You

Share the knowledge of how to build a lifelong, romantic love with this gift book that highlights the trusted concepts of *His Needs, Her Needs.* Perfect for weddings and anniversaries!

ℛ Revell *a division of Baker Publishing Group* www.revellbooks.com

TO HELP YOU START AND
Romantic MARRIAGE

Walk down the aisle with confidence! *I Promise You* shows engaged couples four promises you can make to your future spouse that will establish your love for a lifetime.

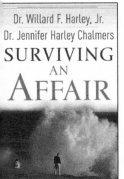

Surviving an Affair

A guide to understanding and surviving every aspect of infidelity—from the beginning of an affair through the restoration of a marriage.

The One

Here today or here to stay? Find out how to stop the pattern of failed relationships and find someone who will commit to a lifetime of love.

Available wherever books are sold

MARRIAGE BUILDERS®

Building Marriages To Last A Lifetime

Why do people fall in love? Why do they fall out of love? What do they want most in marriage? What drives them out of marriage? How can a bad marriage become a great marriage? Dr. Harley's basic concepts address these and other important aspects of marriage building.

At www.marriagebuilders.com Dr. Harley introduces visitors to some of the best ways to overcome marital conflicts and some of the quickest ways to restore love. From the pages of "Basic Concepts" and articles by Dr. Harley to the archives for his weekly Q&A columns and information about upcoming seminars, this site is packed with useful material.

Let Marriage Builders™ help you build a marriage to last a lifetime!
www.marriagebuilders.com